THE THIRD BANK
OF THE RIVER

THE THIRD BANK
OF THE RIVER

Power and Survival in the
Twenty-First-Century Amazon

Chris Feliciano Arnold

Picador
New York

picadorusa.com • instagram.com/picador
twitter.com/picadorusa • facebook.com/picadorusa

Picador® is a U.S. registered trademark and is used by Macmillan Publishing
Group, LLC, under license from Pan Books Limited.

For book club information, please visit facebook.com/picadorbookclub or
email marketing@picadorusa.com.

All photographs are courtesy of the author.

Map by Jeffrey L. Ward

The Library of Congress Cataloging-in-Publication Data is available upon request.

ISBN 978-1-250-09894-8 (hardcover)
ISBN 978-1-250-09895-5 (ebook)

Our books may be purchased in bulk for promotional, educational, or business use.
Please contact your local bookseller or the Macmillan Corporate and Premium Sales
Department at 1-800-221-7945, extension 5442, or by email at
MacmillanSpecialMarkets@macmillan.com.

First Edition: June 2018

10 9 8 7 6 5 4 3 2 1

For Reyna

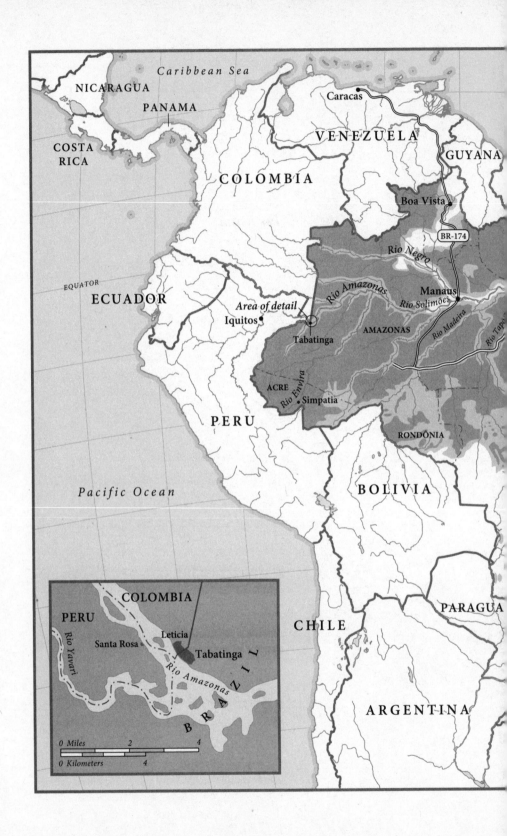

AMAZON FOREST IN BRAZIL

0 Miles 400 800
0 Kilometers 800

SURINAME

FRENCH GUIANA

AMAPA

Atlantic Ocean

EQUATOR

Rio Amazonas

Santarém
•Belém
BELO MONTE DAM
Altamira
Rurópolis
TRANSAMAZÔNICA

Rio Xingu

PARA

MARANHÃO
CEARA

RIO GRANDE
DO NORTE

PIAUI

PARAIBA

BRAZIL
TOCANTINS

PERNAMBUCO
ALAGOAS

MATO
GROSSO

BAHIA

SERGIPE

DISTRITO
FEDERAL
Brasilia •

Salvador

GOIAS

MINAS
GERAIS

MATO
GROSSO
DO SUL

SÃO
PAULO

Belo Horizonte

ESPIRITO SANTO

São Paulo

RIO DE JANEIRO

PARANA

Rio de Janiero

SANTA CATARINA

O GRANDE
DO SUL

Atlantic Ocean

URUGUAY

KEY

Original Forest Cover

Current Forest Cover

© 2018 Jeffrey L. Ward

Contents

God knows how we got through that great mass of water. I advise thee, O great king, never to send Spanish fleets to that cursed river!

—FROM LOPE DE AGUIRRE'S LETTER TO
KING PHILIP II OF SPAIN, 1561

But when death comes I want them to take me and put me in a little boat in this perpetual water between the long shores, and I, down the river, lost in the river, inside the river . . . the river . . .

—JOÃO GUIMARÃES ROSA, "A TERCEIRA MARGEM DO RIO"

PART I

A FINITE WORLD

1

FAN FEST

t was high noon on July 18, 2014 when our 767 touched down at Eduardo Gomes International, the godfather of all jungle airstrips, cut dead center in the Amazon, and waypoint to a city of 2 million people. Across the tarmac, palms wavered like a mirage through the jet fumes.

I was one of a million sweaty gringos landing in Brazil for the FIFA World Cup. An arctic blast of air-conditioning welcomed the new arrivals to Manaus. In anticipation of the biggest public spectacle in the region's history, the airport was undergoing a $100 million renovation, but like most of the country's infrastructure projects, it remained in the throes of construction. The terminal smelled of drying paint, some gates boarded over with red Coca-Cola ads spotlighting the gilded World Cup trophy as if El Dorado had at last been found. Beyond the customs check, a pair of tall, sporty women greeted visitors with complimentary mini Budweisers, making themselves available for selfies. The cold brews went down fast on the way downtown, a ride barely recognizable from my last visit eight years earlier when I'd traveled to Brazil for the first time to see the country where I was born.

The city had mushroomed like never before. Just beyond the airport perimeter stood a fresh Subway franchise, sandwich artists squeezing sauces on canvases of bread. A recently paved and painted four-lane highway unrolled into the city, flanked by business hotels, night clubs, and love motels. The road led to a knot of overpasses and underpasses, the latest attempt to wrangle the city's notoriously chaotic streets. Trees had been supplanted by billboards: 3G cell phone service, cosmetic dentistry, and home appliances with easy monthly payments. Motorcycles, buses, and American sedans zipped from lane to lane as if testing the asphalt for imperfections.

At first glance it seemed as if the World Cup in Manaus was already fulfilling its economic promise, against all odds and the will of the chiefs at FIFA, who had consulted their maps and spreadsheets and determined that the capital of Amazonas state was no place for the Cup of Cups. They said that Brazil could feasibly host matches in eight stadiums. Ten at most. Brazil's national organizing committee disagreed, proposing an audacious seventeen-stadium network that would span every region of the fifth largest country on Earth. Even on paper, hosting matches in the remote interior looked like a disaster. Coastal Belém was the ideal rain forest host city. A no-brainer, as the Americans would say. Positioned at the mouth of the mighty Amazon River, Belém would fit seamlessly in the itineraries of athletes, tourists, and journalists, a quick flight from the beachfront cities of Fortaleza, Recife, and Salvador. Manaus was, well, Manaus. Aside from BR-174—the cratered route to Caracas, Venezuela, that closed at sunset to accommodate nocturnal wildlife and native tribes—the city was accessible only by plane or boat. Manaus wasn't even a soccer town. Its biggest team, Nacional, hadn't competed in Brazil's highest league since the waning years of the military dictatorship in the 1980s, and its neglected 12,000-seat stadium hadn't been filled to capacity for years.

Think of the athletes, those pampered, world-class specimens, flying four hours in-country to play a sweltering match in the middle of nowhere. Temperatures in Manaus hover in the nineties year-round, day and night, even during the six-month dry season. Imagine penalty kicks by players on the verge of heat stroke, goal-keepers plagued by prehistoric insects. There wouldn't even be enough bandwidth for networks to broadcast the spectacle. No, no, no. The answer was no.

But Brazil's President Lula had Manaus circled on his map.[1] And, as President Obama quipped at the 2009 G20 summit in London, Lula was the man.[2]

The man: Luiz Inácio Lula da Silva. The myth: Lula. The legend: Born in the northeastern state of Pernambuco in the drought-stricken 1940s, Lula didn't taste bread until the age of seven, when his family climbed aboard a dusty flatbed pickup headed a thou-sand miles south to São Paulo, Brazil's steel heart. The Silvas set-tled in its crowded slums. Young Lula dropped out of the sixth grade to shine shoes on the street, bankers and lawyers tossing him coins on their way to their deco high-rises. At fourteen he began working the graveyard shift in a deafening auto plant. By 1964, the year of Brazil's military coup, he was nineteen years old, a vet-eran press machine operator at Volkswagen. During one bleary shift, as Lula reached inside a faulty press to make a repair, the operator lost control. The contraption smashed the pinky finger of Lula's left hand. He waited until his shift ended before heading to the hospital. When at last he arrived, the doctor grimaced. It was too late to save the finger. Off it went.

Decades later, Lula would tell the story on late-night talk shows, funny after all these years, shitty luck that men who wore overalls could recognize. Here was a president who understood everyday Brazilians—and fought for them. During the height of the military dictatorship, when dissenters faced beatings, shock torture, or worse, Lula was a hard-drinking labor leader who stood up to the military men and the factory bosses, raising an army of workers with his gravelly voice.

In 1980, he founded the Partido dos Trabalhadores (PT)—the Workers' Party—which would swell into a national political movement in the years to come, capable of paralyzing the country's automotive industry on behalf of steelworkers. In 1987, as the military men loosened their grip on the government, Lula rose to congress as a champion of the working class. In 1989, he ran for president in the country's first democratic elections in decades, campaigning on a leftist platform inspired by Castro's revolution in Cuba. He lost. Instead of running for reelection to congress in 1990, he toured the country to galvanize the PT, sharing beers, barbecue, and sugarcane rum with workers struggling under 2,000 percent annual inflation. According to one government economist at the time, "Money was like ice melting in their pockets."[3]

In 1994, Lula again ran for president, this time against Fernando Henrique Cardoso, the former minister of finance who tamed Brazil's runaway inflation by replacing its fickle currency with the real. Pegged to the U.S. dollar, the real stabilized markets, attracted foreign investment, and helped Cardoso defeat Lula in the biggest landslide in Brazil's electoral history.[4] In 1998, Lula challenged Cardoso again, criticizing the privatization of the publicly owned telecommunications, mining, and steel industries, but he was spurned by capitalists leery of handing the country over to a self-styled revolutionary who wore Che Guevara T-shirts to rallies.

Soon after the 1998 election, Brazil's economy was infected by the financial contagion in Asia and Russia, a crisis magnified by its ballooning public debt, which had risen to almost 50 percent of GDP. When Cardoso left office in 2002, Lula seized his chance, rallying frustrated Brazilians around a call for sustainable development and a commitment to social justice. "The country can no longer cope with a third lost decade," he wrote in a "Letter to the Brazilian People" outlining his vision for the twenty-first century. "Brazil needs to navigate the open sea of economic and social development."[5]

Hungry for change, Brazilians marched to the polls. Even those who couldn't read could identify the name of their champion on the ballot: Lula. As president, he pledged to give millions of forgotten Brazilians the dignity of work, a steady income, and a comfortable home. A corruption scandal threatened to derail his mandate when investigators discovered that the PT was paying politicians to join its coalition, but Lula dodged the worst consequences, just in time to catch the commodities wave of the 2000s. In the spirit of his friend Hugo Chavez and his inspiration Fidel Castro, Lula doubled down on investments in public health, education, and the national oil company Petroleo Brasileiro, turning Petrobras into a symbol of national wealth and pride. Brazil would never turn around its fortunes by relying on rich countries. It needed to turn its gaze toward fellow developing nations that relied on Brazil for oil, corn, soy, beef, and its iron ore, red as blood.

Millionaires became billionaires. Hundreds of thousands of families living on less than $2.50 a day rose to a burgeoning middle class, many experiencing steady food, electricity, and indoor plumbing for the first time. Bolsa Familia, Luz Para Todos, Agua Para Todos—20 million people cleansed by flowing water and credit, lifted into the light of prosperity.[6]

Lula had been born in a forgotten region, and under his watch no region would be forgotten again. For a century, generals and industrialists had struggled to develop the interior of Brazil. Penetration roads. Telegraph lines. Airstrips. Highways to nowhere. Yet the Amazon remained a backwater. No more. Order and progress would rule the day. God and workers would erect street lamps where once there were candles. God and workers would bring clean water where once there was sewage. God and workers would build riverside schoolhouses where once there were brothels. The Amazon would rise in the twenty-first century as a national treasure. Brazil would pay off its debts to the International Monetary Fund, cement its investment-grade credit rating, and take its rightful place on the world stage alongside the United States, Europe, and China. Lula traveled the world, charming heads of state, even trying to broker peace between Israel and Palestine. By 2009, Lula was sitting side by side with Obama, who marveled at Lula's 70 percent approval rating, affirming what millions of Brazilians already knew: "This is my man."

And so it was settled: if the Brazilian organizing committee wanted to host the Cup of Cups, it would host matches not only in its famed coastal cities and economic hubs but in the bosom of the world's greatest forest. Lula had transformed the country and passed the baton to his handpicked successor, Dilma Rousseff, a fellow leftist guerrilla, tortured at the hands of the military regime, now Brazil's first woman president. When 150,000 visitors arrived in Manaus, they would not see an isolated port city kept on life support by tax incentives. They would see the meeting of the waters, the dark coffee of the Rio Negro and the milky cream of the Rio Solimões, coalescing into the almighty Amazon. They would photograph a glorious white suspension bridge, one of the longest in South America, spanning those waters like a promise. They would carry that image to the four corners of the earth, a message from the country of the future: Brazil is bringing light to the jungle.

. . .

In every host city, World Cup projects were over budget and behind schedule, with most good news dwarfed by political scandals and security crackdowns. Journalists swarmed like mosquitos. Rio de Janeiro lured the most international media with its beatific landscape, legendary soccer stadium, and alluring beach culture, a dream assignment for any writer with a staff job. Then there were freelancers like me, filing stories in host cities like Manaus, where there wasn't as much competition.

Brazil is in my blood. I was adopted from the southern city of Belo Horizonte as an infant, during the waning years of the military regime. When I returned twenty-five years later, the experience stirred something dormant inside me. I'd been daydreaming about this summer since the announcement that Brazil would host the World Cup, with the Olympics to follow in 2016. This was a chance to experience a turning point in the history of my birth country. I spoke serviceable Portuguese and carried two passports: the Brazilian citizenship of my birth and the U.S. citizenship I scored at age thirteen at the sleepy federal courthouse in Portland, Oregon. I'd be lucky to cover my expenses, ducking out of my day job to fly to Brazil with a notebook full of ideas and a camera. What I wanted was some kind of quasi-spiritual experience to help me at last understand where I came from.

I spent the first week of the group stage in Belo Horizonte, soaking up the ambiance, barbecuing with my birth family, and helping my Brazilian brother Ramon with his grocery deliveries while he counted down to the imminent birth of his first daughter. Nobody could understand why I would head up north instead of enjoying the rest of the World Cup in Belo Horizonte, or at least digging for stories in São Paulo or Rio de Janeiro. Anywhere but Manaus.

"It's a better place for me to work," I said. "There won't be as many journalists."

"Just be careful," said Ramon. Like most Brazilians, he'd never been to the Amazon. "It's different up there."

Moeses Martins lives with his wife and three children in a house on stilts along one of the hundreds of *igarapés*—little rivers—that course through Manaus like veins. On a lazy Saturday afternoon during the group stage of the World Cup, I stood on the plank walkway outside his front door, watching home videos on his cell phone. Fifty years ago, when only the most affluent neighborhoods in the city enjoyed electricity and indoor plumbing, thousands of migrants homesteaded on the marshy banks for ready access to clean water and a limitless supply of catfish. Now a reflective orange sign in the middle of the *igarapé* warned against bathing, drinking, or fishing.

Inside, Moeses' wife, son, and daughters relaxed in front of the television, their attention divided between the World Cup match on the screen and the parched gringo talking to their dad. Tomorrow night the United States and Portugal would square off a few kilometers up the road at the Arena da Amazônia, a barely finished $300 million world-class stadium built in the shape of an indigenous basket from materials sent across the Atlantic and upriver from Portugal.

Booms and busts were as natural in Manaus as the rise and fall of the river. During development fevers in the capital, builders jostled for position along the main waterways and avenues; when the fevers inevitably broke, the sprawl could fall to ruin within a few rainy seasons, reclaimed by the forest. With each new cycle came a cyclone of construction with no regard for the vanity projects of dead mayors.

These days a bird's-eye view of Manaus was as tangled and frenzied as the jungle. Over time the city had been divided into crude quadrants—the northern zone, the southern zone, the eastern zone, and the western zone—but only one law seemed to govern development in the city now: the law of gravity, wastewater flowing ever downward to the *igarapés* while bankers chased capital in the wealthy neighborhoods, financing condos and malls on higher ground.

"You have to see this one," said Moeses. Shirtless and in shorts and flip-flops, he leaned against the railing, thumbing through the pictures on his cell phone, a mix of tender family moments and neighborhood catastrophes. Behind him, the creek running through Bairro São Jorge was high but placid. The rains had tapered off and the water was dropping every day. By December it would be a trickle dammed up with trash.

Moeses is in his thirties, like me, but he's had to work thirty times harder in his life and it shows. Like a lot of people in this neighborhood, he came to the capital from a village in the interior, looking for work. Those villages can be as far as twenty-six days away by slow boat. Many of the migrants only make it home again for their mother's funeral.

"Here it is," he said, tapping Play on a video shot from the exact spot where we stood. "This was just last month." The creek was raging, old tires and home appliances tumbling in the current. During the flood, which lasted for days, swells overtook the banks and swept away whole chunks of his neighbors' houses. Green anacondas and spectacled caiman swam through the living room where the kids now fidgeted in front of the television.

Moeses' daughter toddled outside and hugged his legs, smiling up at me. "Oh and this one," Moeses said, pressing Play again. The second clip made the first one seem pedestrian. Across the water, an electrical transformer was in flames, igniting nearby homes and sending plumes of black smoke across the neighbor-hood of São Jorge.

"The World Cup is for rich people," Moeses told me. "The pol-iticians haven't done anything they said they were going to do."

Despite being in the heart of Earth's largest watershed, one in four homes in Manaus lacks running water. Its century-old sewer system accommodates less than 10 percent of the population, leav-ing many residents vulnerable to hepatitis, acute diarrhea, and intestinal parasites in a city where many neighborhoods lack hospitals and many hospitals lack doctors.[7] Moeses and his kids—and families in homes like this across Manaus—are part of the 90 percent who grow nose-blind to the waste outside their windows.

On TV the crowd cheers a goal in the match between Germany and Ghana, an unlikely thriller, live from Fortaleza. "It looks like you guys still enjoy watching the games," I said.

"Yeah," Moeses said. "I mean, what are we supposed to do? I love football. And I have to take the kids to Fan Fest."

That's why, on match day in Manaus, while thousands of drunk, flag-waving foreigners funnel into the city's new stadium, Moeses and his wife dressed the kids in national green and yellow and caught a sweltering bus to Ponta Negra Park to wade into the FIFA Fan Fest, a riverside extravaganza overlooking the Rio Ne-gro and the triumphant new suspension bridge that connected Manaus to nearby Iranduba by road for the first time.

The dark jewel of modern Manaus, Ponta Negra is an enclave of luxury apartment towers, the tallest buildings for thousands of miles, the perfect neighborhood for the international soccer fan-dom to colonize for the world's biggest sporting event. When I first visited years ago, before the initial pillars of the bridge were sunk into the muddy river bottom, the natural riverbank was long and sandy, and on a clear day, you could imagine yourself in Rio de Janeiro, sunbathing under a bright blue sky as the black waves of the Rio Negro lapped the shore. Over time the city dredged the river to expand the beach, inadvertently creating pockets of quicksand that periodically sucked swimmers to their deaths. To this day, swimmers hug the shore, distrustful of the new sand.

Drownings aside, it was all part of the Ponta Negra master plan. During the economic boom of the 2000s, developers targeted this zone as the place to inflate a bubble of creature comforts for the wealthy, far from the troublesome smells and shadowy alleys of the city's old neighborhoods. When Manaus was chosen as a World Cup host city, Ponta Negra construction kicked into hyperdrive. A chic new shopping mall opened a portal to first-world capitalism, complete with monthly rotations of pop culture exhibits in its causeways. Visitors could satisfy hungers they never knew they had at McDonald's ice-cream kiosks, a steakhouse, a twelve-screen cineplex, and dozens of immaculately lit, frigidly air-conditioned retailers where shoppers conspicuously consume Nikes, Dolby Surround Sound systems, and Ford sedans, sparkling like game show prizes at a dealership on the bottom floor. Satiated shoppers could walk it off at the nearby promenade and take in the splendid view: pop concerts pulsing at the amphitheater, yachts bobbing on the water, parasailers banking across the sunsets.

At Fan Fest, Fuleco the Armadillo, the cartoonish yellow and purple World Cup mascot, welcomed Moeses and his family to the celebration. Parking attendants waved towels to lure drivers into their parking spots where, for a few coins, their cars would be kept safe from harm. Thousands of fans filtered through security gates at the amphitheater where matches were projected on a screen the size of a building. Along the mosaic walkway, riverfront restaurants dished up Italian food, hamburgers, ice cream, and cold beer.

For all the bright lights and laughter, there was an undercurrent of potential catastrophe, unsteady elements mixing for the first time. Officers toyed with their stun guns, crackling blue in their hands. A surveillance truck towering with satellite and radio antennas beamed feeds to a central location in São Paulo, where intelligence agents from across the world monitored events in every host city, scanning for threats. Across the country, protestors were marching against FIFA and the government. Black bloc anarchists were smashing luxury cars in Rio de Janeiro. Dissidents in São Paulo were being seized in their apartments. But at Fan Fest in Manaus, the match was ending and the free concert was about to begin, power chords carrying across the river where houses like the Martins home twinkled on the far bank.

Serpents in his living room be damned, Fan Fest was a gift for Moeses. "My kids are never going to see anything like this again in their lives."

Not long after Fan Fest, at a World Cup street party near Praça da Saudade, I played bingo with an elderly woman who told me she barely recognized her own street. The city of Manaus had sponsored a competition to see which neighborhoods had the most World Cup spirit. The winners were deemed *Ruas da Copa*. The woman's neighborhood had won a small budget for party supplies to deck out the streets with green, yellow, and blue paint, streamers, and balloons, plus AV equipment for live entertainment.

"It's strange," she said as our host plucked bingo balls from a wire basket, calling numbers through a brand-new PA system. "I remember when this street first got electric lights."

Electricity or no, few World Cup visitors would stray far down streets like this, instead orbiting the stadium in districts like Vieiralves, a posh neighborhood of real estate offices, plastic surgeons, and English schools that had become an epicenter of tourist hotels, restaurants, and bars tailored to foreign tastes. One old dance club had been renovated into an American football–themed bar named Touchdown, complete with faux reserved parking spaces for global superstars like Tiger Woods, Kobe Bryant, David Beckham, and more, just in case they ever showed up. Crowds of drunk tourists overflowed into the street, while extra police kept the peace, some perched in makeshift watchtowers.

"It feels safe to me," said a software engineer in a U.S. jersey, on his way from one bar to the next. "I mean, I'm from Chicago, and it feels way safer here."

Others would find beds in the city's historic center where dozens of hourly love motels had been converted to traditional lodging to accommodate the surge in visitors. On the evening of the big U.S.-Portugal match, the city's elites gathered alongside foreigners outside the historic Teatro Amazonas to get smashed and take snapshots with whoever was overheating inside the Fuleco the Armadillo costume.

The watch party was a modern daguerreotype of the city during the rubber boom. In the late nineteenth century, as the Industrial Revolution fueled unprecedented demand for rubber, the barons of Manaus enjoyed a lavish lifestyle of yachts, champagne fountains, and pet lions—and enough extra money to send their laundry to Europe. At the time, public services in Manaus were state of the art: a tram system, piped gas and water, and one of the world's first street-lighting systems.[8] In commissioning a Portuguese architect to build the Teatro with materials mostly imported from Europe, the state governor, Eduardo Ribeiro, scoffed at the cost. "When the growth of our city demands it," he said, "we'll pull down this opera house and build another."[9]

The glow of the opulent Teatro Amazonas briefly recast the city as the Paris of the Tropics. More than a century later, the Arena da Amazônia infused the elites of Manaus with a renewed sense of hubris. In the buildup to the games, a viral video on social media showcased residents dancing across the famous landmarks of Manaus, lip-synching to the song "Happy" by Pharrell Williams as if introducing themselves to the world.

Those who weren't mingling with gringos were selling to gringos. The influx of tourist dollars had turned any local with a Styrofoam cooler into an entrepreneur, wandering the crowds with drinks, smokes, and candy for sale. Vendors looked stunned by the price they could command for a reasonably cold can—three or four times what any Brazilian in their right mind would pay. Wandering the plaza, it seemed the target audience for the World Cup was PE teachers—fit, jocular men from around the planet, testing out their same tired pickup lines on Brazilian women.

"I heard girls in Manaus are easy," said one PE teacher from Australia, whose pickup lines didn't make it look easy at all. In all likelihood, he would end up paying for his own story about sex with a Brazilian girl. It was all part of the package, the chance to swoop into the Amazon for a couple days, see a match, take a day or overnight trip into the nearby jungle for some wildlife photos, and get back in time for beer and *bom bom*.

When the U.S.-Portugal match ended in a dramatic 2–2 draw, a clutch of fans draped in American flags swarmed the neoclassical statue in the center of the plaza, singing "Seven Nation Army" to celebrate, as if paying homage to the White Stripes who had rocked the Teatro Amazonas in 2005.

In the coming days, the international media formed a consensus that the World Cup in Brazil was a success. Sure, the stadiums weren't completely finished, but the matches were rousing, and the Brazilians had been gracious hosts, even as their impotent national team stumbled toward a humiliating 1–7 loss to Germany that portended dark days to come.

The night before the last match in Manaus, I unwound with two friends on their balcony on the seventh floor of an apartment building near the stadium. She was a TV reporter; he was an art photographer. My stories were filed, my edits were turned in, and at last I could catch my breath after two weeks of hustling. We swapped cameras, flipped through each other's pictures, talked music and politics, and passed a skunky joint until the air was thick with smoke.

Soon we heard sirens. From the balcony, we could see a glittering motorcade escorting a charter bus to the stadium. I counted sixty police vehicles before I lost track in the river of blue and red lights. A helicopter traced their every turn with a spotlight. It was the Swiss national team en route to the stadium to practice for its match the next day against Honduras, the final game of the World Cup in the Amazon.

On the living room television, there was breaking news: an accident along the river. Earlier that afternoon, a tugboat had collided with a small bridge, collapsing the structure and crushing a critical water line. By match day, 300,000 people in thirty neighborhoods were without water service. The president of the local water-and-sanitation company was on vacation, but he announced that he would return immediately to find a solution. Until then, he advised citizens to start saving water. There was no telling how long it would be before the system was fixed.

2
ISOLATION

A thousand miles from the glowing basket of the Arena da Amazônia, the Ashaninka of Simpatia slept, nested on the misty border of Peru and Brazil. Seven days upriver from the nearest road, the villagers belonged to one of South America's largest tribes, scattered from the Andes to the Amazon watersheds. Keen hunters, fishermen, and farmers, Ashaninka boys learned to fashion arrows and dig canoes from trees while girls learned to plant tidy gardens and weave beautiful robes. Villagers painted their faces with red and black dye to express their moods, as varied as the monsoon clouds that passed over their territory.[1] When villagers fell ill, family members hurried them downriver to the nearest doctor, bartered for gasoline along the way, and paddled if the motor gave up the ghost. When villagers died, they were laid to rest in Eagle's Canyon where the sacred birds collected the dead and the dead rose again as eagles.[2]

On this night, on the outskirts of their settlement, where the clearing met the sandy bank of the Rio Envira, a band of intruders forded the current and crept into the Ashaninka village. They were isolated Indians from a tribe deeper in the jungle. They had come before, seldom taking more than they needed—a cast-iron pot, a hatchet, a mirror—but years ago, the strangers plucked a three-year-old girl from her hammock. Sawatxo was never seen again.[3]

As daybreak lit the river, the Ashaninka woke to fresh barefoot prints around their huts. Women scrambled for their children. Men readied their bows and knives. The *isolados* usually kept their distance from Simpatia, trespassing only when the river was at its nadir. There was enough forest on this reserve for all tribes to live how they wanted, unmolested by the loggers, traffickers, and guerrillas who had tormented the region for years.

Now Ashaninka territory was under threat. The *isolados* had been encroaching for weeks, circling closer each time for reasons nobody in the village could explain. The Ashaninka dispatched scouts to trace the footprints before they disappeared in the rain. A trail of broken branches and discarded fruit pits led to the tiny campsite. Warm ashes, a damp matchbook. Fish bones crawling with ants. A stash of venom gleaned from the skins of striped frogs, the final touch for deadly arrows. Most peculiar among the evidence, as if it had fallen from the sky, a souvenir wallet emblazoned with the crest of the Corinthians of São Paulo, soccer champions of a city across the continent.

Some of the men of Simpatia were ready to defend their land by force, but they had yet to see the intruders face-to-face. Their chief urged calm. The village schoolteacher radioed FUNAI, Brazil's National Indian Foundation, charged with defending the rights and interests of the country's first peoples and protecting the majority of the planet's last tribes living in voluntary isolation from the modern world. Many of those survivors hide here in the western-most state of Acre, a remote borderland in the Amazon basin where the lines between nations are blurred by ancestral claims.

For a generation FUNAI's policy toward these communities has been unambiguous: do not initiate contact. This no-contact philosophy was a belated corrective to centuries of intrusion, exploitation, and infection that had decimated South America's indigenous population from the Age of Discovery to the present day. Modern medicine seldom worked its miracles fast enough to prevent a common flu from annihilating an 11,000-year-old culture. Since 1987, FUNAI has made only five encounters with isolated tribes. In the decades since, Brazil has emerged from a military dictatorship to a democratic and economic power while dozens of isolated tribes hunt—and are hunted—in the remote interior.

Instead of forcing contact with tribes as it had during the second half of the twentieth century, FUNAI keeps a respectful distance, monitoring tribes by plane, satellite, and the gossip of settled groups like the Ashaninka. By gathering proof of Brazil's isolated tribes, FUNAI hopes to sway policymakers in the capital, Brasilia, to increase funding for their protection and expand the borders of indigenous reserves in the Amazon. Veteran FUNAI frontiersman and activist José Carlos Meirelles has spent more than twenty years monitoring the tribes of Acre. Years ago, on the Rio Xinane three hours east of Simpatia, Meirelles helped establish an outpost to monitor local communities and discourage traffickers from using their waterway as an artery for illegal cocaine, timber, and firearms trafficking. In 2004, Meirelles and his team at the base were ambushed by an isolated tribe. He took an arrow to the face, clear evidence that *isolados* sought to avoid outsiders at all costs.

Soon even the most remote forest reserves were no longer a refuge from the outside world. In 2011, FUNAI was forced to abandon the Xinane base when it was surrounded by dozens of heavily armed drug traffickers. Meirelles and his team radioed the Brazilian federal police for help. The traffickers would surely open fire on any hostile Indians in order to secure their trade route.

A week later, federal police arrived at the outpost by helicopter. By then only a single trafficker remained, lugging a backpack of shotgun shells stolen from the base. A broken arrow at the scene suggested that the traffickers and the tribe had crossed paths. It was impossible to know how many may have been killed. The federal agents left quicker than they came.[4,5]

"Since nobody from the Brazilian government is prepared to stay, we made the decision to come here," Meirelles wrote at the time, holding down the base with four other FUNAI staff. The Ashaninka sent a handful of men with rifles to provide reinforcements.

"We are completely surrounded," wrote Meirelles' FUNAI colleague Carlos Travassos, head of the Department of Isolated and Recently Contacted Tribes. "We have nowhere to run. And we will not run until something is done."

For a time there was no further trace of the traffickers or the tribe they encountered. FUNAI and the Ashaninka may have prevented an imminent massacre, or they may have been too late; either way there would be no long-term solution without more federal support. Year by year, pockets of the protected Amazon were falling under the domain of smugglers. Loggers harvested illegal hardwood, sawing down an average of twenty-four trees of no commercial value for every coveted load of mahogany. Drug traffickers used the thick canopy as cover for cocaine manufacturing until it was time to ship their product from clandestine airstrips cut into the jungle. Governments on both sides of the border lacked the will and resources to combat the threats. Unknown numbers of tribes have paid the price in blood.

For the last of the Amazon's isolated Indians, the turn of the twenty-first century was the latest chapter in a saga of hiding. They had escaped to these distant tributaries of the Amazon fleeing centuries of slavery, rape, and massacre by early European invaders and later-day rubber barons. Modern loggers and traffickers have been no less ruthless. Generations of isolated tribes have proven their resilience, teaching their children and grandchildren to evade the white man, to kill or be killed, but poison-tipped arrows are no match for automatic rifles.

The chief of Simpatia told his people that if their isolated neighbors were daring to come so close, it could only be out of desperation. FUNAI warned that contact was imminent.

"It's not normal for such a large group to approach this way," Meirelles said. "Something serious must have happened."[6]

On June 13, 2014, as South America plunged headlong into the first full day of the World Cup, the village schoolteacher in Simpatia radioed a distress signal to FUNAI. Armed with bows and spears, four young *isolados* had brazenly waded across the river in broad daylight. The Ashaninka chief implored families to retreat to their huts. There was no telling how many other invaders lurked in the underbrush across the river. A loose arrow can never be taken back.

The trespassers strode from hut to hut, helping themselves to machetes and metal pots, trying on garments hung out to dry. The clothing worried FUNAI most. A single T-shirt could carry enough infectious agents to wipe out the entire isolated tribe, who had no defenses against modern contagions, even those as common as chicken pox, the flu, or a cold. Officials assured the Ashaninka that a response team was on its way, but since the Xinane River outpost had been abandoned, it could be weeks before a team could reach Simpatia.

In the meantime, officials at FUNAI tried to pinpoint which tribe might be encroaching on the Ashaninka. Anthropologists suspected the *isolados* may have been scouts from a small group that FUNAI had been mapping since 2006 and spotted once before by aircraft in 2008. Flyovers were typically a means of last resort for monitoring isolated tribes. They were expensive, complicated missions with no guarantee of success. Above the hypnotic green static of the forest canopy, it could be nearly impossible to spot tribes who kept on the move as a matter of survival. Successful sightings presented an existential dilemma. The spectacle of an airplane roaring overhead terrified tribes with only the vaguest notions of the outside world. Large tribes tried to repel the otherworldly beast with spells and arrows. In aerial images from 2008, the tribesmen believed to be the ones invading Simpatia are seen glaring skyward, painted head to toe with bright red dye, firing arrows to warn against further trespass. Some anthropologists consider such hostility a positive sign. Tribes on the verge of extinction are prone to cowering at the sight of aircraft. At least this community was confident enough to defend itself. Documenting the location of these reclusive survivors is vital to accelerating the designation of protected lands that could save them from oblivion.

In the era before FUNAI's no-contact policy, flyovers were the least risky and most effective way to introduce isolated tribes—known as wild Indians back then—to the outside world. In the 1940s the federal government created the Central Brazil Foundation with a mandate to open the heart of the country to development. Step one was to cut a network of airstrips to be used for emergency landings, supply drops, and weather stations. The mission was spearheaded by three brothers from São Paulo: Claudio, Orlando, and Leonardo Villas Bôas. Leading a three-year expedition into the scarcely explored headwaters of the Xingu River in the eastern Amazon, the Villas Bôas brothers made first contact with an entire generation of isolated tribes. The profound experience inspired their lifelong devotion to indigenous rights, but they believed that securing those rights required relocating tribes to reserves safe from the relentless march of development. There was only one way to preserve those ancient ways of life: drastic intervention.[7]

The Villas Bôas brothers turned the age-old practice of Indian pacification into a daring art form. According to chronicles of their missions in the 1960s, Orlando and Claudio attempted to reach the Txikão Indians of Mato Grosso state, a warrior tribe succumbing rapidly to disease and violence on the lawless frontier. With no time to waste, the Villas Bôas brothers chose to "soften up" the tribe by air-dropping gifts. Much as the first Europeans in the New World had exploited the Indians' fear of firearms, the Villas Bôas brothers capitalized on the shock and awe of modern aviation, buzzing the Txikão village with a cargo plane in the bright light of day.

Women and children scampered for cover. Men fired arrows at the winged beast. Its rear end gaped open. Packages crashed to the ground. When it retreated over the horizon, Indians stepped cautiously toward the bizarre remnants, probed them with spears, sniffed for signs of danger. Before long, curiosity overwhelmed fear. They sliced open the parcels. Inside were shiny silver pots, soccer balls, and bricks of brown sugar tucked alongside pictures of the Villas Bôas brothers. The tribe tapped the cookware, tasted the sugar, and stared at the strange two-dimensional images, bewildered by the lack of an image on the reverse side.[8]

Flyovers were a risky gambit. American missionaries had tried a similar tactic in Ecuador in the 1950s. That tribe suspected the photographs were the work of sorcerers. When the missionaries landed their plane on the river a few days later, they were speared in the chest. The Villas Bôas brothers had better luck and more experience. When they landed their Piper Cubs outside the Txikão village, holding machetes and mirrors aloft as gifts, they were welcomed peacefully. Soon they convinced the Txikão that their survival depended on leaving before bulldozers devoured every tree in sight.

By the twenty-first century, the Brazilian Air Force was using high-altitude planes with thermal-imaging capabilities to locate tribes without interfering with their daily lives, but identifying and classifying those tribes was as complex as finding them.[9] Anthropologists examined hairstyles, body paint, and agricultural and architectural practices, retracing the evolution of communities that had fissured, fused, and fissured again in the centuries since Europeans fractured their world forever. For the teams who studied these tribes, monitoring their movements was a delicate balancing act. Even after isolated communities became accustomed to the shock of an occasional low-altitude flyover, they struggled to explain what they were seeing. After being contacted, one tribal leader asked an outsider if the planes were traveling on invisible roads in the sky. No matter how the Indians explained these astonishments, those uncanny forces could only be the work of the same whites who brought deadly spirits and slavery to the forest. Over the centuries warnings about white men had spread to the farthest territories. The distant roar of a machine was enough to uproot a village and push its families ever deeper into the riverine borderlands.

As remote groups became harder to locate and verify, some South American governments denied they still existed. President Alan García of Peru insisted that the romantic figure of the jungle native was merely a ruse to prevent oil exploration. Daniel Saba, the former head of the Peruvian national oil company, found the possibility ridiculous: "It's absurd to say there are uncontacted peoples when nobody has seen them."[10]

In the face of such willful ignorance, close-up images of isolated people had more than just anthropological value—they could prove to the world that these tribes were not the stuff of legend. In 2011, FUNAI took a calculated risk, releasing the first-ever aerial footage of an isolated village.[11] From a Cessna circling nearly a mile away, anthropologists filmed the group at high-zoom. A village tucked below the canopy, rows of thatch huts roofed with palm fronds. Naked villagers gazed skyward from a garden brimming with papaya, manioc, and hundreds of annatto shrubs, source of their brilliant red body paint. The tribe seemed robust, healthy, masters of one of the most foreboding ecosystems on the planet.

Released by the NGO Survival International, the short film startled policymakers into action and reignited a debate that had been taking place among environmentalists and anthropologists for more than a century: Should governments extract tribes from their remote villages to help them resist the triple threats of trafficking, disease, and exploitation—or should they expand and protect the patchwork of reserved forest, trusting its first peoples to ensure their own survival?

The images broadcast worldwide by the BBC had the desired effect, stunning viewers and spurring the Peruvian government into action. Visible in the footage was a piece of cast-iron cookware and a machete that dispelled the longstanding myth that these tribes have never had contact with the outside world. On the contrary, their isolation is voluntary, driven by warnings passed down through generations about the hordes of slavers invading their forest. If these tribes have iron tools or machetes, they have been won in battle, stolen from settled groups, or acquired through the sparse trading networks of the remote interior.

"They should be free to choose whether to make contact or not," FUNAI's José Carlos Meirelles told viewers over the roar of the Cessna. "If illegal miners or loggers contact these people, they won't shoot images, they will shoot guns."

3

A WAY BACK FROM OBLIVION

While the Ashaninka of Simpatia guarded their children from the intruders, I obliviously soaked up coffee and air-conditioning at the Cultural Center of the People of the Amazon, a museum in Manaus commemorating the indigenous heritage of the entire basin, from Brazil, Colombia, Peru, Venezuela, Ecuador, and Bolivia to the smaller nations of Suriname, Guyana, and French Guiana. Built in 2007 near the city's industrial district, the center's full-scale replica of indigenous huts and interactive exhibits invited visitors to experience the ingenuity of the Amazon Indians firsthand, just not during the World Cup. For these two weeks, the state of Amazonas had commandeered the center's offices as a pop-up headquarters for foreign journalists, staffed by communications pros who would make sure our stories portrayed the region in a flattering light.

Drenched in sweat, I arrived by mototaxi and handed my ripe helmet back to the driver, who zipped on to his next fare. In the foyer, a bank of HD televisions intended for educational videos instead broadcasted a group stage match unfolding a thousand miles away in São Paulo. A guard leaned against his security hut, smoking a cigarette and watching the action. I followed the posted arrows to a conference room labeled with a freshly printed sign: OPEN MEDIA CENTER.

For a writer racing to a deadline, the Open Media Center was an ideal pit stop, home to free Wi-Fi, forced AC, and a refrigerated water cooler, which gurgled as I chugged cup after cup. The staff wore bright yellow shirts, emblazoned with the state logo and the World Cup mascot, Fuleco the Armadillo. Naturally, any news tips they gave would point you to the stories Fuleco the Armadillo wanted you to hear. State-sponsored media excursions should be greeted with a double dose of skepticism. A triple dose in countries with a semi-free press, like Brazil. Yet in a few minutes, I would join a group of international reporters on a trip across the river to watch the Brazil-Cameroon match with the Tururukari-Uka tribe, a village welcoming its first foreign visitors to a carefully curated experience of their history and culture.

In recent years, ecotourism had blossomed in the Amazon, at a cost to the forest and the dignity of its tribes. For a reasonable fee, countless guides in Manaus could take visitors out for an overnight glimpse of the rain forest just beyond the city. More sophisticated tour operators coordinated large group trips to remote lodges for a more immersive experience of the forest, its animals, its tribes, and even their psychedelic spiritual rituals. Along the way, those outsiders carried technology, pop culture, drugs, and alcohol to communities only a generation or two removed from ancient customs. Some nefarious gringos pay top dollar to plunge deep into the wilderness, where they can poach jaguars and caiman or satisfy carnal appetites free from the watchful eye of the authorities. Government officials worried that an influx of hundreds of thousands of foreign men during the World Cup would aggravate the insidious, age-old exploitation of women and children on the river. Our visit was a chance to see the government's vision for a gentler, sustainable ecotourism.

Besides, story or no story, after a week of World Cup fever, this was an escape from the sweltering city in an ice-cold charter bus.

Our chaperone was Rodrigo, a handsomely scruffy twenty-something who helped coordinate the Open Media Center and its crack team of interns. He greeted reporters at the folding door of the bus, looking a touch hungover behind his sunglasses. I stepped aboard and found a window seat. Aboard were two Chinese journalists—a young woman from an independent blog and a young man from the state media agency who refused to acknowledge the independent blogger. There were two middle-aged Portuguese men, a reporter and a photographer, flirting pathetically with the undergraduate interns and the Chinese blogger. Lastly, there was a woman from a Bolivian newspaper, another hangover sufferer. The driver ground the bus into gear and pulled away from the center as the traffic swelled with fans hurrying home to watch the match, Brazilian flags fluttering from their antennas.

Our guide to the world of the Tururukari-Uka was Marinaldo Guedes, a middle-aged man who looked like a cross between an inspirational speaker and a linebacker coach. Turns out he was a little bit of both. A professional executive trainer, Guedes had spent the last two years working with the young chief of the Tururukari-Uka on his leadership skills. In that time, Guedes had become a lay expert on the history of the Omagua ethnic group, and as we labored through prematch traffic, his college-aged daughter, Loanna, passed out a two-page oral history of the tribe, which she had painstakingly translated into English for her father.

Guedes stood in the aisle, bracing himself against hard turns while he spouted facts about the tribes of Amazônia. As recently as the 1960s, he told us, anthropologists had presumed the Omagua were one of the ethnic groups that had nearly vanished, but since then, they have bounced back and become leaders in indigenous politics. Loanna served as a translator for those on the bus who didn't speak Portuguese.

It was my first time crossing the magnificent Rio Negro Bridge. When I first came to Manaus, it was only possible to cross by boat or costly ferry. Now four lanes of traffic breezed over the 2-mile-long suspension bridge while cargo ships and water taxis streaked across the river below. At last we descended onto a highway still under construction. What was once a two-lane penetration road to nowhere was now being bulldozed into a four-lane expressway to nowhere. Already the city of Manaus had spilled over the opposite bank, ushering in a new wave of development with billboards for condominiums, golf courses, and jungle lodges. Here was the rub: since the turn of the century, 75 percent of deforestation has occurred within an estimated 50 kilometers of roads. President Lula knew the statistics and declared it didn't matter: "I don't want any gringo asking us to let an Amazon resident die of hunger under a tree," he told the audience at a 2009 Amazon summit.[1] Now construction workers in blue uniforms milled from machine to machine, burning trees and leveling the red earth. This was all supposed to have been finished before the World Cup, in time for these men to be at home watching today's match with their sons and daughters, but like most World Cup projects in Brazil, it was facing uncertain delays.

Less than fifteen minutes from Manaus, our cell phones lost their signals. The development had receded to periodic gas stations and banana farms, with some parcels of land smoldering from controlled burns while other parcels remained untamed. The utility poles on the side of the road had been planted as recently as 2012, the city's tentacles extending transformer by transformer. With every mile of new asphalt came telephone service and electricity, dragging everyone along this roadway, like it or not, into the twenty-first century.

After an hour-long ride south of the capital, the bus driver let off the gas and hooked a right on a dirt road, nice and slow. The axles groaned on the descent to the edge of a murky bog. The air breaks hissed.

"Here we are," said Guedes, herding us off the bus. The dirt road disappeared into the water where a long canoe sat empty on the shore.

Guedes stood at the edge. "This is the traditional way of announcing your visit," he said. Cupping his hand to his mouth, he hollered into the forest, a wavering of the tongue that sounded like the call of a horny bird.

We listened to the chirping jungle, waiting for a reply. Nothing. Then, just as Guedes cupped his hands to call again, we heard the faint bleating of a World Cup noisemaker.

The Omagua. "Born from water." Like water, free and mighty.

Five centuries ago, at nightfall during the dry season, Omagua men would float silently in dugout canoes waiting for nests of giant Arrau turtles to come ashore. The creatures made land to lay eggs by the thousands, a rich bounty for the tribe. When the female turtles finished their labor, the men swept the shore to collect the warm eggs and flip the mothers on their shells before they could waddle back to the river.

While the turtles squirmed, the braves drilled a small hole in each of their shells. One by one they roped the captives to their canoes like stringing a necklace and towed them to the village. In wooden enclosures beside each hut, the Omagua fattened their fresh stock on foliage, until it was time for harvest: slick eggs, nutritious meat, breastplates to be sharpened and fired into hatchet blades.

For centuries, ingenuity and sound governance made the Omagua one of the most prosperous ethnic groups in the Amazon basin.[2] They supplemented their homegrown supply of turtle protein with crops of maize, manioc, and sweet potatoes cultivated in the fertile river mud. From the forest, they gathered pineapples, guava, nuts, and honey, planting reserve crops along their hunting trails to satisfy warriors on long expeditions. They mastered slash-and-burn farming and milled salt from the ash of burnt palm leaves. In a climate where humans are as inconsequential as ants, they willed the landscape to meet their needs, living in abundance where lesser tribes perished.

From the chronicles of Spanish friars, we know that February 11, 1542, marked the beginning of the end of Omagua rule in the Amazon. On a gray afternoon when clouds rumbled over the canopy, the tribe witnessed the arrival of a strange ship. Sixty ghostly white men in a leaky brigantine, famished, eyes sunken in their skulls. They reeked of fear, no more dangerous than children. Omagua chief Aparia called his tribe to attention. Prepare these visitors a feast.

The Spanish expedition had begun months earlier in Quito, Ecuador, with thousands of soldiers, workhorses, pigs, hunting dogs, and Indian slaves on a quest for the fabled El Dorado, a city so rich with gold that its royals were rumored to powder themselves with glittering dust each morning, only to wash themselves clean at night. The landscape proved more treacherous than any the Spaniards had ever encountered. To hack through this jungle was to seek your own death. Each cliffside pass, each bend in the river only revealed a thousand new trees, armed with thorns, guarded by poisonous orchids, crawling with serpents or spiders the size of the Spaniards' helmets. Ungodly diseases wiped out entire columns of soldiers before anyone could understand what was happening. By night, insects burrowed their way into fresh wounds to hatch eggs and feed on rotting flesh. Soon the original party was fractured in body and spirit, survivors urged forward only by the promise of gold or the threat of execution.

Edible game was scarce, and soon progress slowed to a crawl. A decision point: turn back to Quito or send a scouting party ahead to search for food? Half the group returned to Quito. The other half, led by Captain Francisco de Orellana, assembled a flotilla and forged downriver, desperate to find open land where they could hunt and return to the others with provisions. Along the way, Orellana's party encountered friendly tribes who offered food in exchange for textiles and trinkets. When hostile tribes fired arrows from the riverbank, the Spanish fired back with gun blasts, scattering birds from shore to shore and terrifying the Indians with their first whiff of modern weaponry. In the villages he could pacify, Orellana held ceremonies to formally annex their lands to Spain while the Indians looked on, puzzled by the foreign rituals.

Yet for all the strength of the Spanish firepower, bullets couldn't be eaten. By the time Orellana's party descended into the Amazon basin, they were starved to the point of insanity, gnawing shoe heels as they floated the maddening labyrinth of water and jungle that they would come to call the Green Inferno. How could any man survive, let alone thrive, in this false Eden?

Then came the day of salvation, the day of damnation. Orellana's waterlogged vessel was met by canoes full of Omagua bearing fruit and eggs. For eight weeks the Spaniards called Chief Aparia's village home. Day by day, the Omagua nursed the visitors back to health. Orellana, who had an affinity for native languages, earned their trust through sheer conviction and curiosity. The chief helped Orellana expand his fledgling vocabulary of Tupi words while Omagua men helped the Spanish gather resin to patch up their boats. Chief Aparia could never have known that these few dozen whites were the tip of a spear that would spill the blood of his children, his grandchildren, and generations to come.

Fortified for the next leg of their journey, Orellana and his men drifted another 1,000 kilometers along the river, crossbows cranked, harquebuses loaded, trained on anyone who dared to attack them. They found tribes who made beautiful ceramics, hundred-gallon jars that rivaled some of the finest porcelain in the known world. Village storehouses brimmed with food: cotton, maize, yucca, beans, peanuts, dried fish, and all manner of fruits and vegetables—Eden realized. Their strength and greed revived, the Spaniards pillaged their way downstream until word of their violence outpaced them. Before long they were met at every bend by warriors who attacked with clubs and spears, armored with shields of alligator and manatee skins, fighting to their last breath.

The Spanish drifted on, holding out hope that the river would eventually spill into the Atlantic. Only the overwhelming power of their firearms kept Orellana's expedition alive, stopping attackers in their tracks and scattering the survivors in primal fear long enough for the flotilla to escape. One friar recalled a battle that lasted through the night, arrows flittering from the trees, the ungodly calls of savages like demons in the black. At sunrise Orellana ordered his men to hang the bodies of several Omagua from a tree. The friar, who by then had been stuck by arrows in his ribs and left eye, wrote solemnly of the dangling corpses: "It was done in order that the Indians from here on might become afraid of us."

It was the first of many atrocities that the natives would suffer at the hands of European invaders. By the mid-eighteenth century, when French courtier Charles-Marie de La Condamine toured the Amazon, the Omagua territory along the main river had been abandoned for the interior. La Condamine took note of a peculiar material the Omagua called *heve*.[3] The Indians gathered it from bleeding trees to craft shatterproof bottles, waterproof boots, and bouncing balls for children. Within a hundred years, this curious resin would become an indispensable material of the industrial age—rubber—extracted drop by drop from the veins of rubber trees by descendants of the Omagua, while kin of the original tribe fled deeper into the headwaters until it was thought they had vanished from the earth.

Not long after we heard the call of the World Cup noisemaker from across the bog, a long canoe nudged through the trees, paddled by two young men. One wore a white tunic and a red stripe of paint across his eyes; the other sported a bright yellow T-shirt emblazoned with the image of Fuleco the Armadillo. As they drew closer to the shore, it became clear the young men were boys.

"These two are ten years old," Guedes said without introducing them. "After the age of nine, they are men. There is no adolescence here."

The men welcomed their first load of passengers aboard, one by one, ladies first. The interns stepped into the canoe, which threatened to capsize under their clumsy weight. It took three trips for the boys to ferry everyone to the waterside village. During the wait between trips, we snapped pictures and swatted mosquitos. The bus driver had already settled into a nap behind the steering wheel. By the time I boarded, the pilot up front looked exhausted. I was tempted to take an oar to give him a breather, but he seemed too proud to accept any help.

It was a short ferry through the flooded forest, barbets squawking in the trees. A hand-carved sign welcomed us to the opposite shore, a modest clearing with plank-walled, thatch-roofed huts arranged around an open-air schoolhouse at the center. After centuries of semi-nomadic life, the Tururukari-Uka settled here in 2004 when Chief Waldomiro Cruz persuaded local authorities that his tribe needed a stable home to provide a better education for their children. Now the tribe, which consisted of fifteen families and fifty-six people, farmed, hunted, and fished nearby for sustenance. During the dry season, their plot is about the size of seven soccer fields, including an actual soccer field with goalposts fashioned from tree branches. During the wet season, the water rises high enough that villagers can fish from the windows of their huts.

Today the tribe had arranged school desks, amphitheater-style, in front of a wide-screen television in the shade of palm trees at the heart of the village. Atop a nearby hut, a Sky TV dish pointed to the clouds, harnessing satellites in outer orbit to capture the World Cup in glorious high definition.

We were welcomed by Chief Waldomiro's grandson, Francisco Uruma, a thirty-five-year-old whose quick smile belied his piercing eyes. Shirtless and barefoot, he wore the traditional wooden headdress that his ancestors wore from infancy, tightened around their skulls to mold the long, sloped forehead they considered a mark of beauty. The Omagua abandoned that practice a century ago, but a decorative version of the headdress remains. A few of the village women welcomed us with fruit juice served in gourds. The sweet aroma of roasting tambaqui—a river fish that leaps from eddies to feed on low-hanging berries—wafted from a nearby fire. On the television, the Brazilian national team lined up at midfield for their national anthem, players wiping tears from their eyes as they mouthed the words.

"We apologize for the low volume on the television," said Francisco. "Our chief is sleeping, and he is very ill these days."

• • •

By the time Waldomiro Cruz, future chief of the Omagua, was born in the hinterlands outside Manaus, his mother tongue had been cut from the mouth of Amazônia. To quell Indian uprisings during the eighteenth and nineteenth centuries, Europeans prohibited native languages, forcing ethnic groups from across the basin to blend with other tribes in the region, seeking safety in numbers. Tribes like the Omagua splintered or fled deeper into the rain forest. Sapped by detribalization, hundreds of unique cultures that relied on oral tradition lost their origin stories within two generations.

By the time the rubber boom busted in the early twentieth century, Brazil's plutocratic monarchy had evolved into a plutocratic republic eager to expand federal power. Indigenous communities witnessed their landscape transformed by telegraph lines, airstrips, and penetration roads. Young Waldomiro grew up during an era when a zealous military dictatorship seized control of the country, backed by U.S. agencies trying to keep communism from gaining a foothold in South America. For these midcentury military men, developing the Amazon frontier was a matter of national security. They created the Free Economic Zone Superintendence (SUFRAMA) in Manaus to jump-start its languishing port. The last vestiges of indigenous life in Brazil were soon relegated to distant riverside villages and areas like the Xingu Indigenous Reserve, the legacy of the Villa Bôas brothers, where tribes could find solace in one of the last pristine folds of the forest, removed from their ancestral territory but protected from whites and the modern world.

By 1972, Waldomiro Cruz had seen enough to understand that his people were on the brink. In a final bid to save his family, he left the safety of his home village for a nearby town. For the first time in his life, he witnessed running water, electricity, and automobiles. He begged an audience with the mayor and pleaded for a teacher of indigenous languages to return to his village and revive the weak pulse of his tribe.

Omagua? Nobody believed him. Their staple food of arrau turtles had nearly disappeared from these waters, harvested for lamp oil during the rubber boom. By all accounts, the last Omagua had died decades ago.

All accounts were wrong.

For the next three decades, Waldomiro Cruz helped reconstitute the last remaining Omagua families in the region, traveling from village to village, introducing kin to kin, leading a charge to Brasilia to battle for land rights. The Omagua would not be relegated to a park. They would rekindle their legends in the face of bulldozers and chainsaws.

Today the highest-profile symbol of indigenous culture in the Amazon is the multimillion-dollar stadium erected for the World Cup. Designed in the shape of a woven indigenous basket, the arena was protested by Indian leaders who argued it appropriated their culture. Chief Waldomiro was unable to attend the demonstration, too frail for boat rides and intertribal visits. By then he was resting in a small hut at the center of the Tururukari-Uka village. From his sickbed he gives each member of the tribe a daily blessing. His children and grandchildren worry that he has grown quiet.

"I am trying to prepare myself for the great trip," he tells them.

In the twenty-first century, the survival of the Omagua rests with Chief Waldomiro's grandson, Francisco Uruma, who assured us the Tururukari-Uka will not go extinct under his watch. "I want every child to have a future," he said. "I want them to adapt and be prepared for today's world."

Since 2012, Francisco had been modeling that adaptability by working closely with Guedes, whom he called "Professor." They had met a year earlier when Guedes was researching indigenous culture on behalf of an executive coaching firm in São Paulo. Francisco seemed eager to lead but uncertain about what his tribe needed. Guedes had built his career in corporate training, a world apart from the challenges Francisco's tribe faced, but coaching is coaching, *né*? Besides, the tribe needed all the help it could get, and if it worked, the experiment could prove the effectiveness of Guedes's coaching model. Soon after, Guedes began visiting the village twice a month for one-on-one consultations with the young chief, preparing him to preserve his culture at a time when fiber optic cables were the new penetration roads.

"This is the only tribe in Brazil—and possibly the only tribe in the world—that has enlisted the help of leadership coaching," said Professor Guedes with the conviction of an infomercial pitchman. "We focus on improving Francisco's interpersonal skills, his self-awareness, his self-motivation, and his ability to respond to new situations."

This busload of gringo reporters was one of those new situations, a soft launch for Francisco and his tribe. With the support of Rodrigo and his interns, Professor Guedes and the Amazonas state tourism agency were helping Francisco and his people use the World Cup in Manaus to kick-start an ecotourism business that could help small tribes balance heritage and modernity in the information age.

An important early lesson: tourists don't like mosquitos. The interns had forgotten to pack bug spray. One of the village grandmothers hurried to assist with a natural bug repellant that smelled less noxious than the bottled stuff but didn't seem all that repellant to bugs. No matter. Professor Guedes refocused the group on a super awkward photo-op before the game started. Without asking, the Portuguese photographer jammed his camera lens paparazzi-style inches away from Francisco's face, snapping a dozen close-ups. The village children emerged from their huts and swarmed the photographer's legs, having never seen a camera so large. Those of us with less impressive gear milled about with compact cameras and smartphones, trying to get a shot of the tribe without another journalist in the frame.

We lined up for lunch in the village schoolhouse. Until the age of twelve, the children would take all of their classes here, learning traditional subjects like math and geography alongside the Omagua language, writing poems about their tribal legends, and practicing ceremonies, songs, and dances. Last year, Francisco joined other indigenous leaders in Brasilia to address lawmakers about the need for more land, better services, and a schoolhouse of their own.

"The government doesn't know our reality," he said. "We have basic desires. Water. Health. Education. In Brasilia, I met people who share the same vision. I learned how we can take matters into our own hands."

For Francisco, that meant turning his village into an ecotourism start-up. His goal was for each of the fifteen families to earn $500 per month independently of other tribes to preserve the integrity of their language and culture. Over time, he wanted to invite up to fifty visitors per day to sample their food and drink, witness their dance and music, buy artisanal crafts, and even have their marriage vows renewed by a shaman. I cringed at the thought of the place listed on Airbnb or highlighted in someone's dog-eared copy of *Lonely Planet Brazil*. Even a few dozen people per week would leave a massive footprint on a community this size. Harvesting enough fish and fruit to feed that many guests would scramble their daily and seasonal routines, not to mention the cultural pollution—glimpses of new technologies, medicines, music, and fashion that could no longer be turned off with a click of the TV remote.

After the national anthems were played in the stadium, we all took seats to watch the match. There was popcorn and fresh-squeezed passion fruit juice, served in decorative gourds that made the drinks seem all the sweeter. The fish smelled close to done; we would feast during halftime. Rodrigo and the Bolivian journalist went back for second and third cups of juice in hopes the native fruits might cure their hangovers. Fortunately or unfortunately for them, there was no alcohol among the Tururukari-Uka. Too many tribes have succumbed to alcoholism and drug addiction, and federal law prohibits selling alcohol or drugs to indigenous communities. Naturally thousands of smugglers disobey that law every day, but under no condition will Francisco allow visitors to enter the village with beer or booze, Fuleco the Armadillo be damned.

When the match began, I watched with a mix of wonder and unease, reluctantly banging handmade drums to celebrate Brazil's goals. Cameroon was such a mismatch for Brazil that the tribe began to lose interest halfway through the first period, but Francisco and Professor Guedes knew that cameras were watching. Dramatizing the tribe's adoration of soccer was a way to demonstrate how the community had integrated with the rest of Brazil and the World Cup narrative at large. Francisco goaded his tribe into cheering for the match even as attention was waning, but soon it was halftime and the food was ready.

While we picked through our fish, careful not to choke on the needle-like bones, the children performed dances and songs in the schoolhouse until the Portuguese photographer was satisfied with his shots. Two little girls demonstrated their prodigious ability to shimmy up the trunks of palm trees. The interns had their wrists and faces painted with bright red berry juices. Then, just when

I thought the postcolonial awkwardness had reached its zenith, Professor Guedes kicked it up a notch.

"Come over here," he said, summoning one of the little girls to stand beside him. She held still as he pointed to her lighter skin and eyes as evidence that her blood is not pure Omagua. "You see," he said, "over the centuries, the Omagua bloodline mixed with other tribes." Even as tribes coalesced to resist violence and oppression, they remained keen to the differences between ethnic groups. Now the little girl smiled as if she were living history, superior to any exhibit back at the cultural center.

Where did Francisco's culture end and Professor Guedes's coaching begin? How could any stories we filed about this experience possibly capture this tribe for the American, Portuguese, Bolivian, or Chinese readers absorbing the tale over coffee or tea? Before the match resumed, I snuck away from the group to wander the village unattended. Walking a narrow path between huts, I startled a few chickens and a bony cat. As it turned out, there wasn't just one communal television. Where the land met the water, I heard halftime commentary warbling from a small hut. Inside, I saw another man, about Francisco's age, slung in a hammock, watching the game alone on TV. We locked eyes. His scowl made it clear he was not pleased by our visit.

The second half of the match was getting started. I returned to my seat in front of the TV. Professor Guedes seemed to sense my discomfort.

"I know," he said, looking almost apologetic. "They can show you more than twenty different things about Omagua culture. How they build their houses. How to spear a fish. And here we are watching soccer. But the World Cup has been a good warm-up for them. A chance to see what it's like to have visitors."

To ensure his tribe's future, Francisco was being urged to sell a romanticized vision of the past. What were the consequences of asking these children to perform for outsiders? There was already no adolescence for the Omagua. Will childhood vanish, too? These boys and girls had learned how to pose for cameras. If this ecotourism vision blossomed, soon thousands of their pictures would materialize on the social networks of the world—*hashtag Amazon hashtag Omagua hashtag wow*. Would filtered and tagged tourist pictures be the last evidence of this ancient way of life?

The blowout was nearly complete. The reporters slowly dropped their journalistic guises. Done taking notes, the Chinese state media reporter—who spoke Portuguese more formally than anyone in the village—initiated a game of soccer with the kids and our fellow reporters, dividing everyone into equally matched teams.

Life is too short for feigned objectivity. I stepped on the field, playing keep-away with a little boy who couldn't stop laughing at my clumsy footwork. Yet even as we passed the ball around, my wonder melted into worry. As tribes were encouraged to compete for ecotourists, what lengths would they go to for attention? How long before demand for more Stone Age experiences pushed thrill-seekers deeper into the rain forest to contact the tribes at greatest risk of exploitation?

The Portuguese cameraman recorded video of the match on his iPad. When he knelt down and played it back, the children huddled over his shoulders to watch themselves on video, perhaps for the first time. Professor Guedes and Francisco told us that the benefits of these visits outweighed the potential consequences, but if the young chief had any reservations, he wasn't about to betray those doubts to a gaggle of reporters. I had to wonder what conversations took place in the privacy of Chief Waldomiro's hut. What songs and dances were not for sale?

I'd experienced the theme park version of tourism in the Amazon years before, piranha fishing and caiman spotting and rubber tapping to make souvenir condoms—homogenized thrills that usually lined the pockets of corporate operators in Manaus. Francisco's vision was to showcase the daily life of a single tribal group, and if there proved to be an appetite for that experience, at least the profits would go directly to the families in this village. When he talked about Omagua culture, he spoke not about the past but about the future. But maybe their future was the past in a friendlier disguise.

When it was time to part ways, the boys began ferrying the visitors back across the dark water toward the waiting headlights of the charter bus. The mosquitos redoubled their efforts to suck us dry. Before the canoe even reached the opposite bank, everyone was sorting through the pictures on their cameras, touchscreens aglow like will-o'-the-wisps on the marsh.

"What happens when the kids grow up and leave the village?" I asked Francisco as I waited for the boys to return. "It's great that they want to go to college, but will they come back?"

"The way of life is different now," he said. "When they leave the tribe to study, it's hard to return and become farmers." That year alone, six young members of the Tururukari-Uka would graduate from the university in Manaus. Another was a literature student in Belém who performed traditional Omagua poetry and dance on the side. Yet another was studying law. "Our vision is for our children to go to the city and show people our way of life, to learn how to become doctors and teachers and lawyers, then come back and help our tribe in other ways."

Francisco's teenage nephew Tashira was training to be an archer at the 2016 Olympics in Rio de Janeiro, dreaming of being the first indigenous athlete to represent Brazil in the games. It was Francisco who taught the boy how to shoot in the way of their forefathers, using a weapon fashioned himself, the way Uncle Francisco had been taught by Grandfather Waldomiro, the way Grandfather Waldomiro had been taught by his own grandfather, bow fishing on the river at dusk when the tambaqui flickered in the eddies like flecks of gold and silver. There wasn't much time left for teaching, but there were so many lessons left to teach.

"Our culture will not fall into oblivion," Francisco said as I stepped into the canoe. "Twenty years from now, when my grandchildren are alive, I don't want them to know their people only through books."

4

SITE X

In the village of Simpatia, the Ashaninka lay awake in their hammocks, ears keen to the calls of honeycreepers and spider monkeys chattering in the canopy. Any sounds peculiar to the hour could be harbingers of an ambush. FUNAI had assured them that support was on the way, but for now the government was only a crackling voice on the radio.

At last on the morning of June 26, 2014, the villagers heard the drone of a distant motorboat. A small FUNAI team, accompanied by veteran frontiersman Meirelles, rounded the bend in the river. At the sight of outsiders, the tribe that had been raiding the village dissolved like specters into the forest.[1]

It had been almost two weeks since the original distress call. The abandonment of the nearby Rio Xinane outpost may have cost FUNAI the opportunity to make timely contact with the isolated tribe. If the *isolados* returned home with infected clothing, disease could sweep through their entire village. More likely, though, they were still lingering on the outskirts of Simpatia, taking measure of the new arrivals. There were stories of other isolated tribes who had surveilled their settled neighbors for weeks from the cover of the bush; when at last they emerged, they knew the names of every settled tribesmen.

If FUNAI sent a team into the forest to look for the tribe, it would only spur them to flee deeper. There was nothing to do but wait. Meirelles and the FUNAI team passed time among the Ashaninka, gathering testimonials, updating their records, looking for any new traces of visitors up and down the riverbank.

A hemisphere away, the University of Missouri anchors the city of Columbia, a bastion of undergraduate hijinks, first-tier research, and college football pageantry surrounded by farmland parcels neat as the squares on a waffle iron. In the unassuming offices of the Department of Anthropology, associate professor Robert S. Walker and his team of student assistants keep watch over the last of the Amazon's isolated tribes, analyzing geospatial data with the potential to determine their fate.

A bearded father of two, looking like a lumberjack who traded his axe for a library card, Dr. Walker is the director of a project that studies the protection of isolated tribes, sponsored by *National Geographic*, his university, and a crowdfunded network of small donors.[2] He and his research partner, Dr. Dylan Kesler, a quantitative conservation biologist who studies bird migrations, examine high-resolution satellite imagery to find, assess, and map isolated villages pixel by pixel, applying the same technology that millions of commuters use every day to the most remote swaths of the Amazon rain forest.

Their methodology blends cultural anthropology, open-source and commercial satellite imagery, and good old-fashioned math. Aside from the occasional tree fall, there are few reasons for clearings to exist in the dense interior of the Amazon, other than human settlement. With that in mind, Walker and Kesler estimate that on publicly available Landsat 8 imagery, measuring 30 meters by 30 meters per pixel, as little as two contiguous pixels of cleared forest is evidence that a small tribe may be settled nearby, practicing slash-and-burn agriculture. Once they have zeroed in on a potential village, they task a commercial satellite to capture updated imagery of the focal areas, then overlay polygons on the results to measure clearings, houses, and gardens. In their final analysis, they use moderate resolution imaging spectroradiometer (MODIS) data from NASA to verify that fires in those areas have been detected. Graphing the results, the team can reliably estimate the size of villages and track whether they are growing, holding steady, or at risk of imminent extinction.

According to Survival International, the Brazilian Amazon is home to at least a hundred isolated tribes—more than any other region in the world.[3] So far Walker and his colleagues have collected between ten and fourteen years of data on eight isolated groups in the rain forest. Their charts and graphs tell the story of tribes fusing and fissuring through peace and war that can ultimately benefit their genetic viability. Other groups shrink and grow as a result of threats from the outside world that force them to abandon their agricultural practices and merge with other dwindling tribes in hiding. Based on their data, Walker and his colleagues are making the case that advocates of no-contact policies toward isolated tribes are dead wrong. When a tribe is in danger of being wiped out, they argue, governments should proactively contact those groups under tightly controlled circumstances before it's too late.

For many tribes, time is already running out. As the genetic pool shrinks and communities resort to a life on the run from loggers and traffickers, they rapidly lose technological, linguistic, and cultural knowledge. According to Walker and his colleagues, organizations like Survival International are blinded by romantic notions of indigenous life, recklessly gambling that these tribes can withstand the triple threat of development, disease, and black markets.

"The common assumption that all contacts with the outside world are devastating is not necessarily true," Walker, Kessler, and Professor Kim Hill of Arizona State University write in a 2016 paper.[4] Based on the most recent imagery, Site X, a tribe fleeing loggers on the border of Peru and Brazil, appear to be hovering around thirty to fifty individuals, the minimal population for a tribe "to have reasonable long-term survival prospects."

Their work suggests that some signs traditionally interpreted as evidence of indigenous communities feeling threatened are, to the contrary, evidence of healthy growth. When tribes go to war, it's part of a fissuring process that's been happening for generations before Orellana and his flotilla of bloodthirsty Spaniards descended on the Amazon. When communities reach a certain size, factions develop and they split in two. When tribes fire arrows at passing planes, they're feeling strong. You only take aim at an unidentified flying object when you believe you're better off fighting than hiding.

Yet if these tribes seem confident, it's only because they have no idea what they're up against. "The evidence that most isolated populations are viable in the long-term appears flimsy," write Walker and his colleague, pleading for South American governments to band together with the UN to develop a cohesive approach to protecting isolated tribes. "Well-organized contacts have the potential to save lives and decrease the risk of ethnolinguistic extinctions."

The notion of proactively contacting tribes horrifies advocates at Survival International who warn that any policy shift in this direction would play directly into the hands of those who wish to open the Amazon to further development. "What tribe would abandon isolation if it could first study Pine Ridge or the Guarani, and if it knew that many of its children would die as a result?" refuted Survival International president Stephen Corry. "There are plenty of contacted tribes who do know what happens and respond by striving to protect isolated relatives from contact."[5]

Yet despite admirable indigenous efforts, no single tribe or government may be strong enough to resist the forces of multinational development. Seven of the eight groups Walker and his colleagues study are listed as critically endangered.

"There is a unanimous consensus that people stay isolated mostly because of fear of extermination and slavery," write Walker and his coauthors. "People want to trade, particularly for access to steel machetes and axes, and they crave exposure to new ideas and new opportunities. Humans are a gregarious species that intrinsically desire and benefit from outside interactions with other groups." In a provocative claim, the researchers argue that tribes would be unlikely to "choose isolation if they had full information."

Three days after FUNAI arrived in Simpatia, the isolated Indians emerged again from the forest. One, two, three men appeared on the steep riverbank, naked save for loincloths. Others soon peered through the trees. Four, five, six, seven in all. There were adolescents among them, two boys and two girls. The men advanced first, wielding machetes, bows, and arrows. One brandished a rifle, although even from a distance it was clear that he didn't know how to use it.

Suspecting the tribe spoke a language from the Panoan family, FUNAI had staffed its intervention team with two Panoan interpreters. From across the river, they greeted the tribe with a mix of encouraging phrases, hoping at least one friendly combination would stick.

In shaky handheld video from the scene, the interpreters cup their hands to their mouths and call across the waist-deep river. The *isolados* call back, waving their arms, singing. One gestures to his stomach as if hungry. Another wades across cautiously, striding against the current. One interpreter steps into the river with two bushels of fresh bananas. On shore, the anthropologists chatter gleefully, on the verge of contact. Off camera, Ashaninka children giggle.

At last the tribesmen meet the interpreter midstream. One takes the first bushel of bananas, then the second, tearing into the food without hesitation. The interpreter offers his hand, but the distrust in the air is heavy, each step toward the modern world a step toward oblivion. At any moment, the *isolados* could scatter into the forest.

FUNAI had precious little time to discover who these people were and why they chose to reveal themselves to the world of bulldozers, chainsaws, and assault rifles. Emboldened by the first moments of the encounter, the other *isolados* descended the bank and crossed the river. Standing a safe distance from the Ashaninka and the FUNAI officials, they wiped their hands in their armpits, then cupped their palms to their mouths, hissing. They gestured toward the men's red T-shirts, clearly fascinated by the bright clothes. One of the FUNAI officials, a white man in dreads, shakes his finger: no. How to explain these T-shirts can be deadly?

Minute by minute, hour by hour, the *isolados'* fear gives way to fascination. The tribesmen linger a few hours in Simpatia, exploring hut to hut, unaware they are being recorded, unaware of the concept of being recorded. The Ashaninka prepare a *caiçuma*, their traditional fermented drink, an offering of friendship. The interpreters ascertain that the visitors hail from a village deep in the forest where as many as sixty others live. Throughout the afternoon, the *isolados* saunter between Ashaninka homes, still carrying spears and machetes. When one reaches again for a blue T-shirt, the interpreters and villagers try to wave him away, but it is dangerous to get too close. Any sudden move could shatter the fragile peace.

In a tense moment near the end of the encounter, one of the *isolados* sees an object too tempting to resist. Ignoring the pleas of the interpreters, he snatches an unattended axe and retreats across the river with his tribe. A small price to pay for a friendly first encounter.

The next morning, the *isolados* returned. The elation of contact was short-lived. Some of the visitors were already coughing, eyes rheumy. The FUNAI team radioed Brasilia, an urgent message for the Ministry of Health: We may be too late.

5

THE REAL JUNGLE

Since before I was old enough to know the cardinal points of a compass, South America has exerted a magnetic pull on my imagination. For kids like me, raised in the glow of 1980s movie rentals, the Amazon was adventure incarnate, a territory so deadly that even farm boys in Oregon committed a few survival tips to memory in case we ever needed to escape a booby-trapped temple, Indiana Jones–style. Catching frogs at the lake, we'd ponder their neon cousins in the rain forest, source of venom for Indians' poison-tipped arrows. (If one even grazed your arm, you'd be dead in less than a minute.) Bucking hay on hot summer afternoons, we'd return the dumb stares of cows across the pasture, imagining them devoured by ravenous piranhas. (Our science teacher never explained why cattle grazed in the Amazon, but we learned that a school of piranhas could pick a cow clean to the bones in less than a minute.) Cooling off at the swimming hole, we'd take a leak midstream, joking about the tiny parasitic fish in the Amazon that was attracted to the smell of urine. (It could swim right up your dick, set its hooks, and lay its eggs in less than a minute, which is why you never piss in the Amazon.)

I tucked those cautionary tales into the myth of Brazil that blanketed my childhood: a wondrous country, full of perils. There was no doubt I'd hit the lotto by being adopted to the United States where exotic dangers were confined to the video store. Beyond movies and TV, everything I knew about Latin America I learned from my parents, who had brought me from urban Brazil to rural America in 1981, at the twilight of the military dictatorship, six weeks after I was born.

With black curly hair and dark eyes, I stood out next to my freckled, blue-eyed mom, dad, and brother. I was only a few years old when my mom tearfully explained in the simplest terms that I was adopted, holding me tenderly by the shoulders as if to brace me for the revelation. When she got it all out, I assured her that I didn't mind and asked if it was time for a snack. She must have worried that she'd told me too soon, but my parents never wanted my history to feel like a secret. They preserved my Brazilian last name as my middle name on my U.S. documents to make sure I never forgot where I came from—and to leave a paper trail of my origins. I never did forget, but I never really cared, daydreaming about Brazil only on the occasional snow day, when I would trace the heart-shaped splotch on the globe the way another child might touch a birthmark.

For someone transplanted from the tropics to the high desert, it was relatively easy for me to blend in. My brother Josh and I grew up on a 10-acre farm, herding sheep, climbing trees, and riding our bikes as far as we could before dark. As soon as I was old enough to choose my own hair style, I buzzed off my curls. A dutiful Cub Scout, I learned knots, orienteering, and celestial navigation, accompanying my dad and uncles on bleary-eyed deer hunting trips at dawn. Once or twice a year Brazil crossed my peripheral vision, usually due to some bureaucratic snafu, like the day in sixth grade when I had to miss school to become a U.S. citizen before my resident alien status expired. When I returned to class the next day, Mrs. McLaren asked me to explain the majesty of citizenship to my classmates.

"How do you feel?" she asked, patriotism welling behind her glasses.

"I don't feel any different," I said.

"Tell us about the ceremony!"

"There was a judge like in *The People's Court*," I said. "Then we all said the pledge. Then they gave us little flags." (What I didn't confess was how my mom had ceremoniously planted that little U.S. flag alongside a souvenir Brazilian flag on my nightstand.)

"The same pledge we say every morning!" Mrs. McLaren said, connecting the dots for the class. "Isn't that amazing?"

"So that means Chris can never be president?" asked Cari, my main squeeze.

"Well, yes. Yes, it does," said Mrs. McLaren, "but that's not the point. The point is, don't you all realize how lucky you are?"

"Speaking of luck," I said, "isn't it time for computer lab?"

Like everyone else, I just wanted to get back to massacring buffalo on the Oregon Trail. I'd already been taught to marvel at the cosmic good fortune of a life in the United States, a life of security and freedom that would never have been granted to me in Brazil. In junior high, I was free to drop out of Boy Scouts. In high school, I was free to get a job bussing tables at an old-fashioned steak house, free to blow my tips on 40s of Olde English, free to smoke weed and drop LSD by firelight at the reservoir. Yet even if I shattered my mind into fractals, kaleidoscoped by *The Jimi Hendrix Experience*, I never let my thoughts spin to Brazil, the most dangerous trip, more mysterious than *The Dark Side of the Moon*, a black hole, too big, too powerful for exploration. If I got too close, it would swallow me.

The first time I traveled the Amazon, I was a twenty-five-year-old English teacher on summer break, adrift and unshaven, backpack stuffed with DEET-soaked clothes and dog-eared books. It was July 2006 and Brazil was on the rise in a new century, transformed by democracy, soaring commodities prices, and the populist economic policies of President Lula. Luxury developments like the Arena da Amazônia and the Ponta Negra promenade were mere blueprints, but Manaus was already in the throes of a new boom.

I'd wanted to take a trip like this since my days at the University of Oregon. Like college students since time immemorial, I'd tried to reinvent myself into someone who could conceivably get laid, embracing my heritage in hopes of enchanting women at parties. Unfortunately, Brazilian culture in Oregon was about as accessible as snow in the Amazon. The Department of Romance Languages offered Portuguese only as a special supplementary course for fourth-year Spanish majors. A yearlong Latin American history series distilled five centuries into two semesters, but whenever I asked about Brazil, my professors—one Colombian, one Cuban—demurred. Brazil was a special exception, they said. We'd circle back at the end of the semester, time permitting. Time never permitted.

As I sought my own answers in books, every passage I highlighted only seemed to underscore how much I didn't know. The history of a nation is more than names and places, dates and events—it's a flow of capital and blood over time, currents of euphoria and fear, victory and grief that bring a country to its present borders. Reading could only take me so far, especially when I was

swimming against the tide of European superiority that perme-
ated so much English-language scholarship about Brazil. I was determined to fill in the gaps with my own observations.

After graduation, I taught high school on the U.S-Mexico border, listening to language lesson CDs on my commute to adapt
my Spanish into mongrel Portuguese. By my second summer I'd
saved enough money for Brazil. I would spend a week in Rio de
Janeiro, fly six hours north to Manaus for a trip into the jungle,
take a boat 1,000 miles downriver to Belém, catch another quick
flight to Salvador, then south again, returning at last to my birth
city, Belo Horizonte.

Before I left, my mom mailed photocopies of all of my Brazilian records in case I decided to search for my birth mother—and
as evidence of my legal status on the off chance I was held up at
immigration coming or going. "We always knew this day would
come," she said. "Whatever you decide to do, we support you."

"I'll see how I feel when I get down there," I said. "I'm still not
sure if I'll try to find her." Looking for my birth mother seemed
like a recipe for disappointment. And I didn't want my mom, my
dad, or my brother to feel betrayed. My meandering itinerary, with
a long detour through the Amazon, was reassurance for my family
and me that the real point of the trip wasn't to track down blood
relatives but to explore a country I'd only seen in photos.

My dad, a Vietnam vet who prefers to leave the past in the past,
urged caution: "Just remember," he said before I took off. "Some
doors, once you open them, they can't be closed."

Like all wannabe explorers, I craved the unknown, even if it was
only unknown to me. On a steamy afternoon in July 2006, mosquitos whizzing in my ears like dentist drills, I wandered the historic center of Manaus to find a guide who could get me out of

the city and into the jungle. The capital of Amazonas state was more concrete jungle than rain forest, traffic jams and jackhammers, shopkeepers trumpeting their discounts through mini-PA systems, a haze of smog below a cloudless sky. Japanese businessmen clustered at corner bars, pecking at laptops and sipping beer from sweaty glasses. Tourists stalked the perimeter of the Teatro Amazonas, straining to capture the once great opera house in a single frame. Others walked the streets spooning up cupfuls of blended açai fruit. Boys and girls in school uniforms ambled across the plaza, clustering at the magazine kiosks to ogle photos in celebrity magazines.

Window by window, I shopped tour companies, offices plastered with snapshots of backpackers like me fishing for piranhas, swimming with pink dolphins, spotting caiman alligators by night, punctuated by professional close-ups of monkeys, sloths, jaguars, and psychedelic birds clipped from the pages of magazines like *National Geographic*. For six generations, gringos had arrived in Manaus hungry for the riches of the interior, except these days, instead of extracting rubber sap, visitors posed with parrots on their shoulders, fed mice to bright yellow snakes, and slunk into alleyways to purchase scraps of jaguar pelt before retreating to sensual massages and American style *banheiros*.

Intoxicated by pride, I decided I was no mere gringo, as if my birthplace and fractured Portuguese entitled me to a more authentic experience of Brazil. I wanted the real jungle, not a luxury tree house, so I went looking for the realest guide I could find. A few blocks off Rua 10 de Julho, I found my man. Operating from what looked like a walk-in closet, he wore a thick pair of glasses with a crack down the middle of the left lens. No brochures, no photos, no English. On a laminated map, he drew the route of his proposed tour with a dry-erase pen, inking a path from the Port of Manaus to a lodge on the bank of the Rio Negro.

"Are we talking about the real jungle?" I asked in Portuguese.

He licked his fingertip and smudged away the original route. After a moment's thought, he drew a new one along the broad Rio Solimões, clear onto the reverse side of the map, then up a few curvy, watery detours to another spot in the heart of the interior. "Rio Arasi," he said, giving me thumbs up. "Jungle *muito bom, muito bonito.*"

"Perfect," I said.

"Just you?" he said.

"Just me."

He seemed puzzled but tallied up some figures on the solar calculator he kept in his shirt pocket. When he presented the total, I negotiated halfheartedly and accepted his second offer. We would leave the next day at dawn.

That night, sweating profusely in an eight-dollar motel room, I sprayed my clothes with an auxiliary coat of DEET, swallowed my malaria pill, and succumbed to uneasy dreams.

Dawn arrived smoky gray, clouds low and motionless over the city as if pinned in place by radio towers. My guide was waiting outside the hotel, yawning behind the wheel of a Volkswagen Gol. Weaving between taxis and buses, we cruised along the river, banks lined with factories, waste lapping the shore. It was my first look at the river. I remember being underwhelmed at first glance by its width, hardly more impressive than the Columbia River back in Oregon, coursing through a sleepy port town. This was before I understood that the power of a river lies in its length, not its width, that its mystery lies not in what is seen but what is hidden.

When the driver deposited me at a floating dock at the Port of Manaus, I realized he was not my guide but a link in the gringo supply chain.

"Wait, you're not coming?" I asked.

"Your boat will be here soon," he said, glancing at the sunrise as if checking a watch.

"How will he find me?"

"Oh, he'll see you."

A few minutes later a water taxi sputtered to the dock. The driver spoke to the *taxista* over the chug of his outboard motor and then handed me off as if passing a baton. Without introduction, the pilot grabbed my backpack, balanced it in the middle of the boat, and pointed me to a seat and a life jacket up front. When I slipped on the life jacket, he encouraged me to use it as a seat cushion instead.

Our crossing gave me a better appreciation of the size of the river. It's never easy to estimate distance across water, but even a few minutes away from shore, the opposite bank seemed no closer. "What are those?" I asked, pointing to a cargo freighter leaving port.

The driver squinted at the ship. "Honda motors," he said.

"Where are they going?"

"Other cities."

I'd read that Manaus was a manufacturing hub for everything from dishwashers to semiconductors, shipped throughout Brazil thanks to the tailwinds of a tax-free zone created to encourage manufacturing and development, but I hadn't internalized the scope of industry in the Amazon until our boat was bobbing in the wake of a container ship.

In the middle of the river, the *taxista* cut the engine so we could observe the meeting of the waters—the point at which the cream-colored Rio Solimões joins the coffee-dark Rio Negro, each river having run its individual course for more than a thousand miles. Both rivers are among the world's longest in their own right. Both are habitat to thousands of species of flora and fauna uniquely evolved to thrive in the precise flow, temperature, and ionic composition of their waters. The cooler, faster Solimões and the warmer, slower Negro run side by side here for almost four miles, light and shadow, murky sediment and decayed leaves, combining to form the largest river on the planet, the Rio Amazonas, source of 20 percent of Earth's fresh water, carrying its own universe of species another thousand miles to the ocean.[1]

Satisfied that I'd taken enough pictures, the *taxista* yanked the motor back to life and ferried us to the opposite bank, where I would wait at a roadside supply kiosk for my next ride.

"He'll be here soon," the pilot said, gassing up his motor.

I lit a cigarette while the *taxista* boarded two more passengers for the return trip. The sun had barely crept over the leafy canopy and already it was too hot for smoking. At last a Volkswagen Kombi the color of spoiled mayonnaise skidded to a stop where the road met the river. The driver, a shirtless boy around twelve years old with a cigarette dangling from his lips, gestured for me to climb in. He must've weighed less than my backpack, which I tossed in the backseat before we sped off.

A seasoned wheelman, he drove one-handed, head tilted back so he could see over the dashboard.

"You like music?" he asked.

"Sure," I said.

Shifting into a higher gear, he rummaged through a collection of cassettes in the console, slipped in a tape, and punched Play. After few seconds of lo-fi hiss, the Kombi was bumping to the bass of Tupac's "All Eyez on Me." Noticing I dug the music, the kid beamed with a satisfaction that can only be achieved by a preadolescent simultaneously driving, smoking, and listening to rap. The dirt road was long and straight. We passed herds of cows wading knee-deep in flooded fields. We passed villages built on stilts to weather the wet season and the dry. We passed yellow school boats docked near schoolhouses. The boy honked at every pedestrian—farmers, nannies, and his jealous friends riding bicycles or donkeys along the overgrown shoulder. He seemed uninterested in conversation until he ran out of cigarettes, at which point he touched two fingers to his lips like, *Hey, can I bum a smoke?*

The kid was younger than my students back home.

"These things will kill you," I said.

He gave me a look like, *Quit bullshitting me.* He was clearly a working man. A working man who deserved a smoke. I tapped a single cigarette from my pack and gave him a light. Why not? He'd already started.

The kid smoked capably, pinching the filter between his lips when he needed both hands to shift gears or dodge puddles. I lit a cigarette of my own, rolled down the window, and let my hand surf the breeze. For the first time in a few days I wondered about my birth mother, about my own hypothetical boyhood in Brazil. When the tape deck began chewing up Tupac, the boy ejected the cassette, wound it with his pinky, and slammed it back in, pumping the volume louder. The trees grew thicker, and without warning he cranked the wheel hard right, power-sliding into a narrow, teeth-rattling cow path. He stomped one of his flip-flops on the brake pedal and we skidded to a stop at a makeshift dock. The boy slid off the driver's seat, opened the back of the Kombi, and hauled out a large Styrofoam cooler.

"You'd better go to the bathroom, *meu mano,*" he said.

What followed was the most glorious outdoor piss of my life, overlooking the Rio Arasi, a quiet tributary of the larger rivers. The canopy was sixty feet high, strands of thumb-thick vines connecting river to sky. The forest was reflected so clearly on the river's surface that if you unfocused your eyes it would be difficult to distinguish the real from its mirror twin. When I finished, the kid offered me a beer from the cooler. We drank wordlessly, listening to the chirp and warble of hidden birds fluttering through the understory.

The spell was broken when the *thwap* of a motor echoed through the trees. An aluminum boat drifted into view, the pilot cutting the engine as he made his final approach. The boy tied the boat to the dock while the pilot leapt ashore and took a quick inventory of the cooler: chicken breast, a plastic bag of silver fish, a carton of eggs, and a small supply of beer floating in melted ice. He pulled a few damp bills from his shorts, paid the boy, and carried the cooler aboard. I tossed my backpack in the boat, and before I could say good-bye, the kid was already reversing back up the road.

The pilot was a young man about my age named Beto, sporting sunglasses and a neon yellow 2006 World Cup Germany hat in support of the Brazilian national team, which was in the midst of a tournament run. We skimmed upriver, the canopy and its reflection surrounding us: green, blue, black. Beto steered with one hand, navigating the creeks like they were neighborhood streets. I stared into the floodwaters, half the forest drowned below us. Only now did it occur to me that this water was already receding, that soon these islands would be hills. Beto carried two maps in his mind, low water and high water, mastered through a lifetime of navigating this river in all seasons and weather. The landscape I saw today was a fraction of the forest, with the rest underwater, breathing in the dark.

After an hour or so of skimming through the trees, Beto nosed the boat into a thicket and onto a muddy shore. Without cutting the motor, he pointed up the trail to an open-air thatch hut with a thin curl of smoke rising from the roof.

"Up there," he said.

Fresh white streaks of rubber bled down a nearby hevea tree. I stepped from the boat and approached slowly, careful not to disturb whatever was unfolding inside.

Then I heard the laughter of Americans on vacation. Inside the hut I was startled to find a white couple in their twenties and a young Chinese woman standing around a fire, watching the person I assumed was their—now our—guide. Dressed in board shorts and Nike sandals, a Nike visor corralling his raven black hair, the guide lifted a droopy strand of hot latex from the fire.

"And there you have a condom," he said in perfect English. "Now you try." He noticed me standing in the entry—the new arrival he had been waiting for. "Oh, you must be Arnold!"

"It's Chris," I said. "Hi."

"My name is Damien," he said. We shook hands and I exchanged introductions with the young couple and the Chinese woman. The Americans were Jeff and Lizzy, graduate students on a research excursion. The Chinese woman was Li Jing, an anthropologist who spoke little but took even more pictures than I did.

"We can start over if you want to learn," Damien said, testing the elasticity of the condom.

"No, that's all right," I said.

Apparently one memorable way to demonstrate the rubber tapping process to gringos was to show them how to make rubbers. Damien coached Jeff and Lizzy through their condomcraft, while Li Jing took snapshots with the intensity of a paparazzo. They held up their finished products for the camera, trading jabs about size. I paced about the hut, listening to the quirky calls of birds from the trees. Overhead, the roar of a commercial jet descended toward Manaus. I'd been duped by the illusion of water travel. As the crow flies, we couldn't have been more than thirty miles from the bustle of the Teatro Amazonas.

The young couple tucked their condoms into Jeff's fanny pack for later. We walked to the other side of the island and, one by one, climbed into a canoe that was tethered there. Damien distributed us evenly by weight to keep the canoe from tipping; then he pulled the engine cord for the jaunt to our camp. I told myself it could be worse. If wherever we were headed was a place where graduate students and anthropologists stayed, then I must have found something resembling the real jungle.

From a distance, our lodge seemed to be built on the kind of shady inlet where I imagined jaguars drank. We moored alongside a warped-plank dock. When Damien cut the engine, I heard death metal raging from the camp, echoing all the way to the canopy across the river: drums, power chords, and growling that must have chilled the spines of every howler monkey within earshot. Onshore was a long hut with a Brazilian flag hung above the entrance, half a dozen hubcaps nailed to the exterior wall, catching the sun. Three hammocks hung inside, veiled in mosquito nets. In the center of the room was a rectangular wooden table with benches on either side. A woman swept the open-air kitchen, greeting us with a thumbs-up. In the corner, a propane stove, an ice chest, and a boom box stacked high with bootleg CDs. Behind the hut, a dirt path forked off toward an outhouse.

"Are there piranhas?" I asked Damien in Portuguese.

"Speak English so that everyone can understand," Damien said.

"Are there piranhas?"

"You guys want to see piranhas?" he said. "No problem." He removed his hat and sunglasses, set his cell phone on the dock, and dove headfirst into the river. We gasped, waiting for blood to pool. After what seemed like a minute, in which Li Jing snapped like fifty shots, Damien surfaced, gasped for breath, and smiled: "When the river is full, like now, the piranhas aren't so hungry. You have to go looking for them. We'll catch some for dinner."

I stripped down to my boxers and leapt off the dock into the dark relief of the river.

"Don't pee in there," said one of the guests onshore, a frat boy rolling a joint. "Bugs will crawl up your schlong!"

"That's a myth," I said.

"No, that's true, so don't piss," Damien said.

The water was warm and buoyant. I stayed below the surface as long as possible, listening for the splashes of the others, but there were none. Here. I. Am. Swimming. In. The. Amazon. When I surfaced, the heavy-metal music was gone, replaced by the warble of saccharine Brit pop: "You're beautiful . . . you're beautiful . . . you're beautiful, it's true."

Fuck's sake. Not one of my Brazilian daydreams had been scored by James Blunt. Some evil marketing genius in London had managed to colonize one of the most remote stereos on the planet and, worse yet, people were humming along.

What can I say? I was young and naïve. I'd told myself that great traveler's lie—I'm not like the other tourists—but like any visitor to the Amazon, I was only skimming its surface. No matter how much I wanted to experience the real jungle, I was as foreign in Brazil as a British pop ballad. The real jungle would always be out of reach, a reminder that my Brazilian blood meant nothing. I was at heart a gringo, sightseeing through a Hollywood lens.

That afternoon we went piranha fishing. Li Jing sat up near the nose of the canoe with her digital camera. Jeff and Lizzy took the middle bench. I sat in the back next to Damien, who steered us into the flooded forest, using a long pole to nudge the river bottom.

The shafts of light through the leafy canopy grew thinner until we drifted into a cool, shaded inlet. Damien passed each of us a thin stick with string attached. He removed a chicken breast from a plastic bag, diced it into pieces with his machete, and tied a chunk to the end of each string.

"So the way you fish for piranhas is you want to trick them into thinking an animal just fell into the water," he said. To demonstrate, he touched his stick to the calm surface and thrashed it about. A few seconds later he lifted the pole. A shiny piranha dangled on the string, razor teeth sunk into the chicken.

"Holy shit," said Lizzy. Li Jing gestured for Damien to dangle the fish her way for a close-up of its beady, blood-lusting eyes.

Now it was our turn. Twenty minutes later, Jeff, Lizzy, and Li Jing had filled a bucket with piranhas. I couldn't manage a single bite. What was I doing wrong?

"You want to hold mine?" asked Li Jing, offering her pole with a fresh, feisty piranha. "We can take a picture?"

"No thank you," I said.

"Maybe we can try another spot?" Jeff said.

"No, no, that's okay," I said. "I think we have enough."

I wanted to push them into the water and watch them get picked clean by the piranhas in less than a minute, but the river was high and the piranhas weren't hungry enough, so I had to settle for seeing them getting eaten alive by mosquitos.

That night, as promised, Damien boiled a pot of piranha soup. The mighty little fish tasted like the chicken we'd used to lure them. He watched us eat, and when we finished, he fixed himself a box of macaroni and cheese of the sort I'd eaten every week of my childhood, the smell of powdered cheddar taking me home to the farm.

Our agenda on day two was a journey deeper into the creeks, a search for the açai fruit, a regional snack that would soon be a globally exported "super food," though it was not so super for the animals losing their habitat to industrial-scale açai cultivation. The morning sun melted across the water like gold. Damien paddled our wooden canoe deep into the forest, stopping now and then to rest his arms and call out perfect imitations of toucans and tamarins and parrots, creatures calling back as if he were a lost friend. He moored us on an island, stabilizing the canoe with his paddle as we hopped out. Then he hacked a path inland with a machete. We advanced into the thick, leaving chopped vegetation in our wake like ingredients for a giant salad.

"Aren't we hurting the jungle?" asked Lizzy.

"We can't hurt the jungle," Damien said, hacking a few extraneous branches from a nearby fig as if to prove the fauna was impervious. He paused and pointed to the treetops. A barrel of spider monkeys scurried across the canopy, mothers leaping from branch to branch with babies around their necks. Maybe Damien was right. We weren't bulldozers. The jungle shrank us to the size of gnats, compressed our human lives to a few dozen flood seasons.

Damien handed his machete to Jeff and unsheathed a smaller one for Lizzy.

"I feel like Indiana Jones," said Jeff, swinging the machete as if he were on a movie poster.

Oh God. I was Jeff and Jeff was me and neither of us belonged on this river, in this country.

We came across an ancient tree with vines like rope. Jeff, Lizzy, and even Li Jing took turns swinging like Tarzan, complete with sound effects, while Damien took pictures.

"Now you, Arnold," he asked.

"It's Chris," I said. "And that's okay, I'm fine." Every bone in my body radiated a childlike impulse to swing on a vine, yelling, but instead I looked away, feigning indifference, face slick with sweat. Damien shrugged, took a swing on the vine himself as if to call me out for my smug pretension. Looking back, I see why Damien cast a suspicious eye on me, a gringo who didn't seem to realize he was a gringo, a total buzzkill, asking sober botanical questions when I should've been intoxicated by vines and monkeys, hacking recklessly with a machete like a real American.

"Up there you can see açai," Damien said, pointing to the top of a palmlike tree. A patch of purple fruit hung beside a clumpy nest. "It tastes delicious, but we have to be careful of wasps. They like açai, too."

Damien snapped a broad leaf from a nearby bush. Clenching the leaf in his teeth, he climbed the tree barehanded, fingers interlocked around the trunk, Nikes providing the grip he needed to lunge higher. The cyclone of wasps gained velocity as he encroached on their airspace. Hugging the tree one-armed, he reached into his pocket for a lighter and lit the leaf in his mouth.

"What are we going to do if he falls?" Lizzy said.

"I could get us back to camp," said Jeff, looking around for our path, which already seemed overgrown.

Damien held the smoking leaf toward the wasp nest, mellowing the swarm. He plucked four açai fruit and dropped them to us before shimmying down to the jungle floor, mission accomplished.

The fruit tasted like honey. It left our lips purple and sticky. I closed my eyes, taking in the warmth of the sun on my face. Damien was right. I needed to chill the fuck out. Then I felt a searing pain in my neck: vengeful wasps, drawn to the açai dribble on my hands and face. "Fuck!"

We fled back down the path, swatting away the buzzing swarm. Damien pushed us off the shore and let the motor rip. As we bobbed and weaved through the flooded forest, flushing birds from the trees, Li Jing snapped a picture of a crimson bite on my neck, already swelling. By the time we reached open water, I was overcome by feverish chills.

"Those bites hurt, no?" Damien said, smirking. "Don't worry. It will only last a few hours. Now you can say you've been to the real jungle."

6

THE BRAZIL READER

A few days later I returned to Manaus with a sunburn, a tender lump on my neck, and a burgeoning notebook of poems about life on the Amazon. Through the unconstrained power of free verse, it had dawned on me, line by vapid line, that a gringo can never tour the real jungle; the jungle is struggle and the tour is effortless. Now I was ready to leave the folly of tourism behind for the open river, a seven-day slow-boat ride a thousand miles to Belém, where the Amazon River spills into the Atlantic.

On the floating piers of the Port of Manaus, men bunched in the shade of riverboats, luggage in tow. Women and children weaved through the crowd, offering beer, nuts, and shrimp on a stick. Our boat was a diesel-powered, four-deck vessel, 150 feet long with a 30-foot beam, a Brazilian flag fluttering from an aluminum pole on the starboard side. The ticket vendor had tried to persuade me to take one of the three first-class cabins on the top deck.

"It's cleaner," he said. "Safer for a gringo."

"No thanks," I said. "I'll take the bottom deck." It was the cheapest option, $21 including meals, on account of the engine noise and diesel fumes. No amount of engine noise could be worse than James Blunt.

"Suit yourself," he said. "Just watch your stuff."

Before we parted ways, he pointed me to a kiosk where I bought a green and yellow hammock and a length of nylon rope. I descended to steerage and found a place among the dozens of people tying hammocks to the overhead rails. My neighbors gave me puzzled looks. To my left, a middle-aged woman sagged in her hammock, cracking nuts in the palm of her hand. On my right, a man about my age hung his hammock as if preparing the gallows.

I hung mine using a knot I remembered from Boy Scouts. When the man next to me noticed, he undid my work and tied it with a different knot. I couldn't tell if it was to save me from a painful fall or to ensure a painful fall.

"Uh, thank you," I said. "Hi, everybody."

My neighbors softened when they heard that I spoke a modicum of Portuguese, considering we'd be sleeping shoulder to shoulder for the next week. As the crew loaded cargo and supplies, I introduced myself and clumsily fielded questions about my purpose on the boat: I was born in Brazil and now I was traveling the country *para encontrar minhas origems.*

"Você é brasileiro?" asked the woman beside me. *"Bem-vindo!"*

You're Brazilian? Welcome home! I'd been waiting my entire life to hear those words. Her name was Zezé. She was traveling to her mother's house some 300 miles downriver. Her teenage daughter was traveling with her; she was somewhere on the ship, soaking up the bustle of the port. The man who'd helped me hang my hammock was Érico. A migrant worker from Belém, he was on his way home to see his wife and daughter. The brief mention of his family made his eyes pool with tears. Zezé offered me a handful of nuts. Érico had boarded with a plastic bag of cold beers. We toasted to a good journey.

When it seemed not one more hammock could be hung—there were some eighty or ninety people on our deck alone—the boat's engines roared to life. We ferried out of the harbor and across the meeting of the waters. The development thinned from cityscape to village, schoolchildren running along the banks, waving, rolling with laughter when the captain blew the ship's horn for them.

A Brazilian flag hung from nearly every hut in support of the World Cup campaign under way in Germany, broadcast to rabbit-eared TVs up and down the Amazon, the fruits of a decades-long effort to bring the vast interior into the fold—roads, telephone poles, and radio linking villages that had never heard the country's national anthem, let alone seen a live football match, however fuzzy it might appear during a storm. Looking out over the water, our stalwart boat was dwarfed by leviathan cargo freighters with containers stacked like Legos, each flying their own national flags, bound for the Atlantic crossing and every corner of the globe.

Leaving the city, the riverbanks grew farther apart until they were no more than green strips on the horizon, an impossible volume of water moving uniformly east, but by the end of the first day the captain had navigated us to a secondary route to escape the wake of the commercial traffic, a slender brown tongue of river two or three times wider than our ship. Kingfishers swooped from bank to bank. All signs of development had vanished, save for the occasional thatched-hut village.

After the first day, I understood why early European explorers called the Amazon the Green Inferno, an endless static scroll of water and tangled green foliage. Only meals broke the monotony. Three meals were prepared each day, and the bottom deck was the last to eat, waiting for the leftovers from the upper decks. When the dinner bell rang, passengers slipped out of their hammocks and unfolded a bar table that ran the length of both sides. Crew members set out a dozen stools. We hunched together, eating family style, passing out plates and cups and silverware, then bowls of rice and beef, then cups and pitchers of watery fruit drink, as if on an assembly line. You ate quickly and surrendered your seat to one of the other passengers who stood waiting behind you. After meals, crew members gathered the dishware, stacked up the stools, and folded up the table until the next meal.

Between meals, I spent my time leaning against the rail, smoking cigarettes, or lazing in my hammock where I read, scribbled doggerel, or honed my Portuguese with Zezé and Érico. We took in the long, liquid sunsets in silence, a hush falling over the ship. At night I returned to my books by lamplight: *The Brazil Reader: History, Culture, Politics,* a fat collection of academic essays; *An Anthology of Twentieth-Century Brazilian Poetry,* edited by Elizabeth Bishop; and the *Oxford Anthology of the Brazilian Short Story.* I still remember the night I first discovered the work of the great Amazonian portraitist José Veríssimo, surrounded by the wisps and snores of other dreaming passengers. "To go rubber gathering, a fatal phrase . . . It is a fever. It is worse than the malaria." His mosaic of rubber season atrocities cast my journey in a new light. Whether *caboclo* or Indian, passenger or villager, everyone on this river carried some memory of those horrors in their blood.

After the sun went down and darkness poured over the boat, I tossed and turned in my hammock, trying and failing to sleep. It wasn't the engine that kept me awake; it was the first-class passengers tearing up the bar on the top deck, a PA system blasting Brazilian pop music over the water and into the forest. By the third night, my flashlight was out of batteries, and now I lay awake in utter darkness, listening to our boat churn down-river.

Rolling out of my hammock, I slunk past Zezé and Érico and followed the raucous laughter and clinking glass upstairs, where few of the lower-deck passengers could afford to drink. An open-air snack bar was decked out with Christmas lights strung over a few plastic patio sets, all pushed together to form one master table of empty beer cans and liquor bottles and glassy-eyed people who shouted and smoked as only the last people awake can shout and smoke. Behind the bar, the server cued up a new DVD, a selection of Zé Ramalho concert footage. I ordered a beer and took one of the only empty seats left in the cluster. They were almost through a third bottle of rum. Above us the Brazilian flag flapped hard from the top of the ship's radio antenna while Ramalho sang his cover of "Knockin' on Heaven's Door."

A group of young Israeli men sat with two young women—college students from Rio de Janeiro. The men had just finished their stint in the army and were now touring the world. The women were visiting the north country for the first time. Before long I was in the mix, shooting rum and stacking empties in the center of the table.

"Where are you going after Brazil?" asked one of the Israelis.

"Nowhere," I said. "I'm just traveling in Brazil. I was born here, but I grew up in the United States."

"You're Brazilian!" said one of the women. Then to her friend in Portuguese: "He's Brazilian!"

"I thought he looked Brazilian," she said.

"We just came from Colombia," said one of the other Israelis. "You have to see Colombia. The beaches. Like no other beaches."

They went on about the countries they had seen, the countries they would see, Brazil just another stop on the way to the rest of the world. After weeks of trying to get by in my broken Portuguese, speaking English was like relaxing into an old recliner. The bar seemed stocked with an infinite amount of rum. At some point before sunrise, I staggered back to my hammock on the bottom deck, trying not to disturb anyone's dreams . . .

When I woke the sun was glinting off the river and my gut felt like a squeezed-out lime.

"You missed breakfast," said Érico. "I tried to wake you up."

I staggered out of my hammock and tried not to throw up over the railing. At a glance it was clear we had floated a great distance overnight. There were only a few single-family huts on the riverbank. When our ship rounded a bend, a flotilla of children in small wooden canoes paddled toward us, flashing thumbs up as if they'd been waiting for us. Leaning over the railing, I looked up to see the top-deck passengers taking pictures. One of the Israelis heaved a plastic bag overboard. The children paddled frantically after the gift: a can of Coke and a bag of chips.

A woman and two young boys paddled directly into the path of our ship. We narrowly missed splintering their canoe. The boy tossed a rope onto the lower deck. Érico grabbed the line and tied it off, and when the rope snapped taut the canoe skimmed securely up to the side of the boat. Hand over hand, Érico reeled them closer as the woman tied several plastic grocery bags to the older boy's arms. Once loaded up, the kid walked the towline like a high wire, arms outstretched, until Zezé received him on our end, his bags overflowing with fresh fruit and dried shrimp.

Hammock by hammock, the boy made his sales while the woman and the other boy in the boat sold cups of fruit and nuts. It wasn't long before they were sold out. The boy on deck wrapped the wrinkled bills and coins in a plastic baggie and secured them to his wrist.

With Érico's help, the boy unfastened the towline. The canoe, unloosed, hit the river with a hard splash, bobbing in our wake as the boat roared onward. The boy climbed over the portside railing, staring down at the churn as if ready to leap. I hurried over to stop him.

"*De onde você é?*" he asked, narrowing his eyes.

"*Dos Estados Unidos,*" I said.

"*Que bufo!*" he said, giggling, as if he knew I had no business here. Without warning he front-flipped into the water. For a moment I was sure he had drowned in the churn, but he surfaced a few yards out and swam quick strokes toward his mother. By then they must have been at least 3 miles downriver from where they met us, a long paddle home against the current unless they could hitch a ride going back.

Not long after, we stopped at a Petrobras station for fuel and supplies. Passengers were allowed to leave the boat for 30 minutes. "Thirty minutes exactly!" the captain warned us over the PA. "These boats don't turn around."

Zezé didn't stray far from the boat. Instead, she purchased a bag of fresh silver dollar fish from a vendor.

"What are you going to do with all those?" I asked.

"You'll see," she said. I followed her to the edge of the dock along with the two women from Rio de Janeiro. Crouching at the river's edge, Zezé took a fish and slapped it on the tranquil water. A moment later, a school of huge creatures nosed to the surface, snapping the fish from her hand.

"What are you doing?" I asked. Zezé handed me a fish. Kneeling, I mimicked her.

From the depths came a pale pink dolphin. It tugged the fish from my fingertips and swam away, quick as a dart.

"*Boto,*" Zezé said, laughing. "River spirits."

• • •

By the third day on the boat I was rereading old pages. By the fourth I was drinking beer with lunch. By the fifth I was drinking beer with breakfast, too hung over to read even if I'd had fresh books.

That night, the ship was halted at a federal inspection point. Soldiers boarded the vessel to inspect cargo and luggage for contraband. Foreign passengers were required to de-board and present visas. I stood on the dock with the Israelis, a couple of drunk Danish guys, and an Englishman on the verge of puking. On the dock, residents of the nearby village materialized from the shadows, selling shrimp and catfish. Zezé and Érico watched from the bottom deck. I felt like I'd blown my cover, exposed as pure gringo.

The next morning Zezé disembarked without saying good-bye. Port by port, the hammocks below thinned out, and Érico moved his bedding to another section without saying a word. One woman offered me a large brown nut and watched with great interest to see if I could crack it. When I couldn't, she plucked it from my palm and cracked it for me. The other passengers chuckled. I wasn't fooling anybody down here. I was an imposter. Fuck *The Brazil Reader*. I could jabber on about colonialism, but I couldn't crack a brazil nut.

By the seventh and final night, the gang on the top deck had accepted the challenge of finishing all the booze on the boat, and by midnight, triumph was in our sights. What I remember I wish I could forget. The Israelis, drunk and on the verge of a fistfight, barking at the bartender as if they owned him. One of the Danish men, curled in the stairway outside his cabin, whispering compliments to an Indian girl who seemed barely a teenager. My own drunken insolence, scaling the flagpole and swinging freely over the dark water as a crew member yelled at me: "Get down from there, you idiot! These boats don't turn around!"

The next morning Belém glistened in the middle distance across a delta so wide it was impossible to see the banks. Érico was gone before I could say farewell. The first-class passengers from the top deck disappeared into the crowd, leaving the boat behind as if it were a theme park ride. I remember collapsing onto an $8 a night hostel mattress, so grateful to sleep horizontally that I ignored the fleas needling my flesh. I remember a thunderstorm so fierce it shook the city, blowing down road signs, white lightning splitting the horizon. The chaos broke as suddenly as it began, and the Brazilians resumed their ordinary lives on the ordinary river they called home. After seven days of water, it seemed impossible there could be more, but I had never been so grateful to see the coast, the Rio Pará pouring into Marajó Bay and, at last, the Atlantic, where it all ended and began. It would be another decade before scientists discovered that the river exhaled its sediment—sand and decayed forest, sewage and industrial runoff—over an enormous coral reef, one of the largest in the world, hidden in plain sight.[1] By then the biome would be on the brink of collapse, bleached and rotting, poisoned beyond salvation.

7

WOLVES AMONG SHEEP

The 1494 Treaty of Tordesillas divided the land, people, and resources of the "New World" between Spain and Portugal along a meridian halfway between Cape Verde and the Caribbean islands where Christopher Columbus made landfall on his first voyage. Lands east of the line were claimed by the Portuguese Empire, lands west claimed by the Crown of Castile. All of the Americas except for the eastern tip of Brazil fell under the domain of Spain. For more than eighty years, the two monarchies adhered to the treaty in relative peace, focusing their naval and military might on colonizing the millions of indigenous people in the new territories.

There was one complication. In 1578, young King Sebastian I of Portugal disappeared during an attack on the Moors in Morocco, leaving no rightful heir.[1] King Philip II of Spain took advantage of the dynastic crisis to seize control of Portugal, forming the Iberian Union. While the Spanish pillaged the Inca Empire in the Andes, Portuguese patriots in Iberia and the New World plotted to liberate their country from a foreign monarch.

The city of Belém—Portuguese for Bethlehem—was founded in 1616 as a military fort at the mouth of the Amazon River. With a superior navy, a century of experience in Brazil, and a fearsome reputation among the Tupi-speaking tribes of the Atlantic coast, the Portuguese soon controlled the Amazon basin. From their stronghold, the Portuguese muscled out colonists from Spain, France, Ireland, and Holland.

When a small party of Spanish friars and soldiers landed in Belém in 1637, they introduced themselves as explorers who had floated all the way from Quito, converting Indians the whole way in the name of their king. Their Portuguese hosts were not amused. Line of Tordesillas be damned, this was their territory.

In Belém, the patriots caught a whiff of opportunity. To keep the friars and soldiers from alerting Spanish authorities, the Portuguese governor kept the visitors under house arrest. Then he dispatched Commander Pedro Teixeira on a bold expedition upriver: seventy soldiers in forty-seven long canoes paddled by more than a thousand Indians. The governor gave Teixeira sealed orders to be opened only after the expedition had passed the Omagua territory near Quito.

It was a grueling eight-month journey against the current—especially grueling for the Indians who did all the paddling. When at last they reached the end of Omagua territory, Teixeira opened the orders: he was to establish a settlement and boundary stones, bearing only the Portuguese coat of arms. The expedition did as commanded, staking out a new claim in secret, 1,500 miles west of the Line of Tordesillas. The Amazon east of its Andean headwaters would soon be the domain of Portugal.

Their Spanish hosts in Quito were suspicious, but they welcomed Teixeira and his men. When Portugal restored its own monarch three years later, the Spanish were too consumed by wars in Europe to contest the new boundaries. A century later, in the 1750 Treaty of Madrid, the Spanish conceded more than half of South America to Portugal. Today Teixeira's original claim still sketches the boundary between Portuguese-speaking Brazil and Spanish-speaking Peru and Colombia, a massive territory— nearly half of the South American continent—that would never have been claimed without the labor of hundreds of indigenous paddlers. As a reward, the surviving Indians were permitted to shoot a few bulls in Quito.[2]

Colonists had always depended on indigenous people for their survival in the Amazon, whether for military expeditions or daily chores. Many believed that after surviving the perilous journey across the ocean, they should be treated like kings in the New World. Their helplessness only seemed to affirm their sense of entitlement. Settlers could barely orient themselves in the dizzying forest, let alone hunt, fish, or cultivate crops plagued by insects and overgrowth. At first they could persuade awestruck tribes to supply food, build weatherproof shelters, or row them to mass—all for fishhooks, lengths of cotton, or metal spades.

Soon the tribes had all the tools they needed. For the Indians, the forest abounded with fruit and game year-round. Cultivating a surplus to ship overseas seemed ridiculous. They had countless better ways to spend their time. Bathing and decorating themselves. Telling stories and teaching their children the ways of the forest. Plotting ambushes to avenge their ancestors. Up and down the Atlantic coast, settlers faced a common dilemma: how to make these new subjects obey?

Missionaries fared no better. While the Franciscans and Carmelites attempted to convert tribes in the upper basin, the Jesuits dominated the lower Amazon, learning the Tupi language and documenting the marvels and horrors of Indian life.[3] Like the friars on Orellana's Spanish flotilla, the Jesuits were impressed by how the tribes managed to live lives of plenty and leisure in such a hostile environment, yet the Indians were shockingly ignorant of God, empty spiritual vessels ready to be filled with Christianity. At first the Indians were enchanted by the friars and their manic rituals—curious variations on their own shamans—but tribes had no respect for the cross and even used sacred objects to adorn their animals. The Jesuits were flummoxed: how to bring these pagans to the light of the Lord?

If anything, violence seemed to consume their lives. The first European settlements in Brazil coincided with a war among the Tupi ethnic groups of the Atlantic coast who fought mercilessly, day and night, rain or shine. "If they struck an enemy's head, they did not just knock him to the ground, but slaughtered him as one of our butchers fell an ox," wrote the sixteenth-century French Calvinist Jean de Léry of a battle he witnessed in the south of Brazil. "These Americans are so furious in their wars that they fight on without stopping as long as they can move arms and legs, never retreating or turning tail."[4]

A German soldier, Hans Staden, captured by Indians at the southern Port of Santos, chronicled the cannibalistic rituals that would come to define the Brazilian Indians in the eyes of Europeans. Tribes worked prisoners of war as slaves for months before ceremoniously killing and cooking their captives, eating all but the brain in drunken revelries that lasted for days. "Although they confess that this human flesh is marvelously good and delicate, nevertheless they feast on it more out of vengeance than taste," Staden wrote after his escape. "Their main purpose in gnawing the dead down to the bones in this way is to fill the living with fear and horror."[5]

What early settlers did not know was that the Tupi were the only tribe in the Amazon basin who engaged in cannibalism, and only after generations of bitter feuds and vendettas. Tragically for the rest of Brazil's tribes, cannibalism gave Europeans a justification to organize a system of oppression that would ensnare every other ethnic group. The Indians were heathens. When forced to work, they were not being enslaved—they were being saved.

A bureaucratic hiccup: enslaving Indians was illegal if you called it slavery. Lisbon was impatient to extract wealth from its colonies, but if settlers and missionaries wanted Indians to work their plantations and fill their soul counts, they needed a legal and moral framework to save the royal family from eternal damnation.

There were two workarounds. First, it was legal to enslave prisoners of a "just war," which was any skirmish with Indians who refused to bow to Portuguese rule or convert to Christianity. With a little ingenuity, these battles were easy to incite, and the Indian men, women, and children who survived could be roped up, dragged back to town, and sold to the highest bidder.

The second way to legally enslave an Indian was to "ransom" one who had been captured by a rival tribe. Presuming those poor souls would be cannibalized, Europeans traded cloth, mirrors, and other goods for the prisoners, who would then be indebted to their new masters for life. Surely the pope would agree that it was better than being eaten. Tapping into the bloody wellsprings of intertribal hatred, the settlers goaded Indians into pillaging the villages of their enemies and bringing back captives to exchange for metal tools and the promise of protection from reprisals. Soon, ransoming expeditions to the upper tributaries were a routine way for colonists to bring tribes downriver. Indians who survived the initial melee and the outbreaks of disease that followed were strong enough stock to be divvied up between the settlers and the missionaries.

The Jesuits assigned Indians to model villages, which were designed to harness the power of Christ to turn heathens into productive subjects of the crown. New arrivals were granted a two-year grace period to learn Christian ways before being put to work in the service of the mission. Naturally, they would be paid, but first they must be clothed, so they were paid in cotton, which they spun themselves. While not legally the property of their masters, Indians were forced to work six, eight, or even ten months of the year, a humble price to pay for salvation.

Before long, competition for Indians pitted settlers against missionaries. From the perspective of settlers, the black-robed Jesuits were cunning businessmen who put undue regulations on the labor supply to fatten their own coffers. The Jesuits loathed the settlers for abusing their subjects to fulfill base desires. "They killed them as one kills mosquitos," wrote the seventeenth-century Jesuit Father João Daniel. "In labor they treated them as if they were wild animals or beasts of the forest . . . they used, or abused, the feminine sex brutally and lasciviously, monstrously and indecently, without fear of God or shame before men."[6]

For Jesuits like Father Daniel, the purpose of punishing Indians was not to extract maximum value before they succumbed to exhaustion or disease but rather to shape the heathens into true believers. "Fear achieves more with them than respect," wrote Father Daniel, a notorious disciplinarian. "Thrashing is the most convenient and appropriate punishment for Indians. . . . Only forty strokes is recommended. . . . If the crimes are more atrocious this can be repeated for more days, together with a sentence of imprisonment. They mind this very much, for they find themselves deprived of their hunting, roaming and other entertainments, and especially of their daily bathing, etc. In truth there is no punishment that tames them better than a long spell in prison, with some good shackles on their feet."[7]

As more ships full of new colonists made land in Brazil, more Indians fell victim to the diseases they brought with them. Soon the demand for slave labor outstripped the supply. "For a man to obtain manioc flour he has to have a small clearing," wrote one missionary. "To eat meat he needs a hunter; to eat fish a fisherman; to wear clean clothes a washerwoman; and to go to mass or anywhere else a canoe and paddler."[8] For settlers struggling with failing crops, African slaves were too expensive, and those who did arrive from the Caribbean were as helpless as whites in the Amazon. In their hunt for fresh bodies, slaving parties ventured farther upriver, resorting to ever more vicious measures. Slavers would erect crosses on shore, and when Indians passed by without supplicating, they were hauled downriver in chains. Over time, enforcement of slavery laws became so lax that trickery became unnecessary. Indian men and boys were branded across the chest with their owners' full names. Women and girls were separated from their families and sold for sex. To incite terror in their victims, one group of settlers barricaded tribesmen in a hut and forced them to witness the rape of their wives and daughters. Other tribes who refused to go were burned alive in their huts.

On the journey downriver, countless prisoners died of beatings, starvation, or smallpox. Slavers would throw feverish Indians overboard before their infections could spread. Mothers and fathers would cast themselves into the river so their children could split their meager portions of manioc flour. Those who survived the descent seldom lived long, their suffering compounded by the pox.

Season after season, hopes for a new Eden in the Amazon were dashed. Heavy rains washed away the fertile topsoil. Ants, caterpillars, and other pests devoured whatever crops managed to take root. Dreams of diamond and gold mines remained dreams. The only precious resources in the rain forest were the Indians themselves, and the fortunes of settlers rose and fell with their headcounts. "Those who have a hundred slaves today will not have six left a few days later," wrote one Jesuit. "Any attack of dysentery kills them; and for any small annoyance they take to eating earth or salt and die."[9]

When the Portuguese Jesuit António Vieira arrived in the Maranhão region in 1653, he was determined to enforce the anti-slavery laws that were almost universally ignored. With rousing sermons filled with threats of fire and brimstone, he appealed to the settlers. "At what price the devil buys souls today compared with what he used to offer for them! All he has to do is offer a couple of Tapuia Indians and he is immediately adored on both knees. What a cheap market. An Indian for a soul!" he preached. The assembled would murmur. "I know what you are going to tell me," Vieira continued. "Our people, our country, our government cannot be sustained without Indians. Who will fetch a pail of water for us or carry a load of wood? Who will grind our manioc? Will our wives have to do it? Will our sons? I answer yes, and repeat again, yes." His conclusion was simple but ahead of its time: "It is better to live from your own sweat than from the blood of others!"[10]

Yet the Lord had endowed Vieira with a shrewd sense of politics: it was no use to appeal to morality alone. The priest reminded settlers that the laws as written were exceedingly generous. There were still legal forms of slavery, and for the love of God, you could still hire an Indian for a length of cloth. Emphasizing these legal workarounds only encouraged settlers to coerce free Indians into claiming they were legal slaves. By threat of violence, captives told inspectors that they had been held prisoner by cannibals beforehand, meaning they should be registered as legal ransoms. Other slave owners would marry free women to slave men so that she and any future children would be legal property.

Any chance Vieira had of shutting down the black market for slaves was hopeless when the ruthless *bandeirantes* reached the Amazon. Hardscrabble pioneers from São Paulo, the *bandeirantes* organized audacious, long-distance slave-catching expeditions— *bandeiras*—to satisfy the need for Indian labor in the burgeoning south of Brazil. Led by white woodsmen and supported by Indian hunters, *bandeirantes* hacked into previously unmapped territories, equipped with shotguns and harquebuses, pistols and blunder-busses, every manner of blade, and enough shackles, padlocks, and iron collars to bring entire tribes to their new masters.[11]

When the infamous *bandeirante* António Rapôso Tavares led his men into Belém in 1649 after a 7,000-mile trek around the pe-rimeter of the Amazon basin—a journey known as "the greatest *bandeira* of the greatest *bandeirante*"—Vieira was impressed by the feat of endurance but horrified by how the slavers treated their catch. "It is as if they were describing the sport of a hunting party," wrote Vieira after the meeting. "The lives of Indians mattered no more than those of boar or deer. All such killings and robbings have been tolerated in a kingdom as Catholic as Portugal for the past sixty years. The killers continue as before without any enquiry or trial or punishment, not even mildly shunned by public dis-favor: nothing but total public immunity."[12]

By then Vieira had lost what remained of his own innocence. The model villages were ravaged by disease. The friars' soul counts were dwindling. As far upriver as the Omagua territory, entire vil-lages were being wiped out by smallpox. "The howling of the sick, and the lamentations they gave for the dead, were such that they seemed to me like the torments of their souls," wrote the Spanish

Franciscan Laureano de la Cruz of an Omagua village in 1647, wiped out in a month. "They took the bodies of the dead, tied in bonds, and threw them into the middle of the river."[13]

Downriver, the Jesuits needed to demonstrate to the crown that their subjects were increasing in number, savages delivered from the Stone Age to the kingdom of the Lord. In an effort to clean up the slave trade, the royal government insisted that Jesuit observers supervise the flow of human traffic down the river, deciding who was a legal ransom and who an illegal slave. Afraid of inciting a revolt among the settlers, and desperate to fill their own villages, the Jesuit friars—including Vieira himself—skewed their accounting in favor of legal slaves. Those who were declared illegal captives were seldom returned upriver to their families; instead they were left to wallow in their own filth on boats and in corrals on the riverbank, kept like livestock, exposed to all manner of weather and disease until they caught such bad fevers that the chiefs would beg the friars for help.

The farther the slaving parties penetrated upriver, the deeper they spread epidemics. "Parents abandoned their children and fled into the forests in order not to be struck by that pestilential evil," wrote the German Jesuit João Felipe Bettendorf. By the 1660s, there was little he could do but take confession from the dying, flesh falling from their bones. "To confess them I was forced to put my mouth close to their ears, which were full of nauseating matter from the pox," Bettendorf wrote. "I rather feared that I would not hear them well, but it was God's pleasure that I heard them better than the others. The rotten smell seemed to me like the smell of white bread when it is removed from the oven."[14]

By the mid-eighteenth century, the Jesuit web of zeal and greed came unraveled when royal officials expelled the friars from

Brazil. Ostensibly, the Jesuits fell out of favor with the monarchy by falling prey to temptation and tarnishing the reputation of the crown with their greed. Government inspectors wrote scandalous reports of model villages where women and children bathed naked in plain sight of the friars, paddling young priests up the river as if they were kings while their congregations toiled in miserable huts. In truth, the missionaries had cornered the market on the only profitable trade in the Amazon—Indian labor—profits that Portugal needed to restore its fading glory. The Jesuits weren't the only offenders, or even the worst, but their secrecy aroused suspicion among the colonists, and they were easy scapegoats in their ominous black robes. In 1757, the government issued a decree releasing the model villages from missionary control. Within three years, more than 600 friars were removed from their villages. According to the new legislation, Indians would now be free to control their own destiny.

Naturally, they could not do so without the support of Europeans, so a second law established the *diretório*—the directorate—a system in which a white "director" was assigned to each model village, not to offer religious instruction but to help the Indians learn to make the most of their land. "From such fruitful and beneficial labors, the Indians themselves will derive profits that they will doubtless produce," wrote the architect of the legislation. "Those profits will make these hitherto wretched people into Christians, rich and civilized."[15]

Now the Amazon needed a proper capital. The royal government funded public works projects to transform Belém do Pará into a city worthy of a European empire. For too long, the city had been subject to the whims of the rain forest climate—deluges in the wet season, dust in the dry. The architect, António José Landi, reimagined the city, designing elegant cathedrals, cobblestone streets, a drainage system, and a governor's palace that was the envy of the colony, all built by Indian labor. Hundreds of mango trees were imported from Asia, a finishing touch that earned the city a deceptively pastoral nickname that persists to this day: Cidade das Mangueiras, City of Mango Trees.[16]

The human landscape would also need to be redesigned. One clause of the new directorate legislation required Indians to adopt European surnames. Another demanded that they wear modest clothing, free of the ornate decorations that were so integral to their individual identities. Another clause tore at their social fabric, decreeing that Indians live in separate houses instead of the large communal huts that wove their tribes together. Ultimately, the goal of the directorate was to merge the Indian and white races. Directors urged white settlers to live among the Indians and marry interracially.[17]

The directors themselves were plucked from the ranks of the military or the inner circles of Portuguese nobility. They devoured the lion's share of the profits, capitalizing on the European craze for chocolate and sugar. Their instructions made it clear that Indians were not yet prepared to be paid in money. For now cotton cloth would remain the prevailing form of payment. Soon the directors lorded over detribalized communities with an even greater reliance on slave labor than before. Unlike the Jesuit friars, who at least claimed to be building their villages in service of the Lord, the directors were rapacious men, free to shape their dominions to meet their desires. They forced Indian men to leave their homes to serve at the whims of new white settlers who received "licenses" to keep Indian laborers. The settlers subjected Indians who did not meet their cocoa, sugar, cotton, and herb quotas to sadistic and often fatal punishments. They forced tribesmen to undertake suicidal expeditions down dangerous rapids in pursuit of rare herbs, leaving their wives and children behind under the gaze of the director.

One visiting Benedictine bishop, João de São José, witnessed firsthand the trespasses of a director he called a "wolf among my sheep." Warped by isolation and power, the man had "persuaded himself that the first fruits of the purity of virgins about to marry were his due."[18] Despite the efforts of Bishop São José to seek justice for the tribe, no record exists of the director being punished.

Word spread to the farthest villages: being captured by whites was a fate worse than death. Witnessing their tribes ravaged by massacres, slavery, and plagues, countless Indians took desperate measures. Pregnant women took poisonous herbs to prompt miscarriages. Mothers drowned themselves along with their children to escape lives of slavery. Men committed suicide by eating earth, swallowing their tongues, or, in the eyes of missionaries, simply "giving up the ghost" rather than risk being "ransomed" from rival tribes who would at least assure them an honorable death.

"Whether they eat you or not is all the same to a dead man," one slave told the Frenchman Yves d'Evreux. "But I should be angry to die in bed, and not to die in the manner of great men, surrounded by dances and drinking and swearing vengeance on those who would eat me before I died. For whenever I reflect that I am the son of one of the great men of my country and that my father was feared, and that everyone surrounded him to listen to him when he visited the men's hut, and seeing myself now a slave without paint and with no feathers fastened to my head or on my arms or wrists—when I think all this I wish I were dead—and I regret my life."[19]

In the face of endless atrocities, many tribes rose against their oppressors. Though the marauders must have seemed supernaturally powerful, with their firearms, tools, and terrible epidemics, cunning tribes turned the invaders' vulnerabilities against them.

Revenge was rare but sweet. During one early encounter with Spanish conquistadors, a tribe offered to row a regiment of soldiers across their river. The soldiers gladly climbed aboard the long canoes. Halfway across the water, the Indians removed plugs from holes they had drilled in their boats. The tribesmen leapt overboard, swimming effortlessly to shore while the Spaniards drowned in their cumbersome armor. A few soldiers managed to reach dry land, only to be slaughtered on the riverbank.

When the notorious slaver António Arnau raided the Rio Urubu, he demanded that the Aruak tribe bring him hundreds of captives from rival tribes. The Aruak chief understood that the white men would come for his people next. One morning, the chief appeared in the Portuguese camp with a group of women, tied up as an offering for Arnau.

"Here are the slave girls you wanted," said the Aruak chief.

Eager to meet his new concubines, Arnau left his tent without any weapons. The Aruak chief "struck one blow on his head that immediately split it into two parts, and another on the mouth that broke his teeth and jaw."

The women had been bound with rotten rope. Hands free, they attacked the slavers while reinforcements volleyed poison arrows from the trees. When the Europeans fled for their lives, they were met by a secondary ambush that left few survivors to tell the tale.[20]

Many Indians fought for freedom until their last breath. Chief Ajuricaba of the powerful Manau tribe became a legend in 1728 when, after trading with the Dutch, his people were hunted down in a "just war" declared by the king of Portugal. When Ajuricaba and his allies were finally caught, they were chained and sent downriver. Along the way, Ajuricaba stirred his men to rise up. With chains as their only weapons, the prisoners attacked their captors on the open water. The canoe threatened to capsize as the Indians struck and choked the slavers with their metal bonds. It was not enough. Seeing his fellows bloodied and beaten, doomed to slavery or execution, "Ajuricaba leapt into the river with another chief, and never reappeared dead or alive."[21]

In modern Brazil, Chief Ajuricaba remains a symbol of Indian courage: death before slavery. Unfortunately, acts of resistance seldom kept the slavers at bay for long. For many tribes, the only hope was to flee up the tributaries, setting their home villages afire to leave no trace behind.

Only a few generations after Orellana and his flotilla marveled at riverbanks teeming with Omagua villages, the main river of the Amazon was a crypt. For tribes like the Ashaninka, fascination with the white man hardened into fear, an instinct that was sharpened over centuries. By the 1970s, tribes on the borderlands of Brazil and Peru still panicked at the site of Europeans, terrified that they would be boiled alive like their ancestors, their fat spooned from the cauldron to lubricate rusting guns.[22]

To this day, stretches where villages once thrived are overgrown, indigenous graves reclaimed by the forest. Even settled tribes like the Ashaninka of Simpatia limit their contact with the outside world. For an isolated tribe to emerge from the forest after all these years is an act of desperate hope.

In the summer of 2014, when Dr. Douglas Rodrigues of the Federal University of São Paulo touched down in a helicopter in Simpatia, the villagers marveled at the astonishing wind. A seasoned medical doctor with long salt-and-pepper hair, Rodrigues had been practicing in isolated communities since the 1970s when the legendary Villas Bôas brothers were still alive to champion indigenous rights. Back then his wife and children worried whenever he packed his bags for the jungle. Now his children were adults and his wife had grown accustomed to his field work. Over the years his hair had turned grayer, but a mission like this could still get his blood up like a med student on his first trip to the frontier.

It was July 6, 2014—almost a month since the isolated tribe first appeared in Brazilian territory—and the seven *isolados* had receded into the forest a week earlier with a stash of stolen clothing. The garments may have been carrying infectious agents even before the sickened braves took them away. If not, they would almost certainly be infected by the time the *isolados* returned home with their own worsening symptoms. For tribes with no tradition of wearing clothing, a T-shirt could become a deadly vector point, a cataclysmic gift passed throughout the village, worn for a time, passed along again, unwashed. If so, FUNAI's worst fears were almost certain to come true. Without immediate intervention, there could soon be a wave of secondary complications like pneumonia. Ninety percent of the village could be dead within weeks, an existential blow to the reproductive viability of a sixty-person population, rendering their language and culture essentially extinct. The survivors would be left to agonize over why the spirits had taken their loved ones, why they had been spared, where they were supposed to go now.

For days the FUNAI team and the Ashaninka had been calling out to the tribesmen, but to no avail. The *isolados* would only be found if they wanted to be found. The only hope was that they would choose to return to the strangers who had sickened them in the first place. By the grace of God, three days after Dr. Rodrigues arrived, three of the seven tribesmen announced themselves to the search party. All three had fevers and acute respiratory infections. Their immune systems had never encountered anything like this before. Through the interpreter, they confessed that they had been struck down by a curse.

The first priority was to locate the other four before they retreated to their families. The tribesmen helped them track down the others nearby. A boy and a girl among them were suffering from conjunctivitis so severe they were nearly blind.

After hours of conversation through an interpreter, Dr. Rodrigues and his team persuaded the *isolados* to accept food, fluids, and fever reducers. That was only a start. They needed time and space to recover before they returned to their village.

Where to set up an effective quarantine in one of the most remote corners of the planet? The only option was the abandoned Rio Xinane base, three hours upriver in the heart of the drug-trafficking corridor where just three years earlier a tribe like this one had been massacred.

No time, no choice. It took half a day to coax the *isolados* into the boat. They had never traveled this river.

As their conditions worsened, there was little they could do but trust this foreign elder. He was always watching one of them, scribbling constantly on parchment. His companions listened to voices crackling through a most peculiar black box. They spoke back as if answering ghosts.

One by one, the *isolados* climbed aboard, bracing themselves. The boat roared to life, lurched away from shore, scattered swallows from the trees. The wind cooled their fevers slightly as they snaked around the bend, then another, another, ever more forest, ever more river, beyond sight of any landmarks they could recognize.

8

THE DEVIL'S PARADISE

In the vacuum of the Amazon, screams can go unheard and sins can go unpunished. The illegal loggers, wildcat miners, and drug traffickers of the twenty-first century are the latest in a ruthless lineage, exploiting the rain forest and its people for profit; yet in the history of the region, the lust for one commodity scarred the human landscape like no other.

"To go rubber gathering. . . . A fatal phrase, which at certain seasons of the year runs from mouth to mouth in the wilderness," wrote nineteenth-century literary portraitist José Veríssimo of the rubber boom in the Amazon. "It is a fever. It is worse than the malaria."[1]

Demand for rubber began as a novelty. Early nineteenth-century visitors to Belém noticed that policemen walking the streets of the coastal port town stayed bone-dry on rainy nights, protected from the elements by waterproof capes and galoshes. The garments had been crafted from a peculiar resin the Omagua had been tapping for centuries, the sap of *Hevea brasiliensis,* a tree with smooth gray bark that rises more than 100 feet into the canopy.

In an ecosystem of hostile pests, fungus, and disease, hevea trees cast their seeds wide for survival. Even where rubber trees grow abundantly, in the constant rain and heat of the southern Amazon, only two or three tappable trees might be growing in a hectare—and tappers had to know where and when to look for precious rubber.[2] For this reason, early tapping operations were mostly small-scale family affairs. When the colony of Brazil splintered from the Portuguese empire in 1822, independence bred new patriotism in the southern cities of Rio de Janeiro and São Paulo, but the Amazon remained a backwater, populated by detribalized Indians and mixed-race river folk jaded by centuries of abuse at the hands of white overseers. Rubber at last seemed to give them an opportunity to seek their own fortunes in the forests they knew by heart.

During the dry season, tappers—known as *seringeuiros*—would wake before dawn to walk hand-cut trails in their territory. Along the way, they would slash the trunks of hevea trees and hang tin buckets to collect the precious white blood, drop by drop, moving from tree to tree to tree, trekking five or more miles through the forest each day to tap up to 150 trees, then walking the route in reverse to collect the day's harvest. Back at camp, they would build a fire to harden the sap in plumes of smoke, rolling the fresh latex into balls that could be hauled out of the woods at the end of the season. By nightfall, shoulders aching, eyes and lungs swollen from toxic smoke, skin itching from the bites of mosquitos and wasps, they would fall asleep, often on an empty stomach. To spend a season in the jungle was to flirt with starvation: the lack of easy game during the dry months could reduce the tappers to bones. But come the wet season, tappers could return to town with enough money to feed their families for a year while long rains washed away the aches of their labor.[3]

Before long, foreign exporters were shipping rubber to Europe, where entrepreneurs were crafting fine weatherproof garments for wealthy clients. Yet the material still suffered from instability. It grew tacky in heat, hard in cold weather. When an American inventor, Charles Goodyear, accidentally touched a batch of hot rubber to sulfur, he unwittingly changed the course of history in the Amazon. Miraculously, the rubber was stabilized in the reaction. Goodyear named the process "vulcanization," after the Greek god of fire.

Within a generation, the resin that Omagua mothers and fathers had used to fashion bouncy balls for their children became one of the most widely used commodities of the industrial age. Rubber gaskets for steam engines and pumps. Rubber belting and tubing for factory machinery. Rubber-coated carriage wheels, railway buffers, and telegraph wires. In 1845, a pneumatic wheel was patented in England, fueling demand for air-filled rubber tires. Thousands of new rubber tappers—and the traders who supplied them—were drawn into the forest in search of fortune. By 1853, export-scale rubber depots were belching smoke along the banks of the Rio Negro. In Pará, nearly every able-bodied man moved his family to the forest to seek their fortune in the rubber trade. "Mechanics threw aside their tools, sugar makers deserted their mills, and Indians their forest clearings," wrote one visitor, complaining about the outflux of labor so severe it caused a food shortage back in town. "Sugar, rum and even manioc flour were not produced in sufficient quantity."

The true boom had yet to begin.[4] In 1888, John Dunlop, a veterinary surgeon in Belfast, created the first detachable pneumatic rubber tire to help his son win a tricycle race. Bicycles became the latest European craze to redefine life and labor in the Amazon. Easy and affordable transit for the masses, soft-wheeled bicycles replaced the old boneshakers rattling along the streets of London.

The same year, André and Edward Michelin founded their tire company. The brothers soon won a motorcar race from Paris to Bordeaux, gliding on inflatable tires, ushering in the modern age of the automobile. World demand for rubber soared—and the Amazon had a monopoly.[5] South American land barons and Caribbean slave masters could not resist the siren call to the depths of the great river.

If geography is destiny, then Manaus was born to be the rubber capital of the world. A former military fort positioned at the meeting of the Rio Solimões and the Rio Negro, the fishing village of Barra was renamed Manaus in 1850. Soon it mushroomed into a hub of trading houses and shipping ports that directed cargo to the mouth of the Amazon and beyond. In the 1860s, it was a 3,000-person settlement that turned to muck in heavy rain; by 1890, 10,000 residents from all over the world were chasing rubber fortunes in the burgeoning capital; at the height of the boom a decade later, it was an orgiastic city of 50,000 where any desire could be fulfilled for the right price.[6]

The rabid growth would set the precedent for the booms and busts of the centuries to come. In 1893, shortly after Brazil shed the yoke of its monarchy, Eduardo Gonçalves Ribeiro, a young colonel with a meticulously engineered handlebar mustache, became governor of Amazonas. Following in the footsteps of previous governors in the Amazon, Ribeiro was fixated on legacy projects that would shape the jungle boomtown into a city that resembled a proper European capital. He planned a grid of cobbled, tree-shaded avenues. As if on cue, rubber barons erected palaces from stone imported by freighter. In trading houses across the city, accountants cooked the books, sweating in their suits, parting their hair and sporting thick mustaches to set themselves apart from the clean-faced Indians.[7] The sum of their calculations was one of the world's most modern cities, briefly known as the Paris of the tropics.

And what is a city without fine art? The crown jewel of Manaus was the Teatro Amazonas, a monument for the ages, built from opulent materials imported from the four corners of the globe. Ironwork arrived from Glasgow, tiles from Alsace, marble pillars from Carrara. A three-story neoclassical hall with a colonnade terrace and curved portico, topped by an art nouveau cupola, gleaming with the blue, green, and yellow of the new national flag, proof that Brazil had finally tamed its savage interior. What its theater lacked in size, it made up for in baroque finishings. Mirrors from France, chandeliers from Venice, Italian tapestries, framed by a 65-foot-high curtain that glorified Lara, the Tupi Indian water nymph. Inaugurated in 1897 with an Italian company's performance of Ponchielli's opera *La Gioconda,* the theater portended a new era of high culture and boundless prosperity. The French geographer Auguste Plane proclaimed: "The most refined civilization has reached the Rio Negro!"[8]

Manaus was one of the first cities in Brazil to have electric lighting and telephones. In 1900, it opened its boulevards to one of the world's finest tramways, with green American streetcars. In 1902, engineers devised a magnificent floating port to accommodate the seasonal rise and fall of the river. Waves of fish broke each morning, tiger catfish, silver arowana, and tambaqui slipping across imported marble slabs at the new municipal market. In 1908, the customs house opened its doors, a perfect simulacrum of the one in Bombay, built from red granite used as ballast on ships from England.[9]

Those ships returned to Europe with more rubber than the Omagua could have dreamed of harvesting. In 1880, 7,000 tons of rubber were exported from the Brazilian Amazon. Seven years later, exports had risen to 17,000 tons. By the turn of the twentieth century, exports would average 34,500 tons per year.[10] There was a new food chain in the rain forest. At the top, barons and speculators, drunk on newfound wealth, crowding bars, literary salons, department stores, and floating brothels. Each day more ships dropped anchor in the port, unloading chandeliers, gramophones, grand pianos, and fine furniture and then loading up the season's take of rubber for the return voyage along with loads of laundry to be washed at home in Europe.

"No extravagance, however absurd, deterred them," wrote historian Robin Furneaux. "If one rubber baron bought a vast yacht, another would install a tame lion in his villa, and a third would water his horse on champagne."[11]

Year after year when the river receded, thousands of tappers ventured deeper into the forest in search of "black gold." Lured by dreams of vast profits, they purchased supplies from clever traders who paddled from camp to camp, offering shoddy equipment, meek provisions, and the company of women at outrageous prices. The traders sold brittle tools, rifles designed to fail, and cans of spoiled meat from the Port of Manaus, where men poked holes in the tins, released the noxious gas, then soldered them shut. The starving tappers had no choice but to choke down the rancid food. Many of these tappers were illiterate river folk or detribalized Indians who could not do the arithmetic to settle their own accounts, placing their faith in the bosses and traders whom they relied upon for necessities and human contact. Trapped in a cage of debt, they began each season poorer than the one before until at last their creditors ordered them back into the forest with threats of violence to their families, abducting their wives and daughters to settle unpaid tabs.

The rubber barons learned that cultivating trees in plantations was a fool's errand in a biome as unforgiving as the Amazon, so profiteers plunged into the headwaters in search of new trees and fresh tappers. Brazil and Bolivia warred over the western border-lands that would one day become the state of Acre, home to the Ashaninka and the village of Simpatia. The farther the rubber men traveled into the interior, the harder it was to recruit labor. The deeper they explored, the more they relied on indigenous workers, plying them with gifts of alcohol and working them to the bone on a brutal quota system. One American observed detribalized tap-pers wincing as they sipped rum by firelight after a long day's work. His host confessed the drink was kerosene. "It won't hurt the Indians."

The dark spirits of the eighteenth-century directorate rose again in twentieth-century rubber stations. Indigenous tappers were sent on dangerous missions, while their wives and children were held hostages to the lust of the station directors. For tribes like the Oma-gua, rubber was a death sentence: more than 250,000 indigenous slaves were driven to their death during the boom. In a frenzy to meet their production quotas, barons and their enforcers built an economy fueled by atrocities. The notorious Suárez brothers threat-ened their slaves with rape and progressive amputation: a finger, then a hand, then an arm, until slaves met their targets or died from the effort. Those who did not provide were beheaded or left to die of starvation in the stocks, a warning to others.[12] Souls who per-ished quickly were fortunate.

In the Putumayo region of Peru, not far from the border where the Peruvian, Colombian, and Brazilian Amazon converge, the ruthless baron Júlio César Arana seized control of an area the size of a small country, bringing an entire ethnic group under his domain. Before his arrival, the natives in the area were known for their kindness and community. Tribes sent messages from village to village using percussive pipes at the top of their huts, played like xylophones to summon neighbors to dances and feasts. In the age of Arana, they sent warnings: hide your children.

In the gray haze between countries, Arana had a stranglehold on transportation to and from the region, controlling its only access points to the Peruvian trading hub of Iquitos. In this distant region, an inferior species of rubber trees needed to be felled instead of tapped, backbreaking labor in the heat of the jungle. Each rubber station was controlled by a director handpicked for his ferocity. Child soldiers were employed to round up stray laborers. Arana worked his slaves to the brink, ordering terrible, often fatal floggings, leaving scars known as "Arana's mark."

Eager to establish himself in Europe, in 1907 Arana and his associates listed the Peruvian Amazon Rubber Company on the London Stock Exchange, attracting more than £1 million from speculators drawn to rubber like piranhas to blood. Then in 1909, a young American engineer named Walter Hardenburg traveled through Arana's Putumayo region. It had been fifty years since slavery had been abolished in the United States, and twenty-five years since slavery had been abolished in Brazil, yet Hardenburg's disturbing accounts exposed some of the worst episodes in colonial history.

In "The Devil's Paradise: A British-Owned Congo," Hardenburg's chronicle for the muckraking British magazine *Truth*, he described the treatment of Arana's slaves in detail: "They are robbed of their crops, their women and their children," he wrote. "They flog them inhumanely until their bones are laid bare. . . . They do not give them any medical treatment, but let them linger, eaten by maggots 'til they die, to serve afterward as food for the overseer's dogs. . . . They mutilate them, cut off their ears, fingers, arms and legs . . . they torture them by means of fire and water, and by tying them up, crucified head down . . . they grasp children by the feet and dash out their brains against walls and trees . . . they have their old folk killed when they can no longer work and finally, to amuse themselves, practice shooting, or to celebrate, they discharge their weapons at men, women and children, or in preference to this, they souse them with kerosene and set fire to them, to enjoy their desperate agony."[13]

In the wake of the report, the British directors of the Peruvian Amazon Rubber Company dispatched a commission to investigate, led by the Irish-born diplomat Roger Casement, the investigator who had plumbed the atrocities of King Leopold's Congo. Ostensibly, the commission was tasked to report on the treatment of the Barbadians working there as subjects of the British Crown, but in his report, Casement could only describe the magnitude of the injustice by coining a new phrase: "Crimes against humanity."

In the isolation of the Putumayo, Arana's private empire had festered, his station masters using the quota system as a sadistic game. Boys and girls as young as six or seven were forced to carry balls of rubber that exceeded their own weight. Slaves were flogged or held in stocks regardless of age or gender. Wives were raped in front of their husbands, six-year-olds beheaded in front of their mothers. The worst of Hardenburg's claims were proven true. One station master flogged a woman's back into strips of flesh, then poured vinegar and salt in her wounds. Station directors doused disobedient workers with kerosene and set them ablaze, delighting in their screams. Those who dared to flee were hunted down and tortured in front of their kin, witnesses to the wrath of Arana.

"Such men had lost all sight or sense of rubber gathering," wrote Casement. "They were simply beasts of prey who lived upon the Indians and delighted in shedding their blood."[14]

Casement's investigation of the Putumayo sparked worldwide outrage. The report earned him a knighthood, yet justice in the Amazon was characteristically slow and human rights violations did little to quench the thirst for rubber. By the time a follow-up investigation ensued, the most egregious offenders had fled to the next frontier.

A crisis of conscience will never end a boom. Only supply and demand—and a brazen act of theft—closed the curtain on the gilded age in Manaus.

In 1874, as part of a mission to see if Brazilian rubber could be cultivated in Britain's southeastern colonies, Henry Wickham was deployed to the Amazon under secret order to secure 10,000 rubber tree seeds.

"Fortunately, I was left quite unhampered by instructions as to way or means," he wrote to Dr. Joseph Hooker, director of the Royal Botanic Gardens at Kew. "A straight offer to do it; pay to follow result. Now with that opportunity, question came home to me, how on earth to bring it off?"

Wickham caught an oceangoing steam ship that ran directly from Liverpool to the upper Amazon and disembarked where the main river meets the Tapajós. There he enlisted as many Indians as he could on short notice and raced to collect and preserve as many hevea seeds as possible in the few days before his steamship passed downriver again for the return journey across the Atlantic. With help from the British consul at Belém, Wickham managed to sneak his payload past customs, explaining that he was carrying a sampling of exceedingly delicate specimens for the queen's own royal gardens. A week later 700 seedlings were budding in a terrarium in Europe. It would take twenty-five years for this first crop to mature, but when it did, rubber production in Malaya soon eclipsed production in the Amazon.

Between 1910 and 1915, the price of rubber exported from the

Amazon cratered 80 percent. Rubber stations shuttered. The skies cleared of smoke. The forest crept back into Manaus. The barons vanished so quickly that some of society's finest gentlemen only announced their departures in newspaper advertisements.[15]

9

QUARANTINE

When Dr. Rodrigues and the *isolados* arrived at the FUNAI base on the Rio Xinane, troops of squirrel monkeys froze on their branches at the sound of the outboard motor. Army ants and tiger beetles kept on with their work. The forest had retaken the outpost; vines and undergrowth camouflaged the dilapidated wooden structures, the only neat rectangles for miles in any direction. Abandoned since the narco attack of 2011, the site had once been a storehouse for basic provisions on the western border. Its modest garden provided fruit and diversion for the station agents. Its satellite dish was an island of telecommunication in a sea of radio silence. Its flagpole was the final landmark of federal power before the Peruvian border, flying the green, yellow, and blue that some citizens on the fringe of the country had never seen before.

Before the FUNAI team unloaded, they inspected the area to make sure nobody was squatting. There had been reports that traffickers were still using the base as a pit stop for long journeys down the Xinane, but Dr. Rodrigues and his team had no choice. These were the only facilities for hundreds of miles fit for a makeshift hospital where the isolated Indians could be quarantined from further infection. There was no telling how long they might need to stay, whether the respiratory complications would develop or subside, or when they would be well enough to return to their village. But there was no point in speculating—the risk of extinction was right there in their chests, a wet wheezing in Dr. Rodrigues's stethoscope. Until the respiratory symptoms cleared up, the best thing the Indians could do was stay hydrated and calm.

Despite the urgent medical situation and the risk that traffickers could return at any time, it was tranquil at the outpost, almost impossibly still compared to the noise of São Paulo where Dr. Rodrigues taught at the federal university. He was among the world's foremost experts on indigenous health, yet he had only treated isolated Indians on three other occasions since the 1970s. Even if the base lacked supplies, such close quarters provided a precious opportunity to study the tribe, their physiology, behavior, and worldview. At the same time, the team had to be vigilant about the basics, taking every precautionary measure to keep from introducing new infections to the group. Through interpreters and hand gestures, the team managed to learn in broad strokes what had driven the tribe from their village. Traffickers armed with automatic weapons had unleashed a torrent of bullets and set fire to their huts. These young *isolados* fled to seek help from their settled neighbors in Simpatia. The oldest of the scouts was still in his twenties.

First things first. Dr. Rodrigues and his assistants opened files for their new patients, jotting names, approximate ages, symptoms, and medication regimens, snapping digital headshots for future reference.[1] One by one the *isolados* stepped into the modern world of recordkeeping. Dyky, an eighteen-year-old boy with a moderate respiratory infection. Xinatxakaiá, a nineteen-year-old boy, presenting white phlegm and a mild fever, but otherwise improving. Pûwû, a twenty-year-old female, running a bit of a fever, early signs of urinary tract infection. Pánaro, an eighteen-year-old male, a touch of fever and phlegm, and a mild allergic reaction to paracetamol—use dipyrone instead. Káda, a twenty-year-old male, feverish, but already on the mend. Hainuno, a fourteen-year-old boy, mildly feverish, nothing too serious. Thirteen-year-old Tosku, a girl with a mild fever and conjunctivitis in both eyes, growing anxious as her symptoms worsened.

"I'm going to die," Tosku told the interpreter, convinced she was cursed. "I got close to the others and now I'm going to die." Unlike settled Indians who understood the basics of modern medicine, these youngsters had a primitive sense of illness. Supernatural forces and witchcraft explained every phenomenon. The fever reducers were beginning to do their work, yet some patients were hacking and coughing, still hexed.

The team had to do their best to keep Tosku's panic from spreading to the others—it only made things worse. Seeped in fear, none of the *isolados* had been eating or drinking, suspicious that a wicked batch of eggs had spurred their fevers and eye infections. Without food and water, the regimen of fever reducers, vaccinations, and antibiotics would be of little use. Dr. Rodrigues and his team pleaded with them to eat rations of unfamiliar food, the only way to regain strength.

Morning, noon, and night, Dr. Rodrigues pressed his stethoscope to their warm chests, closing his eyes to hear their hearts and lungs. Three of them presented symptoms of pulmonary fluid. These patients he monitored more closely, taking temperatures every hour on the hour, making sure their fevers ticked below 37 degrees Celsius and stayed there.

What was racing through the minds of these youngsters during those strange days, fighting against spirits with the help of a white shaman? Among the items they had brought from their village was a Corinthians wallet—a souvenir of one of the country's most famous soccer clubs—yet they knew nothing of São Paulo or any other city. They had come out of the forest seeking help. They had found it. A few short days of tender care cannot dissolve ten generations of mortal fear, no matter how miraculous the white man's remedies or how kind his tone. Tosku's eyes were so infected that her lids were practically glued shut by the discharge. She was blind and terrified, but her companions would not let her get too close to the strangers.

When at last Dr. Rodrigues convinced the *isolados* to let him clean and treat Tosku's eyes, she improved almost immediately. This was a turning point in relations between the tribe and the strangers. Now they trusted Dr. Rodrigues to administer the antibiotic azithromycin to keep harmless phlegm from worsening into pneumonia. Day by day, the young Indians shook their symptoms. Regaining energy, they grew rambunctious, eager to try on uninfected modern clothes. The group gathered around a fire, roasting piranha, modeling their fresh outfits, thumbing through the doctor's notebooks as if they could somehow divine his secrets.

Dr. Rodrigues and his team knew the tribespeople needed time to recover fully—at least three days without presenting signs of infection before it would be safe to let them return home. Only then would there be zero chance they would doom their village with a disease agent. For now they would sleep uneasy nights in the noisy jungle, ears tuned to the stroke of outboard motors on the dark water.

In the early 1980s, outsiders came for oil in the territory of Peru's Nahua tribe. More than half of the Nahua perished. In the 1990s, outsiders came for mahogany trees in the territory of the Murunahua. More than half of the Murunahua lost their lives. While isolated tribes may be able to ward off trespassers with arrows and spears, they remain helpless against the invisible invaders from which they never developed immunity: influenza, measles, and pox—infections that still have the same catastrophic potential as they did in centuries past.[2]

By the grace of God, the *isolados* under Dr. Rodrigues's care had only contracted severe colds, not influenza, and help had arrived before the infections could ripen. By the third day at the Xinane base, their symptoms had almost entirely receded, fevers broken, eyesight restored. Sick of the white man's food, the Indians were restless and eager to hunt. At midday they took their bows and spears into the forest.

Hours later, Dr. Rodrigues and his party heard shouts from the jungle. *"Chara, chara!"*

It was one of the few words they shared with the interpreters. It signified something good. Dr. Rodrigues and his team followed the calls into the thick jungle. There they found the tribe waiting.

The *isolados* had prepared a feast of gratitude. Grilled armadillo, roasted birds, bananas cooked to perfection, all arranged on a table of banana leaves. Years later, Dr. Rodrigues remembers it as one of the best meals of his life.

"I don't have a picture," he said, "but I'll always keep the image in my mind. Gourmet! Absolutely marvelous."

The culinary and cultural exchange was a momentary distraction from the challenge at hand: How would the doctors deliver treatment to the other surviving villagers without risking the transmission of infection? Where exactly was the tribe living and how long would it take for the *isolados* to trek back to their village? Nobody dared speak it, but there was even doubt whether anyone back home was still alive. These youngsters could be the last of their people. At best there were only a few dozen individuals left on the planet who spoke their language. To return for survivors was to risk a hail of gunfire.

Through one of the FUNAI interpreters, Dr. Rodrigues proposed a plan: the tribespeople would return to their village as stealthily as possible, gather up their mothers, sisters, and brothers. In one moon, they would bring them here to the Rio Xinane base to be immunized against the most dangerous of the white man's curses: influenza and chicken pox.

Before the *isolados* departed, Dr. Rodrigues gave a primer on influenza and how it is spread. He warned that if the tribe did not return to the outpost, the entire village could be in peril. At last the tiny group slipped back into the forest with supplies for the journey home. The Ashaninka of Simpatia could breathe a sigh of relief, but for their isolated neighbors, this was only the next chapter in a struggle for survival. They were on the run again, no telling who might give chase.

On July 14, nine days after he arrived, Dr. Rodrigues flew home to São Paulo. In the din and smog of the city, still processing the beauty and terror of the encounter, he typed up his report for the Ministry of Health. This was the first time that twenty-first-century Brazilian doctors had treated an isolated tribe face-to-face. So far they had luck on their side. There was no more time left to lose. There were preparations to be made before they met again. If they met again.

The *isolados* returned before the next moon. On July 26, 2014, on the white man's calendar, less than two weeks after Dr. Rodrigues and the FUNAI team released the isolated tribesmen from quarantine, the young Indians began leading their kin through the forest to seek help at the Rio Xinane base. It's impossible to know how they convinced their loved ones to come out of hiding, how they explained the bizarre magic they would encounter downriver, but in all likelihood the plea was simple: if we don't go, we will die.

It was an existential calculation, at once an escape and a surrender, running away from the killers who stalked them, toward the whites they had avoided for centuries. Generations of their elders had observed the outside world from just beyond its borders. Now the fears that had kept the tribe in isolation all these years—slavery, rape, massacre—were outweighed by the fresh trauma of violence. The whites plundering the forest were determined to exterminate their tribe; the whites at the river base were determined to stop that from happening.

Day by day, more men, women, boys, and girls appeared on the river as if they had slipped through a portal in time. Within two weeks, there were twenty-four all told, ranging from middle age to infants, equally dazzled and disturbed by the sights, sounds, and smells of the modern world: steaming ice in white foam coolers, rainbows of motor oil on the river surface, minty sticks of gum in the mouths of the white-cloaked outsiders who spoke a most sonorous tongue. A quiet fear lingered, whispers among the tribe: do not let the children out of your sight.

This time the government had made every possible preparation. Dr. Rodrigues and a team of interpreters, anthropologists, and FUNAI officials convened in the town of Cruzeiro do Sul beforehand to formulate a plan. Their objectives were simple: vaccinate the tribe against the most potentially lethal diseases; draw blood samples to begin developing a comprehensive profile; create medical records for individuals; conduct interviews to draw a genealogic tree, discover their ethnic group, and pinpoint their reason for contacting the Ashaninka.

For two days in Cruzeiro do Sul, the team gathered supplies and packed vaccinations in thermal boxes. They were prepared to take off for the Xinane base on the morning of August 8, but the helicopter had been dispatched to another emergency on the river. Every day counted. The team returned to the airport the next day for a sunrise departure, only to reverse course when a storm turned them back. Each lost hour could mean a lost life, but they would be no use to anyone if the helicopter crashed.

At last, on August 10, they woke early to clear skies. It was an anxious flight to the upper Xinane, the river and the trees wavering beneath their rotors as the pilot made his descent, slow and easy. At any moment the tribe could question their decision and vanish into the forest.

On the ground, the team unpacked their supplies and fired up their generator. Indians looked over their shoulders at the glass vials, rubber gloves, and filtered masks. How could the team convince the tribe to accept vaccinations? How to even explain their purpose?

The team's only choice was to demonstrate first on themselves. A nurse allowed the Indians to examine the medical equipment as they pleased while an interpreter explained how the potions worked. The tribe watched with skepticism. Nothing they had observed from a distance could have prepared them for this sorcery: syringes, needles, tubes of dark blood, remedies the interpreters promised would protect them from dangers they could not see until it was too late.

The next morning, Xinatxakaiá, one of the young Indian men who had witnessed Tosku's eyes healed by Dr. Rodrigues, volunteered to give it a try. The others watched as he accepted the vaccinations, the nurse pricking him in the arm like the sting of a wasp. For a day and a night they waited, the team praying there would be no adverse reactions that would frighten the rest of the tribe.

At sunrise, aside from a little pain at the injection site, Xinatxakaiá said he felt fine. His family discussed how to proceed. There were those among the tribe who still gazed at their caretakers with doubt and fear.

After some murmuring among the elders, at last it was agreed. There would be no injections for the two littlest ones, just toddlers. They were too young for such strong medicine. The rest of the tribe would open their veins to the strange needles.

While the medical team administered vaccinations and kept watch on a few cases of common cold, the anthropologists and interpreters went to work drawing a tree of the twenty-four members of the tribe, their names, approximate ages, and relationship to each other, taking careful note of the distribution of age and gender. When one of the women presented a spike in temperature after her vaccinations, the anthropologists recorded the forest herbs she foraged in hopes of treating her own ailment. Day by day, the interpreters apprehended new words, casting a wider net as they sought to uncover the story of the tribe.

The tale was grim. These people called themselves the Txap- anawa. None of the adults among them had surviving parents. Over time they had lost their family to common illnesses: diarrhea, malaria, flu. Others had been killed in territorial disputes with other tribes. The worst of it came not long ago: the attack by log- gers who had torched their village, forcing the scouting party to seek help in the village of Simpatia.

With its already depleted families diminished further, the tribe was on the brink of losing their reproductive viability. One of the women had taken two husbands, contrary to their tribal custom, to command the loyalty of more men to provide for children. They had survived their first outbreak by a stroke of good fortune. The virus the young scouts originally contracted was a mild rhinovirus or adenovirus—essentially, a bad cold. An outbreak of influenza might have had irrevocable consequences. Even now a case of the sniffles was circulating around the Xinane base team. The Ashaninka had arrived with a sick child of their own who was being kept in separate quarantine for fear that an errant cough or sneeze could threaten the entire ancestral line of the Txapanawa.

Today, the *isolados* could marvel at these new wonders. Tomorrow, they had a decision to make: settle near the base or return home?

If the tribe chose to resume their nomadic life, Dr. Robert Walker and his team at the University of Missouri would be watching by satellite. Of the eight groups under the gaze of the research team, seven are considered critically endangered, none more so than Site Y: a tiny village of the Yanomami ethnic group in the state of Roraima, Brazil.

This community of Yanomami lives on the edge of extinction, their blood, their song, their words for the moon and its phases all in danger of being extinguished. Should they be extracted from the jungle, saved from the slavers they have been warned about since childhood? Would a controlled contact be tantamount to an alien abduction by a well-meaning but overwhelming force, a space age version of the Villas Bôas brothers' controversial pacification and relocation projects?

The question strikes at the heart of an age-old debate in the New World: what should be done with the Indians? In centuries past, discussions orbited the question of how many lashes would properly motivate the Indians without killing them. In the centuries since, the conversation had barely evolved: should tribes be exterminated, pacified, relocated, or reeducated? Nowadays there are some who argue that if isolated tribes can survive in protected quarters—and even serve as stewards of the rain forest—they should be moved from their ancestral territories to strategically chosen reserves in hopes they will never wander back to civilization.

Stephen Corry of Survival International argues that Walker's approach is shortsighted. "Let there be no doubt: isolated tribes are perfectly viable, as long as their lands are protected," he wrote in a scathing response to Dr. Walker's research. "To think we have the right to invade their territories and make contact with them, whether they want it or not, is pernicious and arrogant."

"It's a nice myth," says Walker of the Noble Savage rhetoric, "but it's not facts. We can't keep them in a zoo."

Walker and his team argue that contact is already happening, that more contacts are inevitable, and that modern medicine can make controlled contacts significantly less risky than in the past. Anthropologists can debate the issue in abstract terms for another generation while the juggernaut of progress renders the whole discussion moot. Two multibillion-dollar transcontinental transportation projects—the 1,600-mile Interoceanic Highway and the 3,300-mile Twin Ocean Railroad—will make the penetration roads of the twentieth century look like wagon trails.[3] Until then, cocaine smugglers and chainsaw teams on the borderlands are not going to tolerate arrows and spears while policymakers and academics analyze the data and argue over its implications.

Should tribes be left to fend for themselves and die in the way of their forebears? What of their lone survivors, the last of their people? What right do governments have to rip villagers away from the rivers where they were born? What price will be paid if they are left to fend for themselves against smugglers wielding weapons of modern war? If outsiders expose them to vaccinations, antibiotics, and DNA testing, what other marvels should the Indians be shown? Does respecting their self-determination mean leaving them alone, or does it mean showing them the modern world—and letting them choose their future?

The Txapanawa did not wait for the white men to settle their debates. After a glimpse of the dangers and wonders of the twenty-first century, they—the last of their kind—chose to return to their forest, their era, their way of life. They were grateful to meet their neighbors, but now they wanted to go home.

FUNAI told the tribal leaders that the Xinane base would remain open to them. If they encountered a health problem, an invasion, or any other danger, they could always come back. Yet everyone must have known at the moment of departure the tribe could not keep outrunning bullets.

The group waded back into the forest. Only the spirits could keep them safe. Dr. Rodrigues collected his papers, snapped a few last photos, and returned home. Back among his books and file cabinets at the University of São Paulo, he composed his second report. In the commotion of Brazil's World Cup collapse at the hands of Germany, the headlines from the upper Xinane faded from the papers. Now and then, Dr. Rodrigues's thoughts would flit back to that marvelous feast, the smell of roasted armadillo on a table of banana leaves, laughter erasing fear as the sun filtered through the understory.

That winter at the University of Missouri, Dr. Walker and his team convened to discuss a batch of new imagery—a disturbance at Site Y, the Yanomami roundhouses. Their small clearing had been abandoned. Flyovers confirmed that the village, once a thriving circle of huts, gardens, and children learning to hunt, was overgrown. The current location of the villagers was unknown. Intelligence on the ground confirmed invaders nearby, wildcat prospectors on a quest for gold.

PART II

HOW MONSTERS ARE BORN

A MESSAGE FROM THE FEDERAL PRESS AGENCY IN BRASILIA

from: Chris Arnold ███████████████████████

to: ████████████████████████████████

date: Thu, Aug 13, 2015 at 8:34 PM

subject: Re: Press tour ao Encontro das Águas, 20/6, 9h / Press tour to the Meeting of the Waters

Dear ███████

My name is Chris Arnold. You may remember me from last June. I was one of the American journalists that you worked with during the World Cup in Manaus.

I'm writing to share some good news. I'll be returning to Manaus next week to write more stories about the Amazon. I was wondering if you're still working in the press office of the State of Amazonas. If so, I would be grateful for your assistance. Amazonas is full of exciting stories, and I'd love to ask you some questions.

Sincerely,

Chris

from: █████████████████████████████

reply-to: Chris Arnold ████████████████

date: Fri, Aug 14, 2015 at 6:24 PM

subject: Re: Press tour ao Encontro das Águas, 20/6, 9h / Press tour to the Meeting of the Waters

Dear Chris,

I don't work in Manaus, I was only there during the Cup. I work at the Federal Press Agency in Brasilia, the capital of Brazil.

I'm sure you can find the two press officers from the Cup on Facebook. ████████ and ████████████ They are from Manaus and work there. But as a former reporter, I can suggest umpteen places where you'll find better stories. Far beyond the Amazon.

The indigenous population there is shrinking every year because of alcohol and teen suicide. The Indians don't see any hope for their way of life. Their traditional food supplies have vanished. I was in Xingu National Park 20 years ago and saw little Indians eating potato chips

So, here are a few ideas:

-Have you heard of the Pantanal? It's a wetlands eco-system with alligators in droves and gorgeous birds like the tuiuiú. Google some pictures.

-Here's another idea about the history of the Brazilian people. You already know about the Indians, but blacks are more prevalent in capitals like Salvador where the African

culture was born in Brazil. You can taste some of their traditional dishes and watch presentations of Candomblé.

-If you want to see the European traditions in the south
of the country, visit Rio Grande do Sul, where you'll find cities full of the descendants of the Italians and Germans.

-And there's nothing like a walk back in time in colonial
Brazil. The historical cities of Minas Gerais will make you
feel like you're in a scene from an epic movie: Ouro Preto,
Tiradentes, Diamantina. All the luster of the country's gold
rush, beautifully preserved.

-Another gem is Paraty, in the state of Rio de Janeiro, a
beautiful colonial city near the sea.

-São Paulo and Rio are must-sees, as are the beaches
of the Northeast. And Brasilia has one of a kind architecture,
as it was designed specifically to be the capital of Brazil. (It
celebrates its 55th anniversary in April.)

So there you have it. I hope you find other trips to take in Brazil
and that you can see many things beyond Amazônia.

Manaus is undergoing a huge surge in violence with
sometimes six murders in a night. The rich people of the city
exterminated more than 200 parakeets that were inconve-
niencing the idiots in their gated condominiums. (They hung
poisoned nets in the trees to catch the birds.) It's a horror.
The police rape girls on the bus lines.

Get out of there, buddy. Indians are a worn-out cliché. Go
see the real Brazil. Sorry to be so harsh.

Trust me.

Hugs,

███████████

███████████

Brasília

10

BITI'S GANG

A year after the World Cup, shit had gotten worse in Manaus. Whole families were out of work. The lucky ones who still had jobs could afford less each payday. Beans, clothes, gas—everything was getting more expensive by the month. Lately it seemed like people only talked about debts, the Ultimate Fighting Championship, and dirty politicians. *Lava Jato*—the Jet Wash scandal—proved what most Brazilians knew in their gut: the country was led by bandits. For years the fat cats at Petroleo Brasileiro, the state-run petroleum enterprise, had been letting other fat cats gouge the enterprise on contracts, using the dirty money to buy real estate, toys, and friends in high places. The graft ran straight to the top. Now the streets were full of protestors saying enough is enough. Even Lula and President Dilma were under the microscope. Hundreds of millions in public money showered on rich crooks while workers could barely keep up with the bus fares.

If there was one good thing about the heat wave pouring over Amazonas, at least it gave people something to talk about besides corruption. Lately there was hardly any rain, not even a breeze to blow away the alien haze over the city, a blend of exhaust, factory pollution, and wildfires burning up the forest. The overcrowded prisons were overheated, with inmates killing each other like mad rats. Even Facebook was sweltering. In one viral video, a woman cracked an egg on a pan in the street, zooming the camera in slowly, the shadows of her friends bobbing on the pavement, nervous laughter as the yolk fried in the sun. People posted snapshots of bank thermometers on the fritz, digital displays gone haywire as if the heat were beyond measure.

To take a bus during rush hour was to climb aboard a torture device, passengers crammed like cattle, headaches on the way to work, brawls on the way home. The *Diário do Amazonas* sent a cub reporter to investigate the outrageous temperatures on public transit. Even the air-conditioned executive buses registered 28 degrees Celsius. On the common line, the mercury touched 45—113 degrees Fahrenheit. A doctor warned that young children and old people should avoid the bus if possible. Make sure to drink two liters of water a day. Three liters if you have a long commute. Eating extra fruit couldn't hurt, either.[1]

Otherwise, pray for rain.

On the afternoon Biti and Foro decided to execute the plan, the sky was white hot at the edges. Two weeks they'd been following this guy. They trailed him in stalled traffic, heat-struck drivers roasting behind their steering wheels. They trailed him in afternoon thundershowers that brought people out into the street for a moment of sweet relief. They trailed him too close for comfort, ducking to avoid his gaze in the rearview mirror. By now they knew his routine, his shortcuts, his favorite stops for a little coffee and chitchat.[2] They knew that when he stepped into Banco

Bradesco on Avenida Leopoldo Péres, he'd come out with a sack of cash for some dude in Educandos.

Who knows why Biti and Foro decided today was the day? Perhaps Biti had the final word. She was baby-faced but she was the eldest, a big sister who could slap you at any moment. The gang took her direction; six people split up into three cars. Maybe one of them had cold feet after too many days of surveillance. Are you sure there'll be enough cash for all of us? Or maybe the heat was driving everyone bonkers. How long can we keep following him, anyway?

Whatever it was, it was on Friday, July 17, just before three o'clock.

Foro and Biti rolled into the parking lot in their little black Volkswagen Gol. All clear. Foro messaged the others. Biti stepped out and crossed the tacky asphalt, trying to act however people acted when they had banking to do.

Inside, the lines were bunched up behind the few cash machines that worked. Through the second set of doors, the tellers were swamped, business owners making end-of-week deposits or withdrawals, checking their phones while they shuffled ahead like zombies. The bank tellers helped old pensioners count their money. They helped young workers understand why their paychecks seemed to be shrinking, with interest on old loans deducted from their wages like tiny cuts—loans to buy microwaves, washing machines, refrigerators, motorcycles, debts from last summer or the summer before, when they had a job, when their currency was worth more. Debts from the high times, when banks like this one sent boats out on the river to teach Ribeirinhos how to use an ATM, how to swipe plastic and get what you needed like magic, how to score a free TV if you signed up for a satellite dish. Debts from the low times after that, future paydays borrowed, spent, boiled, and eaten.

Biti fell into line behind the target. Did he notice her? Maybe he was too hot to notice anything.

Finally it was his turn at the counter. He handed the girl a slip of paper. She read it and tapped her keyboard. The target glanced, gazed up at the security camera. Would he suspect something when he turned around?

And there's the money bag. No use guessing how much the teller was putting in there. The fact that there was a bag at all said enough. Even divided among the six of them, it would be more cash than they'd seen in their lives. The target said thanks and headed out like it was no big deal.

Biti tapped a message into her phone. Here he comes.

He pushed open the door, white bag in hand. Stepping into the bright lot, he took a bit of the cold air with him.

For Sergeant Afonso Camacho, private security was a side gig. These days everybody could use a little extra money. For twenty-four years he'd been serving in the state military police, lately at the 5th Military Police Academy,[3] teaching kids who had their eyes on the future. Good kids. The sons and daughters of other military police. With the support of their parents, he helped forge that raw material with discipline, honor, and good hard exercise. Some kids needed more forging than others, spent too much time playing video games or chasing girls. Others watched too many cop movies, not realizing that movies teach you nothing real, not even how to inspect and clean your weapon. Sergeant Camacho taught his students that it took more than a crisp uniform or a gun to make a soldier. You needed to see the country and your fellow citizens with a sense of duty. He commanded respect from his cadets so that one day they too could command respect.

But let's face it: respect didn't pay the bills. That's why, like a lot of police, Sergeant Camacho had a second job transporting cash. In a city like Manaus, if you had a lot of cash to move around, there were ninety-nine reasons to hire a cop like Camacho. The city was growing, so the gangs were growing, and if you were robbed once, you were marked as easy money. Military police could legally carry a gun. If it came down to that, Camacho would use his weapon to keep your hard day's earnings safe. And you didn't need to look further than the newspaper to see that there were only two kinds of cash in Manaus: stolen cash and cash that hadn't been stolen yet.

When Camacho stepped outside he ran into two men—boys, really: baseball caps, jeans, sunglasses, one in a striped shirt, one in a black shirt. They announced their intention, pistols like wasps. By the time he drew his .38, they'd each stung him with a bullet, one in the arm, one near the heart.[4]

Camacho collapsed in the shade of a pickup truck. *Meu deus.* Adrenaline spiking, he fired back from the ground. Missed. He was living the very ambush cadets were warned to avoid. Caution. Vigilance. Situational awareness. He was a failing grade in a basic security training scenario. *Hit bad, fuck, hit bad.*

The attackers were still on the other side of the truck. One snatched the money bag. *Let them go. It's over. Just let them go.*

But where was the honor in that?

Camacho took aim and fired again. Missed. The boy in the striped shirt took a step back as if he'd forgotten something.[5]

At nightfall a new clip interrupted the procession of heat wave memes on Facebook. A cell phone video taken in the parking lot of a bank in the *centro.* A woman huddles behind her dashboard.

She tries to keep the camera steady, but the footage trembles, filtered through a dirty windshield. Two men dash away from a truck, one clutching a white bag. The other turns around as if he's forgotten something. He bends down, grabs a gun and cell phone from a guy lolling in the forgiving shade of a pickup truck. Then a farewell shot to the head.

The person capturing the video ducks under her dashboard, worried the robbers might notice a witness and shoot, but there is no time for more trouble. They slip into a getaway car and skid out of the lot into a river of rush hour horns.

Customers and tellers peek out of the air-conditioned bank. The door opens, leaking cold air into the afternoon. They stand over the body, glancing over their shoulders.

Within the hour news crews were sneaking around the crime scene. The body was covered with a thin foil blanket to reflect the sun. A police helicopter thwapped overhead, combing the alleyways for suspects. The paramedics loaded the body and left in such a hurry that they got into a fender bender right there in the parking lot, pinning a TV cameraman's leg so that he too had to be transported for medical attention while the footage went back to the studio.

The evening news fanned the flames of speculation. Police sergeant killed execution style. Point-blank range. Sixty grand stolen. What was a cop doing with so much dough?

The footage loops back to the start, multiplies across TVs and phone screens, and loops back to the start again—one, two, three thousand times—all afternoon and into the night, point-blank shots, farewell slugs, robbers running out of the frame.[6] Eyewitnesses say there was a woman involved, but Biti and the guys have already divvied up the bills and gone their separate ways up and down the river.

11

MAXIMUM POWER

On the afternoon Sergeant Camacho was killed, the inmates at the prisons on the outskirts of Manaus had their hearts focused on their upcoming weekend visitations, the chance to slip into a fresh uniform and lay eyes on familiar faces: mothers and kids, sisters and wives, those girls from the corner who know how to save a man's life with a blow job—and how to sneak an ounce or a razor past the x-ray machines.

Every Saturday and Sunday, hundreds of women and children in the capital crowd into northbound buses, lumbering along BR-174, that strip of patchy highway that runs 2,234 miles straight to Venezuela. It's a long, hot ride, past the Pioneer factory, the Whirlpool factory, the SC Johnson factory, the luxury golf resort, the landfill where cell phone signals flutter and the rumble of logging trucks scatters the vultures picking through the refuse before it gets buried.

Out here the concrete gives way to jungle. Military police run exercises on the margins of the road, firing live ammunition and tossing grenades into the trees. The women and children step off the bus at the intersection of the highway and the natural gas plant at the 8-kilometer marker. Even though they are only 20 kilometers north of the city, a heat wave like this can make a two-hour trip feel like a sweltering ride all the way to Caracas.

Joining the procession, the weary visitors carry packages up a gentle slope where three private prison facilities are nestled in the forest, one after the other on the left side of a single-lane penetration road, flanked by guard towers and concertina wire.[1] First is the Instituto Penal Antônio Trindade (IPAT), which opened its gates in 2006 to alleviate overcrowding in the system. Originally built to house 736 inmates awaiting trial, ten years later the place holds 1,006 inmates in three blocks. Second is the Centro de Detenção Provisória Masculino (CDPM), erected in 2011 to handle overflow from IPAT. Built for 810 inmates, five years later it houses 1,383 pretrial detainees. The detainees here might be accused of anything from robbery to murder to missed alimony payments. Those convicted will move to the last unit on the road, tucked into the jungle more than a mile off the main highway, Complexo Penitenciário Anísio Jobim (COMPAJ), a former agricultural penal colony turned maximum-security prison where 1,821 inmates are kept in confined and semi-open spaces designed for 1,072.[2] All told, the three units on this road, the largest in the Amazonas state prison system, are grinding along at 161 percent capacity. Their only relief in sight is a barren clearing near the main highway where São Paulo–based prison management company Umanizzare will eventually build a fourth unit to capture the overflow.

For Umanizzare each prisoner is like an annuity, adding to the income stream from their Amazon portfolio where the prison population has nearly doubled since 2010 in response to a crackdown on drug trafficking. Nationwide, only 3 percent of Brazil's prisons are privately operated. In the Amazon, almost 40 percent are private enterprises, bolstered by the support of local, state, and federal politicians who accept the company's campaign donations and parrot its talking points: these facilities are bastions of hope and rehabilitation, offering legal assistance, health clinics, self-improvement classes, and arts and crafts to bandits who had never learned to respect their mothers or teachers.[3]

When it comes to private security, you get what you pay for. At the primary gate a security team inspects everyone's identification, noting place of origin and time of entry. Approved visitors proceed through a second gate and shuffle through a line to present themselves for a second time, fake IDs being one of the most basic disguises of prostitutes, messengers, and assassins. From there, visitors proceed through a third gate, where they are separated into two lines—one for men and one for women. Everyone gets an intimate pat-down, a close inspection of any packages, and a cursory wave of the metal detecting wand. Agents withhold any electronic devices and flip through the pages of any books or magazines. Then it's through the fourth gate for taste tests and x-rays. All food and drink is placed on a plastic table for a trio of inspectors. Every bottle of Coke gets poured into two little cups, one for the visitor, one for the guard to make sure it's not poison, liquor, or drugs. If there's a child present, all the better. Offer the kid a taste and watch the mother's eyes. Then visitors put their purses and bags on the conveyor belt for an x-ray gaze; nail files, razors, and executive pens glow electric blue on the monitor, begging to be seized before they end up in someone's neck. If guards want to use metal knives and forks during meal breaks, they have to bring their own set of cutlery from home and keep them in little pouches in a secure locker area near the staff dining hall. Not a single scrap of metal makes it past security—at least not unless it's been paid for.

This wouldn't be a prison without contraband. The guards

catch everything except what they aren't supposed to catch. A rock
of cocaine swimming in a Coke bottle. A cake with pineapple
frosting, nineteen candles, and a blade. Clamshell phones tucked
between a child's legs, allowing cartel lieutenants to connect with
their men as easily as they would from a stronghold in the city.
Prison officials will tell you these oversights are simple human er-
ror. What they mean is that, now and then, someone might look
the other way. A new vendor might deliver a cart of laundry or a
bag of beans or rice or beef. It takes a lot of deliveries to cook 3,000
meals a day plus special turkey dinners for Christmas. It takes a
lot of female guards to search so many female visitors, and what
kind of woman wants to work in a place like this? Even the honest
ones might not want to search as deep as you might need to search
or touch a child where she should never be touched. Even in an
ideal world of fully staffed and funded prisons, the cartels will always be better staffed and better funded, engineering new ways to
get what they need inside. Mold cocaine into a baby doll. Fly a
pistol over the fence with a drone. *Inovação, meu mano.*

These days it's harder than ever to keep order inside. Prisoners
are stacked like sardines, mattresses strewn across the floor of every
cell block, each one a hiding place. If guards have to focus on one
threat, they focus on the cell phones, nerve centers for death and
deals across the city. The men might not have enough beer inside
these concrete walls, but they have an abundance of time. Time
to dwell on broken promises, to stoke old rivalries and dream up
new ones, to hatch plots and avenge the betrayals of another man
in a similar cell up the road—or on a corner on the outside. Time
to wait until just the right time, to place a phone call, to arrange
the threats, amnesties, and payoffs necessary to unleash blood fury
right under the nose of the warden. Dial up your man, pass the
phone like a hot potato. If a guard sees something, tell him you

see something, too: his mother soaking beans in the kitchen, his wife painting her nails, his daughter walking home from school.

The chirping forest beyond the fences belies the turmoil inside the units. In the dank cells of COMPAJ in 2002, Gelson Carnaúba, the drug boss known as "G" who controlled traffic in the southern zone of Manaus, orchestrated a rebellion to avenge the death of a fellow inmate who had been beaten and tortured by guards. Armed with a revolver, knives, and hammers, G and his men killed twelve inmates and a prison guard during a twelve-hour skirmish, the catalyst for a chain reaction of riots and escapes on the prison road that continues to this day.[4] On visitation weekends, those riots feel like a false memory. In the main yard of IPAT, a few prisoners punt around soccer balls, scanning the line of new arrivals for familiar faces. Vendors in the parking lot huddle under the shade of canvas tents, coolers sloshing with half-melted ice. They sell energy drinks, water, and chips to the thirsty pilgrims whose arms ache with offerings: small televisions, newborn babies, plastic containers of freshly made pastries.

After an hour or more of security procedures, the visitors get a few minutes of time. There are those who know their loved ones are not innocent, but don't they all believe their loved ones can be redeemed? Why else bring homemade cookies, fragrant soap, school art projects? The men whisper with their families, play solemn dominoes with their sons, watch TV in their cells when there is nothing left to say. Some prisoners have been waiting more than six months for their sentencing. Depending on the crimes and the ruling, they may ultimately just move down the road, making new friends and new enemies along the way, deeper into the forest, a longer walk for their loved ones until one day not a soul will make the trek anymore and the only solace left will be prayers.

. . .

The riot at COMPAJ landed G in a federal prison in the south of Brazil, cut off from the river that fed his empire, from his lieutenants and foot soldiers, from the crooked authorities who looked the other way while he expanded his operation from within the walls of a lax state prison. In 2006, G crossed paths with a long-time rival who'd also been shipped to the federal pen, José Roberto Fernandes Barbosa, known as "Zé Roberto da Compensa," the boss who controlled traffic in the western zone of Manaus. Now the sworn enemies were locked up alongside leaders from Brazil's oldest and most organized criminal operations—Comando Vermelho (CV) of Rio de Janeiro and Primeiro Comando da Capital (PCC) of São Paulo—both eager to build bridges in the north.[5]

Organized crime has festered in Brazil's prisons since the years of the military dictatorship, when everyday smugglers and thugs were imprisoned alongside dissident artists and academics. Between torture sessions at the hands of the guards, the prisoners exchanged lessons. The criminals learned the importance of organization, strategy, and alliances. The guerrillas learned how to harvest the enormous profits to be found in the narcotics and firearms trade. One man's bank robbery was another man's expropriation. Destabilizing the military regime served both sides. By the turn of the century, even as Brazil grew into a young democracy, its prisons remained cradles of organized crime, cities within cities where criminal leaders recruited new talent, directed traffic, and ordered murder, torture, and extortion inside and beyond the walls. On the outside, they were enabled by local politicians eager to keep violent crime confined to the penitentiaries and poor neighborhoods—and to grab their share of power, profit, and influence.

When it came to operating a sophisticated international syndicate, G and Zé Roberto had some catching up to do. The factions in the south of Brazil had diversified their businesses over the years, creating new markets beyond drugs and guns. In the most disenfranchised neighborhoods, PCC and CV could provide residents with basic utilities, cable TV and broadband internet, loans, protection from police intimidation—and jobs on the corner. At a time when President Lula's policies were enriching the elites and elevating millions to the middle class, the largest "gangs" were creating a second state for those still left on the bottom. They could even influence the real state by guaranteeing votes from their people.

Up north, G and Zé Roberto had been embroiled in petty local turf wars, trading bullets with rivals and cops across town. Now leaders of CV and PCC—themselves rivals who had forged a tenuous alliance—took the young bosses from the Amazon under their wings. Look at the big picture, *cara*.

G and Zé Roberto were quick studies. For all their differences, they had one thing in common: northern pride. PCC and CV had built their nationwide networks by absorbing local and regional crime families, making them offers they could not refuse. Now after years of bloody competition, the two biggest gangs in Manaus had reached a fork in the road: remain at war over the river or form an alliance that could rival PCC and CV.

And so it was that in a federal prison cell a thousand miles from their home territory, the Familia do Norte (FDN) was born, its creed etched in a handwritten statute that would soon govern who suffered and who thrived in the Amazon.[6]

From the union of the children of this land is born the "Family of the North," whose purpose is to seek peace, justice, and freedom for all those who dream of the equality of men. And from the synthesis of our ideas it is agreed that all members of this family are subject to the rules and guidelines of this statute and of the directives that emanate from our council.

Article 1: We are all equal without distinction of any kind and our freedom of conscience and belief is inviolable. We ensure that everyone has the right to peace, justice, and freedom.

Article 2: Our struggle is against the oppressors and those who disrespect the rights and dignity of human beings. Injustices, encroachments, rapes, email or inequalities of any nature inside and outside prisons shall not be permitted.

Article 3: Among our brotherhood, respect for loyalty, fraternity, and transparency will prevail, and it will be the duty of all to respect order and hierarchy in the family.

Article 4: The family members of the union will be protected and respected. And the family of one will be the family of all.

For many of Brazil's elites, the revolutionary rhetoric of factions like the Familia do Norte is merely propaganda disguising a ruthless crime syndicate. In the neighborhoods where those factions operate, many residents believe Brazil's elites are the real enemy. No matter whether you consider them gangs or militias, the Familia do Norte is the rabid underdog in the South American drug wars, armed by the communist rebels that lord over Colombia's cocoa fields.

At the turn of the twenty-first century, while cocaine use in North America dropped, the use of cocaine in Brazil nearly doubled. The country grew into the world's second largest market for the drug, flooding the Amazon River with narco traffic.[7] By consolidating resources, G and Zé Roberto established a near monopoly on one of the most coveted smuggling corridors in the world: the Solimões River from Tabatinga to Manaus, a key waterway for cocaine manufactured in Brazil's neighboring countries.

The FDN knows the Amazon the way a spider knows its web. By night, while riverboats and freighters chug up the Rio Solimões toward the Colombian border, they cross paths with clandestine traffic headed downriver, destined for Brazil's capital cities or the wide-open Atlantic, where their cargo can be offloaded for the discotheques and boardrooms of Portugal. Along the way, smugglers skirt past military checkpoints and navy patrol boats using miniature submarines or riverine bypasses that only appear for a week or two during the wet season. Others cross by small aircraft, taking off from impromptu airstrips hacked into the Peruvian and Colombian jungle, flying low over the canopy, landing and unloading without making a blip on Brazil's border radar. Just as many tons cross the old-fashioned way—right under the noses of federal officers—hidden in bushels of fruit or the bellies of livestock, disguised as consumer staples like shampoo and children's toys, or molded carefully into the hulls or motors of their boats. If anything draws the suspicion of the authorities, the smugglers soldier on by bribe or by force, unafraid to empty the clips of their assault rifles on federal police or pirates from rival groups.

It takes a family to bring product a thousand miles downriver and into the right hands. Boat captains willing to bend regulations. Merchant marines willing to toss bodies overboard. Porters who know which crates to deliver to which stalls at the market in Manaus. Thousands of brothers and sisters, each with a price: checkpoint agents, missionaries, poachers, financial analysts, traveling shoe salesmen.

It takes a family to keep everyone safe on the river, in the streets, throughout the cell blocks. In the Amazonas state prison system, every inmate undergoes triage upon arrival: medical, psychological, and legal. Officials ask them to reveal their gang affiliation so they can be placed in a friendly cell block, which makes life easier for everyone. Sometimes new inmates lie to get closer to their enemies, but inmates will finger an imposter on sight if they don't kill him first. When new detainees get to their cell block, they undergo a second interview with an FDN "sheriff" and with Rafael, the FDN's IT guy, who enters key information into a laptop: name, neighborhood, family members, crimes committed. If the new inmate isn't already working for a boss in his neighborhood, he will be assigned one, along with a password. They will wait six months to a year for a trial, lifting weights, getting tattoos, and boosting their boss's team in the prison soccer league. They eat, shit, and breathe the doctrine of the FDN along the way, enjoying drugs, girls, and cell block parties as rewards for their loyalty. Upon release, they use that password to log the purchase and sale of cocaine, crack, and marijuana, leaving a portion of the profits in a neighborhood box on the tenth of every month.[8] By 2015, the FDN was collecting more than R$100,000—roughly $30,000—from boxes in Manaus each month with the goal of raising the rake to a million. Rafael already had more than 10,000 names in a computer registry, pinging his BlackBerry with notifications—details about family members and rivals—updated daily from the COMPAJ cell that served as the FDN's central command center.[9]

It takes a family to spread goodwill and cheer. FDN profits financed legal assistance for family members in state and federal prisons, financial assistance for families who lost their sons in shootouts with the PCC bastards encroaching on their neighborhoods. Profits went toward improving the conditions inside the prison, smuggling in TVs, snacks, beer, and drugs to keep the brotherhood happy on the inside. Profits financed uniforms for the prison soccer league, team names corresponding to the teams of young men assigned to the FDN lieutenants, including a rising young enforcer, João Pinto Carioca, known more commonly as "João Branco," patron of the squad "Potência Máxima"—Maximum Power—a force on the jail yard field and in the streets of the capital.

Soon there was enough money flowing that Zé Roberto could sponsor a legitimate team on the outside, Compensão, the pride of his old neighborhood. In just one season, Zé spent R$320,000 to boost his team to the local championship, where they competed in front of fans who waved banners that celebrated their FDN patrons like folk heroes.[10]

It takes a family to win a championship, to do it all with enough profit left over for the ten-year-old wearing a Compensão jersey on a corner in Babilônia, slinging grams at 3:00 a.m. during a thunderstorm.

On the afternoon of Sunday, March 9, 2014, in the São Francisco neighborhood of Manaus, only a few miles from where workers were racing to finish the Arena da Amazônia in time for the imminent World Cup, Colonel Oscar Cardoso of the Civil Police sat in front of a roasted-fish stand near his home, bouncing his eighteen-month-old grandson on his lap. A white van turned the corner and skidded to a stop. Four gunmen stepped from the vehicle.

"Everyone out of here," said one of the gunmen, waving the innocents along with his weapon.

"You stay put," said another, handgun trained on Colonel Cardoso.

The customers left their food behind at their tables. The cook abandoned the fish on the grill, smoke wafting into the street.

"Please," said Colonel Cardoso. "Spare my grandson. Let me call his mother."

"Hands where I can see them," said one of the gunmen.

"Take me. Spare him," said Cardoso.

One of the gunmen plucked the child from Cardoso's arms. "No!" said the colonel. "Please!"

The child squealed, squirming in the stranger's grip. The gunman set the baby on the ground, carefully like a melon, then returned to the business at hand. Taking advantage of the distraction, the colonel bolted from his chair. Together the assailants stopped him in his tracks, twenty shots ringing up and down the street. On the sidewalk the baby cried while his grandfather bled out. By the time the neighbors returned to comfort the child, the van was gone and the colonel was dead.[11]

The assassination came as little surprise. For months Cardoso had been a marked man. Lately he had even asked to be relocated to a village—any village—somewhere in the interior where he wouldn't have to watch his back day and night. It had all begun last October when Cardoso, chief of the special task force, was arrested with seven of his men on charges of trafficking, kidnapping, and extortion. For months Cardoso and his men had been squeezing local drug dealers, confiscating their cash, weapons, and drugs—even selling product to rivals—all using the apparatus of the civil and military police to monitor criminals, trace their routines, and abduct them at moments of maximum value. There was so much coin in the game now that even the police needed their cut, but Cardoso and his men crossed the line when they kidnapped João Branco and his wife. They wanted R$55,000 as ransom. When João Branco refused to pay, Cardoso allegedly ordered his men to rape his wife. There was nothing João Branco could do but pay, but six months later he settled the score, ordering the hit on Cardoso from behind bars at COMPAJ.

The police who attended Cardoso's funeral vowed revenge as the casket was lowered into the hot earth.[12] Some believed Cardoso was innocent. He had a reputation for being an active and hard-working officer. Others felt that no matter what he had done, there was no excusing the assassination, evidence that the brazen cartel needed to be put in its place. The other men who were arrested with Cardoso knew they were marked. They requested transfers or special detention—anywhere they could be safe.

A week later, federal police entered COMPAJ to serve a federal warrant to João Branco for orchestrating the assassination of a civil police officer. The charges would almost certainly land him in a federal penitentiary, away from the high council of the FDN and the porous prison environment that allowed him to direct his men with minimal interference. In the predawn hours, federal police readied their forces.

When they arrived at COMPAJ, they discovered João Branco's immaculate cell, empty.[13] His unit was swept perfectly clean, adorned with ceramic tile and freshly painted walls, a cooling fan and a set of bookshelves where he could keep his belongings. When business was booming, you had to stay organized, and João Branco liked to keep lists. Lists of special deliveries to the prison—phones, precision scales, power tools. Lists of special requests for the supervisors: repairing the soccer field outside, TVs for soccer season, physical therapy for his aching knee. Lists of family members and rivals who would stand trial by the strict doctrines of the family. Lists of who would live and who would die. The only thing out of place was João Branco himself. Along with nineteen other men, he had escaped through a sewer tunnel underneath the prison walls and into the forest beyond.

A search of the cell revealed how. Nine different cell phones. Radio police scanners. A police-issue walkie-talkie that investigators suspect he had used to communicate with assets in law enforcement, who told him precisely when to make his break.

The failed arrest only revealed the family's gathering strength. With a sprawling network of business associates, the FDN was like a hydra that only seemed to grow with every severed head. What was once a few old-timers paying local kids to bag dope and keep watch on the corners was now a regional empire. Lawyers. Accountants. Realtors. Thousands of World Cup tourists fattened the FDN portfolio, buying pussy and cheap blow in love motels, sliding their credit cards at burger joints and poker rooms, ordering a second bottle of red wine at steakhouses financed and furnished with laundered funds. If the old Manaus was built on balls of rubber, the new Manaus was built on bricks of coke.

João Branco was not done.[14] In the summer of 2015, from an unknown location authorities suspect may have been in Venezuela, he distributed a blacklist, the names of five rivals who had allegedly raped the mother of one of the FDN's men. Week by week, João checked names off his list, each one a warning shot at the Primeiro Comando da Capital.[15]

The PCC was the unquestioned master of Brazil's southernmost cities, born in the prisons of São Paulo. Until recently it was a blip on the radar here in the north, but lately the PCC were making inroads on the streets of Manaus with an upstart local faction, the Spartan 300, a reference to a bloodthirsty movie from years back, laughable, as if anyone believed they had 300 men on the streets of Manaus. (If they did, they wouldn't for long.)

João Branco was on the run. G was still behind bars in federal prison. Zé still kept dominion over IPAT and COMPAJ, where about 70 percent of the inmate population was FDN. The remainder was split between the smaller gangs and stuck to their own blocks of the unit. The family could get into those blocks if it needed to, placing a call to the right supervisor or taking a sledge-hammer to the right wall if they saw fit to deliver justice. There was only one rule: the FDN makes the rules.

On the afternoon that Sergeant Afonso Camacho was killed leaving the bank in Educandos, Hudson de Souza Lopes was trying to follow the rules. Guys called him "the Giant" because he was big. But big men make big targets, and the Giant was on the blacklist because of his work for the Spartan 300.

At 4:30 p.m., not two hours after Sergeant Camacho was shot down, the guards at IPAT had their hands full. Maybe it was a sloppy shift change. Maybe someone lost his keys. Maybe it was the heat or the anticipation of visitors that had the prisoners in a frenzy. Or maybe the right guard looked the wrong way. What-ever it was, the Giant found himself alone between cell blocks.

By the time he realized nobody had his back, it was too late. A group of rivals seized his arms, brought him hard to the ground.

With a shiv they sawed his head from his neck, a message for the other 299 Spartans. The Giant stared emptily at the fluorescent lights as his life pumped out onto the mattress.[16]

The guards arrived too late. They could only separate the in-mates and confiscate their phones before they could post more pictures to the web. It was already shaping up to be a long weekend. The police hadn't even pinned down who was responsible for the death of Sergeant Camacho. Now this.

The sun sank below the razor wire. New orders pinged the cell towers of Manaus. Revenge for the Sergeant. Revenge for the Giant. Night owls coming awake. Blood bats stirring in the trees.

12

THE BLOODY WEEKEND

The hour had come for reprisal. No time for judges or juries, only executioners. Images of Sergeant Camacho circulated on the social networks. Here he was alive in the classroom with his loyal cadets, now dead at the exit of the Banco Bradesco in Educandos. The posts were shared among family and neighbors, among former students and old friends from boot camp, among on-duty police who spread details about the suspects on their battalion group chats. Images of the Giant spread online before news of his death reached the state authorities. Here he was alive at a party just a few months earlier, now dead on a flea-infested mattress at IPAT, his severed head gazing back at his body. The pictures flitted from phone to phone, his PCC and Spartan 300 brothers vowing revenge, the FDN calling its enforcers to arms. Expect retaliation. Shoot first.

The massacre began after dark on Friday.[1]

10:30 p.m. Jolson Martins Ramos, twenty-seven years old, a fry cook, standing near his motorcycle on Rua Dr. Rezende in

Bairro Zumbi in the Eastern Zone. Two riders on another moto approached as if they wanted directions. The oldest trick in the book. But instead of trying to steal his bike, they shot him down within shouting distance of an evangelical church.

11:01 p.m. Júlio César de Oliveira Bentes, forty years old, sitting on a curb on Rua Marçal in Bairro Compensa in the Western Zone—Zé Roberto's home turf. Two men seared past on a motorcycle and sprayed him with gunfire.

11:30 p.m. Anderson Sales Soares, thirty-two years old, a folkloric dancer who had stopped by the Shadai Café for a cold one after a performance. The other patrons saw the gunmen step out of a red Volkswagon Gol, took cover behind walls, countertops, plastic tables that couldn't stop a rubber bullet. Anderson didn't see them in time.

Around the same hour, twenty-five-year-old Edipo Viana de Souza was killed while standing alone on Rua Umarizal in Bairro Santo Antônio in the Western Zone. There were no eyewitnesses, but the neighbors heard gunshots. Dogs and rats scattered from the alleyways as the vehicle sped away.

In the Southern Zone, twenty-five-year-old kitchen helper Josenilson Dias Bernardo—known as Frango—was killed on Rua Puço Fundo in Bairro Educandos—G's old streets. He was just off work, headed home with his girlfriend. Two cars, silver and red, circled the neighborhood like vultures. One of the cars slowed near the curb, summoned Josenilson to the window. Leaning inside, he was surprised by gunfire.

11:40 p.m. Three young men were talking about girls on a street corner in Bairro São Francisco in the Southern Zone. Twenty-six-year-old Rodrigo Anderson de Carvalho Soares, unemployed. Thirty-two-year-old freelancer Paulo Nazareno de Souza Filho. Their buddy, Junior, tagging along. A motorcycle zipped up the street, one of a hundred motorcycles that passed by that night. This one turned around, riders opening fire. Junior, the lone survivor, rushed to the hospital in shock.

11:45 p.m. In the Western Zone, three more young men talking about girls on another street corner in Bairro Compensa. Twenty-three-year-old Samar Marciel de Souza, twenty-one-year-old Fabrico Cerdeira Dias, and Cristiano da Silva. This time a pair of Volks-wagen Voyages, red and white, rolled down their windows and opened fire. Only one survivor, Cristiano, a slug in the leg.

Midnight. A new day. July 18.

12:12 a.m. Harlem Duque Protazio, a shadow outside a blue house on Rua G in Bairro Armando Mendes in the Eastern Zone. Two men, one motorcycle, seven fatal shots.

12:41 a.m. Twenty-year-old freelancer Frank Silva de Almeida, talking shit with two friends in Bairro Jorge Teixeira in the laby-rinth of the Eastern Zone. A silver car approached like an angel of death. Frank's two friends scrambled to escape. When investiga-tors arrived, the neighborhood gossip queen Sterlite emerged from her house to describe the vehicle. She said the killers were going for a guy who used to live on the street, Neném. Neném was still hanging around, threatening people: don't say a word to anyone about any of this.

12:42 a.m. Diego da Silva Lira, eighteen years old, and twenty-three-year-old fry cook Jhonatan Nobre, both killed in front of a house in Bairro Zumbi in the Eastern Zone. A black car came around the corner, shooting.

1:00 a.m. Álvaro Gabriel Rodrigues Ribeiro, a twenty-five-year-old from Tabatinga, walking down the street to grab a beer after work. A red Volkswagen passed, rolled down the window: Hey! When Álvaro looked inside, he saw men wearing skull masks. Gun-shots. Álvaro ran. The VW raced away. Álvaro looked for a place to hide. The car flipped a U-turn, growling behind him. Wounded, Álvaro slipped underneath a food cart, held his breath, waiting.

Waiting. The car crept past, headlights flaring on the sidewalk. Waiting. The car stopped, a click of doors opening. Footsteps drawing closer. Caught, Álvaro begged for mercy. The gunmen fired at point-blank range.

1:10 a.m. Bairro Tarumã. Twenty-one-year-old student José Luan Ramos Picanço, standing in front of a bakery with his wife, Adriana. Two Voyages, red and silver, approached and opened fire. They missed Adriana. She held her husband in her arms, crying out for help, shushing him, crying out again. José had been arrested before. For theft. For beating her. Back when he was seventeen, he was the wheelman during the carjacking and kidnapping of a civil clerk. They took the victim to a house in Bairro Campos Sales, tied her up while they took her car for a joyride and maxed out her credit cards. The next morning they released her, but how could he ever take part in such a thing? Only God knows the shape of justice, but that night, holding José as he left this world, was Adriana thinking of those old crimes or of the new José, the one trying so hard in school?

1:30 a.m. Antonio André Carvalho Trinidad, walking alone on Rua Margarida do Campo in Bairro Gilberto Mestrinho, the farthest eastern stretch of the city where Manaus hits the national forest reserve. Two men on a motorcycle, gunshots scattering bats from the trees.

Over on Rua das Macaúbas, nineteen-year-old freelancer Victor de Castro Farias was drinking with a girlfriend. Two men on a white motorcycle passed, flipped around, opened fire. The last thing Victor saw was his date running for her life. The gunmen shot five times in her direction. *Gracias a deus*, they missed!

1:30 a.m. Twenty-two-year-old student André Ribeiro de Souza—some guys called him Rato—hanging with friends on Rua Viriato Corrêa in the Southern Zone. A burst of gunfire from a silver Volkswagen Fox. Three other guys were hit, but André was hit the worst. Now their corner was a crime scene, marked off in yellow tape, awash in blue and red lights. A kid found a .40 caliber bullet casing on the street, same as the police used. André died before he could learn that two of his friends had been spotted in an alley near the bank in Educandos where that sergeant was blasted.

2:18 a.m. Twenty-five-year-old freelancer Cosmo Paulo Ramos— Sassa, to his friends and enemies. Sassa had waved down a moto-taxi for a lift home. On the way back, along Rua Laranjeiras in the Northern Zone, the *taxista* noticed something fishy in the rearview mirror. They were being followed. A black Volkswagen Gol. Someone shouted, "There, Sassa!" The Volkswagen pulled beside them at a stop. Someone inside rolled down the window.

"Get out of here," the man inside told the *taxista*. It wasn't a request. The *taxista* fled his own bike, gunshots ringing out behind him.

Across the city, phones buzzing, reporters and EMTs and doctors stirred from their beds.

2:30 a.m. Twenty-five-year-old freelancer Erick Soares da Silva, parking cars with his uncle at a community gathering in Bairro da Redenção in the West Central Zone.[2] It'd been a long night, guarding cars, waving drivers in and out of their parking spots, a little bit more, a little bit more, stop, a fingertip away from someone else's fender, perfect. A four-door silver Volkswagen Gol rolled by slowly, its windows tinted. Erick waved his towel: there's a spot right here.

The driver crept closer. The windows rolled down. Gunfire. Erick and his uncle took cover. Erick didn't find cover in time. The VW fled. Witnesses screamed for help, trying to wave down a police cruiser just a couple of blocks away. The cops didn't race over. They didn't chase after the Volkswagen. They didn't even flip on their lights. Instead they rolled away from the scene, cool as an escort.

2:33 a.m. Eighteen-year-old construction worker Ricardo Araújo Barbosa, partying at Preto's house in Bairro Tarumá in the Western Zone. A dark car pulled up out of nowhere, shooting. The partygoers scattered. The car followed Ricardo. Ten shots later the party was over.

3:00 a.m. Twenty-one-year-old vendor Samorino Maciel de Souza took his last breath on Rua Joaquim Barareiro in Compensa.

5:30 a.m. Twenty-one-year-old construction worker Joeliton Pessoa da Silva was waiting for sunrise on Rua Jesus de Nazaré in Bairro Novo Israel. He never saw it.

5:55 a.m. Daybreak.

13

A SENSE OF SECURITY

Saturday morning civil police detectives pondered the crime scenes like abstract art. They measured bloodstains and skid marks. They counted bullet holes in flesh and stucco, searched cracks in the street for shell casings. They scanned the faces of on-lookers for potential eyewitnesses who avoided eye contact or made too much eye contact. The property owners waited with mops and brooms, at a loss to explain how their security cameras didn't seem to be working—a dead battery, a cracked lens, full tape—any reason to send the detectives away so they could sweep up the glass and scrub the concrete, sending pink soapy rivers trickling downhill toward the creeks.

It was going to be a busy day—twenty-six people killed over-night, some yet to be identified. Just that morning they found a ripe one behind the club on Avenida Sete de Maio. Another no-body was found dead out past the airport, but they couldn't fig-ure a time of death.[1] Even in a city accustomed to homicides, this was some next-level shit: more shootings in seven hours than would usually be recorded in a week. The rumor mill was churning. On social media, the military police warned citizens to keep their eyes open—this was war.[2] Members of the Familia do Norte swore there would be hell to pay for anyone who dared to come into their neighborhoods without permission. João Branco and his lieutenants sent a general alert to the entire family on WhatsApp.[3]

> **WARNING MANAUS:** Yesterday, Military Police Sergeant Camacho was murdered in a robbery in the neighborhood of Educandos, which set off a war between criminals and police. Since then, 24 bodies (as of 11:30 am today, 7/18) were found in various parts of the city. Among them were many known criminals, but unfortunately some innocents and even police officers. In police WhatsApp groups, they are commenting that this is the fault of a possible agreement made between the government and leaders of the criminal factions during the electoral period, which generated chaos in public security. Be very careful when traveling through the streets of the city, stay calm during police approaches and please avoid traveling in more isolated areas of Manaus. Take special care with motos carrying a passenger!
>
> **ATTENTION:** This is not a hoax. If you have doubts read the news in the local papers! I reposted to other groups.

FDN loyalists fed the confusion, flooding the social networks with comments implicating the police. Military families responded with their own accusations, blaming the drug factions for the chaos in the streets. None of the back-and-forth brought back the dead.

• • •

The lawlessness and disorder could not stand. The governor of Amazonas, José Melo, had just won reelection on a law-and-order ticket. One of his first orders of business had been installing a fresh trident of top cops.[4] Sergio Fonte, former federal police brass with a track record of battling narcotraffickers, was appointed the new state secretary of public security, charged with overseeing Colonel Gilberto Gouvêa as commander of the state's military police, and Inspector Orlando Amarel as the head of the state's civil police. Colonel Gouvêa had started his tenure by announcing an ambitious plan for his first ninety days: more street patrols in clubs and bars to search for drugs and guns, more police stationed in front of schools to protect the little ones, and naturally, better working conditions for the police themselves.[5] After all, policing is a tough job, and these are family men who deserve the best physical and psychological care.

A minor incident just a few months after Colonel Gouvêa took his post underscored the need for reform. Three members of the elite Força Tactica—the same task force that Colonel Cardoso was using to extort drug dealers in 2013—were caught on street surveillance video beating two detainees with lengths of lumber. They went maybe a little too far. The victims were just kids, a fifteen-year-old boy and an eighteen-year-old girl, and one of the boards broke over one of the detainee's back.[6] A weak board, no doubt, but you can see why the incident was plastered all over the news, né? Yet Colonel Gouvêa wasn't about to let a few bad apples spoil the reputation of his men. Fact: only 3 percent of the 10,000 members of the military police in Amazonas were currently under investigation. Fact: corruption is a problem across Brazil, not just in the military police. Just look at the headlines if you want more facts. Just not today's headlines, which were already calling it a massacre.

Saturday morning, while messages from the police and the cartel swirled on social media, Secretary Fonte convened a press conference, sitting tanklike alongside Colonel Gouvêa and Inspector Amarel. A unified front, deadly calm. Taking turns at the mic, they confirmed what the bleary-eyed press corps had stayed up all night covering.

"This event is outside of the curve," said Fonte.[7] So far the authorities had gathered that some of the crimes seemed to have some resemblance. The recurrence of two pairs of vehicles and two gunmen on a motorcycle. Rest assured, detectives were already scanning the security footage, and even if the footage was sparse, rest assured, they were working on a plan to integrate the private security cameras into the city's sprawling 230-camera surveillance network, which, rest assured, would come in handy next time.[8]

Colonel Gouvêa leaned into the microphone. "The military police are also keen to find out the motive behind all of the homicides in our city," he said. As of 1:00 p.m., he would ramp up patrols, calling more than 700 personnel to assist in the streets.

Fonte elaborated, pausing now and then to make sure the reporters caught the details. In addition to the colonel's efforts, citizens could expect 140 extra men, in groups of three, to patrol each of the areas where the homicides occurred, mostly in the Eastern and Western Zones. They would board buses, search cars, walk the streets, demonstrating their presence and talking to citizens along the way. An intelligence-gathering operation and a show of force. And no, they hadn't forgotten about Sergeant Camacho. Helicopters would stay in the sky. Extra squads would continue monitoring key roadway checkpoints. Patrol boats would keep racing up and down the river to find the killers.

It was all cold comfort to the families waiting to identify their dead at the homicide investigation unit where the doctors in the morgue were working overtime to keep from running out of fridge space. There were only so many ways to write the same cause of death: hemorrhaging from multiple gunshot wounds. With sterile tools, they plucked slugs from the victims, dropped them into a tin with a clang, .38 caliber and .40 caliber rounds, characteristic of standard-issue police weapons.

By nightfall on Saturday, word of the murders had reached every corner of the city, boat passengers were carrying the news to villages up and down the river, and even the talk show hosts in Rio de Janeiro and São Paulo were discussing the deteriorating public security in Manaus. Despite the damage control by Secretary Fonte and Colonel Gouvêa, the killing resumed.

11:30 p.m. Another unidentified man, shot dead on Rua São Tomé in Bairro Parque São Pedro in the Western Zone.

A third day. June 19.

1:00 a.m. Assailants in a white Volkswagon Voyage chased and shot down twenty-four-year-old civil construction assistant Rodrigo Mendes David in Comunidade Mundo Novo in the West Central Zone. In the Southern Zone, masked gunmen in a red Volkswagen Gol opened fire on eighteen-year-old student Erick Patrick Santos Oliveira at a street party in Bairro Japiim. The victim had no criminal history whatsoever. Relatives rushed him to the nearby hospital where he died shortly after.

2:00 a.m. Twenty-five-year-old Fernando Amaro dos Santos was killed in Bairro Grande Vitória in the Eastern Zone. Neighbors heard the shots but had nothing else to tell the authorities. Around the same time, an unidentified young man was found dead inside an apartment in Bairro Tarumá with three bullet wounds and two bags of dope.

3:00 a.m. Twenty-five-year-old freelancer Thiago Peres Castro was shot dead in Bairro São José in the Eastern Zone.

Sunday morning, Manaus woke to another wave of grisly headlines. Psychic mediums in spiritualism schools across the city shivered in the wake of the dead passing on to the next life. In neighborhood churches, parishioners spoke in hushed tones about the bloodshed. Some prayed for the innocents who had been lost: neighbors, cousins, crushes, brothers, sisters. Others prayed for Old Testament justice—the only good bandit is a dead bandit. Yet a hundred thousand prayers were not enough to stave off another night of violence. On Sunday death didn't even wait for the sun to go down, as if it had its own orbit to satisfy.

5:00 p.m., not long before sunset, thirty-eight-year-old Elissandro das Neves Lima was shot three times by gunmen on a motorcycle circling Bairro Armando Mendes in the Northern Zone. Another unidentified woman shot and killed in Bairro Tarumã in the Eastern Zone, missing one of her hands.[9]

10:30 p.m. Twenty-one-year-old student Wesley Santos da Silva and a friend robbed the Kidelicia lunch counter in Bairro Santa Etelvina in the Northern Zone. The pair tried to get away on a motorcycle, but a vigilante shot Silva four times. His partner escaped on foot.

11:30 p.m. Thirty-three-year-old security guard Luzivan Gonçalves dos Santos was shot dead in the Bairro Coroado in the Eastern Zone.

Day four. July 20.

12:30 a.m. The last day for thirty-six-year-old vendor Sidney Carvalho dos Santos in Bairro Novo Aleixo in the Eastern Zone.[10]

2:30 a.m. Thirty-one-year-old freelancer Renato Simplício Duque in Bairro Novo Israel in the Northern Zone. The killers were returning to the same neighborhoods, a second chorus in the same ballad.

Monday morning, as buses of blanched workers lurched through the smog, the final victim of the Bloody Weekend lost his life, a twenty-year-old construction helper shot and killed in Bairro Jorge Teixeira in the Eastern Zone.[11] It was too late to stop the presses at *Hoje,* the tabloid sold for a dime at every bus terminal in Manaus. The paper was already being tossed from trucks, stacked up in the kiosks, a one-word headline splattered with blood on the front page: Carnage.

One by one the crime scenes were pinned on a map in the homicide unit. It was true: most of the killings took place in neighborhoods known for drug trafficking. Also true: most of the dead had criminal records ranging from petty theft to trafficking to spousal abuse or attempted murder. The war between the FDN and PCC was boiling over in the jails and on the streets. A lot of these guys had it coming.

The war between the gangs and the police had reached a flashpoint, too, but it wasn't up to the military police to decide who had it coming. At a number of scenes, detectives found the distinctive brass shell casings etched with Secretaria de Segurança serial numbers—police munitions. An anonymous member of the military police confirmed to a reporter at *A Crítica* what was better left unsaid: "Every time a PM dies anywhere in Brazil, all police join a campaign to hunt for the criminals involved. By our code, they are called 'Ghost Riders.'"[12]

To some degree, the public understood why police took matters into their own hands. Vigilante groups within the force were an open secret. The police had a right to be angry after the death of their comrade Camacho—a teacher, for the love of God. There would be whispers among the elite: the police were only doing their job, doing us all a favor, exterminating pests. Dealers devoured each other like rats. These so-called Ghost Riders are just nudging things along. Whatever happened over the weekend was natural, like a thunderstorm. It would pass.[13]

The problem was that some of the dead were simply in the wrong place at the wrong time. A handful of the victims—like Anderson Sales Soares, the dancer in Bairro Aleixo—had no serious criminal record. Others had never had any contact with the police until the detectives showed up to snap photos of their body. Not good. On-duty police could count on the shelter of a military tribunal, but the men needed to show some restraint.

The wanton shootings were even more of a threat to the FDN. The weekend massacre had grabbed a headline in New York. A little snippet on the back pages, but still—the *New York Times*, for fuck's sake. The feds in Brasilia would be pissed, which meant all eyes would be on Governor Melo. If Amazonas state couldn't get a handle on the violence, there would be a federal crackdown. Zé could get shipped to a federal prison like G, and it was a hell of a lot more expensive to do business from a federal prison.

The police and the FDN went into crisis management mode. At the advice of his communications officer, Secretary Fonte posted his own message on Facebook to squelch the fearmongering on social media. Don't believe everything you see online.

At the advice of João Branco, Zé sent out a message to the entire FDN network, warning people that innocents were being caught in the crossfire. The family had a duty to keep their neighborhoods safe.

Behind the scenes, João Branco and Zé brainstormed ways to avoid key men being transferred to federal lockup. They could launch a wave of attacks against police officers, meeting force with their own show of force, but that could backfire. They could threaten to incite riots in the prisons. The authorities knew that bloodshed in the penitentiaries would spill over the prison walls. They wouldn't want that—not with the Olympics coming.

Public security officials were one step ahead of them. On the Tuesday after the Bloody Weekend, the Amazonas state secretary of justice and human rights, Colonel Louismar Bonates, extended an invitation to Zé. Let's sit down. Talk this out. The colonel had attempted to negotiate directly with FDN leadership before, but Zé had always sent a lieutenant in his stead. This time Zé accepted the invitation himself.

Colonel Bonates breezed through security at COMPAJ, the private guards looking the other way as he passed by. It's not every day you see top brass on the inside. The colonel and Zé met in the library, the closest thing to a boardroom on the inside, eyeing each other under the buzzing fluorescent lights. Based on the federal investigation, and the subsequent changes to the prison system, the conversation must have gone something like this.

"These killings are bad news for everyone," said the colonel.

"Your men are out there killing innocent people," said Zé.

"They're saying we need to hand you over to the feds," said the colonel.

"That would hurt lots of people," said Zé. He had to be careful not to overplay his hand. What the colonel did not know is that Zé's wife had pressed him to take the meeting. She didn't want him sent away from home again. The kids needed to see their father, even if it was only on visitation day.

"So what can we do?" asked the colonel. "Tell me what you need. More TVs? Soccer uniforms? We can help you."

"We need the pavilion," said Zé.

The colonel scoffed. "Those are the only blocks left for the PCC."

"You say you want to help the situation," said Zé

"We can give you cell block one."

"One and two," said Zé.

"You'd have the whole prison."

"So you're saying you can't help?" said Zé. He let the question hang in the air a moment until commotion outside the library doors broke the silence.

"You have to give me your word," said the colonel. "No more chaos."

"And the soccer field," said Zé. "It looks like shit. We need it repaired."

"I'll have to make a call," said the colonel.

By Tuesday evening, the deal was done. In the newspapers, Colonel Gouvêa credited the tranquility to the security crackdown. The 700-soldier surge was working. Manaus went twenty-four hours without a homicide for the first time in months.[14]

"The city is calming down," the colonel said. "We're doing seizures, roadblocks, and containing the violence. Most of the terror you see is being spread on the social networks, but this is a normal amount of crime for a city of 2 million."[15]

Extra patrol would continue. It was a mixed blessing to see the Força Tactica back in the neighborhood after the beatings caught on film two months earlier. Yet there was no time to ask for forgiveness or understanding. By the end of the month, Colonel Gouvêa would be operating with a blank check. Search teams, helicopters, and K9 units. Operation Ratchet monitored the public buses where years ago police had been accused of raping women on routes in the outer zones. Operation Payback monitored the roadways near the riverbanks now that the water level was dropping. Operation Lockdown focused on the prison road on BR-174 where inmates were already plotting the next wave of retaliations.[16] The overtime was expensive at a time when the economy was crumbling, but chaos would be even more costly.

The Wednesday after the Bloody Weekend, Sergio Fonte was slated to be honored with the Gold Medal of the City of Manaus. In a ceremony hosted by the city commission, great men would honor a future great man for his work as head of the Polícia Federal and his—until this latest mess—auspicious start as secretary of public security. The timing couldn't have been worse, but the award had been announced before the massacre. What were the commissioners supposed to do? They definitely couldn't turn a blind eye. If anything, the ceremony would give the young secretary an opportunity to address the devolving security situation, a chance to demonstrate the clear-eyed leadership that had earned him the award in the first place.

Fonte looked the part, a gleaming medal hanging from his neck as he addressed the crowd. "The fact is that whether it is a fight between organized crime or an illegal reprisal, nothing will prevent us from finding the accused with the same urgency as we identify and arrest the sergeant's killers."[17]

Then it was time for dessert.

It was a good meal, but everyone was feeling the heat, even the drug lords in prison. João Branco's blacklist had exposed how comfortably the kingpins operated from their cell blocks. Now the FDN had complete control of the state prison system, but they had to be careful how they crossed the rest of the names off the list. It was a matter of minor adjustments. João Branco put out a simple order: From now on, any hits inside the prison should take place in the target's cell. Make it look like a hanging.[18]

14

TRÊS FRONTEIRAS

Within a decade of its birth, the Familia do Norte had evolved from a handwritten statute penned behind bars to the gate-keeper of the Upper Solimões region, the riverine frontier that Brazil shares with Peru and Colombia, two of the largest cocaine-producing countries in the world. In December 2015, as the families of the victims of the Bloody Weekend braced themselves for a Christmas of grieving, I took a boat to the sleepy border town of Tabatinga. A federal investigation had recently shed light on the complex web of the FDN for the first time, ex-posing threads that spanned the entire continent, and I wanted to see its hub.

At sunrise on a Tuesday, I stood on a floating dock at the Port of Manaus, trying to wake up with a cigarette and a little coffee. More than a year had passed since the World Cup, and the fes-tivities were like smudged fingerprints on a rearview mirror. The Brazilian real had lost nearly half its value, as if even the finan-ciers of the world were laughing at the national team for its implosive 1–7 loss to Germany in the semifinals. Oil giant Petrobras, embroiled in the Jet Wash scandal, had gone from probing the Amazon basin for fresh oil reserves to laying off hundreds of workers. As investigators turned over stones across the country, corrupt politicians and businessmen scattered like cockroaches, validating even the most wild-eyed conspiracy theorists. Amazonas's governor, José Melo, was feeling the heat of an election fraud probe. From street corners to boardrooms, the line between good guys and bad guys had blurred.

On the docks of Manaus, fishermen unloaded their catch while porters shoveled ice into Styrofoam coolers to be shouldered upstairs to the market. The stalls already smelled of blood. Fishmongers splayed open the morning deliveries with flicks of their wrists, listening to the lotto numbers crackle on the radio as they butchered their way through glistening piles of caprari, pirarucu, jacunda, pirapitinga, and every river monster in between, handfuls of guts tossed aside for the cats.

I was waiting to board a fast boat to the borderland 700 miles upriver. Vendors worked the crowd with supplies for any length of journey, whether twenty-four hours or twenty-four days: hammocks, cigarettes, soda, chips, fruit, liquor, medicine, copies of the morning newspaper. Every morning for more than a century, the *Jornal do Comercio* published the level of the Amazon on its front page below the fold, noting to the centimeter the daily measurement, the high-water mark for the year, the low-water mark for the year, and the ebb or flow since the previous day's edition—precious intel for anyone who made their livelihood on the undulating river.

This time of year the hydrologic touches its nadir in the central Amazon. The cascades of Andean snowmelt have ceased flowing. The monsoon clouds that bunch on the horizon during the wet season dissipate at dawn into brief morning downpours. Entire creeks have evaporated while others have fallen so low they can only be navigated by canoe, hulls scraping the sandy bottom, passengers stepping out to carry their boats through the shallows. The Amazon has receded forty feet from its highest level. Thousands of miles of banks are now exposed for the first time in months, eddies reduced to puddles, puddles reduced to mud, mud baked hard as concrete, cracking in the sun. A few weeks ago, this floating dock would have been bobbing thirty feet higher, at street level; now it rests askew on the sandy river bottom, half in the water, half on shore, passengers descending a weathered cast-iron staircase with their luggage, baskets, and sleeping babies.

Low water changes life for everyone. For people like Moeses Martins who live in the *igarapés*, it means they don't have to worry about snakes and caiman swimming through the window, even if the creek outside is littered with trash. For Francisco Uruma and his tribe, it means they can expand their crops into the lowlands, even if they have to trek deeper into the forest for good fishing. For his nephew, Tashira, sunnier days mean more hours of mastering the carbon-fiber bow at the Olympic Village in Manaus, arms growing stronger in the weight room, even as he learned to adjust for the breeze, one eye on the crisp leaves fluttering from the strangler figs. For the police and the FDN, it means bodies might start turning up, even if they are impossible to identify after a season underwater.

Up and down the port, the bank was strewn with a wet season's worth of remnants that the falling water had left behind to dry: T-shirts and shoes, tires and mangled appliances, splintered canoes and broken toys. Who knew how far these misfits had traveled to get here, how many seasons they may have been tangled on a branch or a sandbar upriver, how many seasons more before they caught the current that would carry them to the Atlantic? It was a graveyard for boats of all sizes. Abandoned riverboats bleached lazily in the sun as if it was only a matter of time before their crews returned to scatter the squatters and begin proper repairs.

Our captain greeted us on the gangplank, wearing a crisp white uniform and a huge grin as if he were living his boyhood dream. More than a hundred passengers took their assigned places among two rows of three seats with enough space in the aisle to give the twelve-person crew of merchant marines room to maneuver. Each seat had a food tray and an outlet for charging electronic devices. Toward the bow, two televisions were already playing pirated DVDs of last summer's U.S. blockbusters. Sternward was a snack bar, a closet-sized galley, two bathrooms with showers, and an open-air seating area with another TV where passengers could take in diesel fumes and the roar of twin jet propulsion.

I found a spot outside on the aft side, near the two giant coolers where our thirty-six hours of food and drink were on ice. Early-bird passengers were bunched up to smoke cigarettes and take in the view as we departed, a few mothers and children, a couple of bookish old men, and a *forró* band wearing their own T-shirts, keeping a careful eye on the merchant marines who tucked their guitars and accordions below with the other cargo.

Lighting a cigarette, I was startled to see a shrink-wrapped box at my feet—a small coffin, labeled with the name and destination of its occupant. I quickly stepped away as if death were contagious. Was I already on my third smoke of the day? I'd quit smoking regularly years ago, but the abundant down time and cheap packs in Brazil always drew me back. I unfurled my cigarette into the river and tucked the filter into my pocket. The two bookish men looked at me like I was crazy for not tossing the whole thing straight into the water when there were abandoned cars rusting on shore.

At last the crew cast off. The engine roared to life, and the boat bobbed away from the dock before the captain gleefully opened the throttle, jets gushing an enormous white wake in the Rio Negro. The water sparkled bank to bank, tugboats sputtering below the Rio Negro Bridge, water taxis fueling up at floating stations where the graveyard shift crews waited for the shift change. Midriver, we crossed paths with cargo vessels; barges of Hondas, Toyotas, and Harley-Davidson Fat Boys, assembled by men who could only dream of owning one; container ships of dishwashers, home theater equipment, and 4G tablets, destined for coffee tables in Ipanema and beyond; a barge lugging a single bulldozer upriver like a dormant yellow dinosaur, ready to munch untold acres of forest when it woke. Within minutes, we were beyond the outskirts of Manaus, the Petrobras storage yard, the navy shipyard, banking southwest into the brown waters of the Rio Solimões. Along the shore, fishermen climbed down earthen ladders carved from the red wall of the river, yanking their motorboats to life.

As the sun broke over the canopy, those of us on the rear deck came to a silent agreement to switch from coffee to beer. Soon we were shouting about politics over the roar of the engines, a cacophony of opinions we would have thirty-five hours to resolve. I sat between two professors from the Federal University in Manaus, participants in a faculty strike who'd decided to use their unexpected sabbatical to visit relatives upriver.

"This country is lost until it learns to value education," one said, wiping the rim of a fresh beer with a napkin. A man on the bench across from us glanced up from the gold-edged pages of his Bible. The professor paused for a breath before drinking, a moment of respect for the dead in the coffin at our feet.

"It's her husband in there," the other professor said under his breath, gesturing toward a widow near the galley who wore an expression of contemplative exhaustion, as if this journey would be too long, yet still not long enough. Relieved that it wasn't a child inside the coffin, I snuck a glance at the label affixed to the shrink wrap. It was addressed to a funeral home in Benjamin Constant, a small missionary settlement up near the triple frontier, named for the nineteenth-century positivist leader who played a key role in the formation of the Brazilian Republic—and the slogan *Ordem e Progresso* —"Order and Progress"—on the national flag.

"They are going home," said the first professor.

It seemed wrong to speak so plainly of the dead in the presence of the grieving, so we drank a while in silence, beers warming in our hands. We picked up more passengers at the city of Coati, where Petrobras extracted oil and gas from the jungle, paying local residents a residual from the pipeline that ran through the forest where they hunted, fished, and swam as children. Now and then a canoe would motor out from some unseen village to catch us midstream, latching on to our hull where a sailor handed over that day's mail. We passed small towns with small ice factories and large towns with large ice factories. When a cell phone tower drifted into view, everyone on the boat hurried to check their phones before the signal was lost again.

The sun arced across the sky. We exhausted the boat's supply of beer before lunch. The kitchen staff began chopping potatoes, onions, and peppers, preparing for mealtime hours when they circulated cafeteria trays of beef, rice, and greens, plastic cups of Coke or guarana to wash it down. At dinner I met a traveling shoe salesman from Santarém who went home one weekend a month to try his luck as an independent record producer. The rest of the time he slept and took his meals on boats like these, selling Chinese-made women's footwear to shopkeepers up and down the Amazon.

"It's tough right now," he said. "The economy is weak, but I can only lower my prices so much before I'm starving, too, *né*? I just have to keep moving and hope for the best."

During another meal I met an eye doctor from Tabatinga, heading back home from a training. "It's not as dangerous as they say," he said. "Just stick to the main roads and be careful after dark."

Sunset on the river was long and luminous. People who had lived their whole lives on the Amazon stepped out to the rear deck to take selfies with the view. The captain was relieved by his first mate. The wife of the man in the coffin was out of tears. Members of the *forró* band were trying to be respectful of the widow, but it was a big band and they liked to stand together, chatting and smoking just a few steps away from her beloved. By dinnertime, when the kitchen staff had to hustle back and forth between the coolers and the galley, folks had lost their reverence for the dead and stepped over the coffin as if it were a dozing dog.

After dinner passengers lined up for showers. The crew lulled us to sleep with soothing Brazilian pop concert videos. Families unrolled blankets in the middle of the aisle, sprawled out for comfort, other passengers tiptoeing around them to use the bathroom. Around 3:00 a.m. the captain relieved his first mate, chatting briefly about the river depths before he retook the wheel. At this time of year we could hit a sandbar, a hulking piece of driftwood, or a smuggler's boat at any moment. Through the night he scanned the river with a hand-turned spotlight, blue on the water like an angel or an alien, his face red in the glow of his nautical instruments.

I retreated to the rear deck, Brazilian flag fluttering overhead. To sleep would be to waste these quiet hours on the river. We passed pulsing cell towers. Lonely houses on stilts, bathed in floodlight. Constellations of Christmas bulbs through the trees, the gift of light from Lula, a miracle, even if it may have cost the young democracy its soul. Between villages, the shore was perfectly black, the wavering silhouette of the canopy against a spectral sky. Snaking upriver, the curves on the route were so elongated that the only way to perceive our change in course was to track the planets on the low horizon, drifting left, right, left again on the cosmic plane.

At first or second glance, Tabatinga doesn't seem like one of the highest-volume drug-trafficking corridors on the planet. With a population of 60,000, the town has sprouted around its military bases, border waypoints where the Brazilian army, navy, and air force flex their muscles for their neighbors. Broken-down Piper Cubs rust on the perimeter of the single-runway airport; soldiers and civilians use the empty roundabout as an impromptu track for evening cardio. As recently as a decade ago, most of these roads were dirt. Thirty years ago, the area was a staging ground for Colombian cocaine kingpin Pablo Escobar whose chief lieutenant built his personal mansion along this stretch of river—a plank-by-plank replica of the Carrington family home from American TV's *Dynasty*.[1] Not long before that, these roads were airstrips where frontiersmen touched down to develop the last Brazilian city on the border. The city has more than doubled in population since 2000. It now has a university, a deep-water port, and an international airport, but motorcycles still outnumber cars ten to one. Families of four share 150 cc bikes, shocks squeaking as they roll over the solitary speed bump that separates Brazil from Leticia, Colombia, capital of the Colombian Amazon, a blossoming city of eco hotels and a quaint tourist port where, for a few coins, you can hire a water taxi across the river to Santa Rosa, Peru, the smallest of the three sister cities, a handful of stray lights twinkling on the far bank.

Despite warnings that I should stick to the Colombian side, my stunted but stubborn sense of Brazilian patriotism compelled me to check in to one of the only hotels in Tabatinga. Then I needed wheels. It turned out a mechanic named Roberto had cornered the market on moto rentals on this side of the border. The only notice announcing his business was a handwritten cardboard sign tacked to his garage door that read ROBERTO MOTOS, followed by his phone number. Around closing time I found him tinkering with a bike on a plywood ramp while two teenage boys washed other bikes under an awning. Inside the garage were row after row of little black motor scooters identical to the one he was working on now.

Roberto, like border dwellers the world over, introduced himself by explaining how he came to live on the border. "I'm Japanese-Peruvian," he said in Portuguese. "I married a Colombian woman. And our two sons were born here in Tabatinga, so they're Brazilian. Ha!"

Apparently, all the motos were reserved by locals home for Christmas, but he flipped through his box of index cards and found one that had just been returned.

"It hasn't been washed yet," he said, side-eying the kids washing bikes.

"No problem," I said.

"My son keeps asking for a raise," Roberto said, jotting down the info from my driver's license. "California, huh? What are you doing here?"

"I'm a writer."

"Huh, well, lots to write about here," he said, handing me back my license. "So I tell my son, 'If you want a raise, wash more bikes.'"

It took Roberto a minute to find a helmet that fit my gringo head. "Your registration is under the seat. And remember: you have to wear your helmet in Colombia."

Soon I was among the meandering flow of motorcycles sizzling below the sodium streetlamps, which were decorated with storm-proof metal holiday bells and candy canes. It only took a few minutes of riding around to get my bearings: the air force base, the naval base, and the jungle warfare base, with handfuls of small businesses like ellipses between them. At the edge of the Brazilian frontier, the National Radio Corporation beamed programming from a tower erected in 2005, the tallest object for hundreds of miles, broadcasting news, sports, and culture with the support of volunteer correspondents in the nine municipalities of the Upper Solimões Region. Beyond the tower, a spotlight panned across the low clouds over Colombia.

At the border speed bump on Avenida Amistad, I stopped to chat with the Colombian border guard, who stood with an assault rifle slung over his shoulder, watching traffic whiz between two orange cones. "It's really peaceful here," he said. "Mostly I just tell people to put their helmets on."

Plopping my helmet on, I crossed into Colombia. The road transitioned from asphalt to concrete. On the first block across the border, money changers were doing a brisk business after dark, attuned to every subtle shift in the trinational economy. I spoke with a woman posted up under an umbrella with her moneybox, changing currency while she bounced her toddler son on her knee. She explained the game. Brazilians go to Colombia to buy electronics, gasoline, Coca-Cola, and appliances from the factory there. Colombians go to Brazil to buy shoes, clothes, and liquor. The Peruvians across the river can't afford to buy much beyond food and gas. With Brazil's economic woes, Colombians are eager to sell their reals for pesos, complicating the flow of local trade. The value of currencies moves as much on rumor as it does on the fundamentals. Every week local bankers meet at the port to settle on the value of the exchange for the week, and it's up to the money changers to push back on people who insist the exchange rate should shift based on radio talk show gossip or the results of soccer matches. After Brazil's World Cup humiliation at the hands of Germany, folks on both sides of the border rushed to unload reals.

The signs on the Colombian side of the border changed instantly from Portuguese to Spanish, and the street food from beef kabobs to *arepas*, as if in the absence of a more formal border crossing, the residents had agreed to draw strict linguistic and culinary lines. The *centro* was only a few square blocks away and I soon tracked down the source of the spotlight, a festival in Leticia's main plaza. By coincidence, I'd arrived on one of the biggest nights of the year in the region: the opening of the Golden Pirarucu.

"What's the Golden Pirarucu?" I asked a vendor, paying for a beer in Brazilian reals.

"Our annual music competition," she said, handing back my change in a mix of Colombian pesos and Peruvian sols.

Named for the largest and most delicious fish in the region, the Golden Pirarucu is a folkloric music festival where artists from the three neighboring countries compete for a life-sized gilded trophy in the shape of the giant fish. Under the dazzling lights of the concrete amphitheater, traditional soloists and progressive fusion bands performed before a panel of judges. The talent on stage was unquestionable, as was the national pride. Around the plaza, the palm tree trunks were painted the Colombian national colors, red, blue, and yellow, but Brazilian and Peruvian food vendors defiantly displayed their national flags at their booths. At each corner of the park, trios of benches were arranged facing each other, each bench painted with one of the Brazilian, Peruvian, or Colombian flags. I wondered if people tried to sit only on their country's bench. Between sets, the MCs speechified about the relative virtues of their countries to cheers and jeers from the crowd. The audience greeted each act with a swell of applause, regardless of nationality. Once the music began, fans from each country whooped and hollered patriotically. Child performers, regardless of origin, received rousing cheers from all.

I watched and listened from an open-air pool hall above the plaza where men shot billiards and drank fire water from tiny plastic cups, as they leaned on a wall plastered with nude centerfolds. For these men, the main event was still a few months away—when the same amphitheater would host the annual regional beauty pageant, in which women from all three countries competed for bragging rights and the grand prize: breast implants. This evening the bartender's daughter was singing in the show. When she took the stage, pool games and drink service halted until her emphatic final note.

"She did great!" said one of the pool players. Drinks flowed again. Billiards resumed.

All night long, an Indian in a brand-new cotton T-shirt tried to win shots of fire water in games of pool. We played a game, and when he beat me, we drank. We played a second game, and when he beat me, we drank. When he was too drunk to win anymore, he pleaded with me to buy him a shot as a gift. I obliged out of a sticky mix of guilt, fatigue, and a sincere desire to bridge national divides; only after he threw back the shot with a grimace did I realize that I had enabled a long-suffering alcoholic.

The first night of the festival ended at eleven o'clock. The amphitheater emptied quickly, fans retreating to house parties and the solitary dance club on the Brazilian side where dancers were shaking their booties to the pulsing beats of a DJ. On my ride home, I passed an Indian stumbling as if lost between countries. I slowed up to make sure it wasn't the same guy from the bar. When I saw that it wasn't, I left him in my rearview mirror. Sifting through a trash basket, the man scored an empty liquor bottle and tipped it back for the last swill of backwash as I sped to my hotel.

· · ·

My mission in Tabatinga was to probe the borderland bureaucracy to verify some of the reports that I'd read in the newspapers back in Manaus. Journalism in the Três Fronteiras region is the province of state-sponsored radio hosts and volunteer correspondents, so stories have a tendency to swell into tall tales by the time they get 700 miles downriver to the capital. My first plan was to arrange interviews with officials on the border. Back in Manaus, I'd followed the formal channels, pestering the state media offices of the federal police, FUNAI, the Ministry of Justice, and the like, but their stalwart flaks refused to put me in contact with anyone in Tabatinga. Against their wishes, I moved on to plan B: reaching out to the local offices myself. But I got caught in a web of auto-replies, no replies, expired email accounts, and spotty internet service in a region that still did official business by fax machine. Finally, I decided to just show up at their doors. That's how I ended up at the office of Carlos Fermina, the public prosecutor of Tabatinga, whose assistant was not expecting a gringo writer to drop by his office unannounced, sweating profusely after a hot moto ride.

"Where did you say you were from?" the assistant asked.

"The United States," I said. "But I was born here in Brazil."

"One moment," he said, phoning his boss. Prosecutor Fermina was merciful enough, or at least curious enough, to see me without an appointment. The assistant escorted me down the hallway, opening the door to a modest office just as Mr. Fermina was slipping into his suit jacket, blinds drawn tight against the heat outside.

"Good afternoon," he said, offering me the seat across from him. Fermina was a resident of Tabatinga since his air force days more than thirty years ago. His officer training was evident in his immaculate desk, anchored by a thick legal textbook of federal and

state laws—the most commonly broken statutes highlighted du-
tifully in yellow.

"Sure, you read a lot of bad stories about Tabatinga," he said,
"but it's actually very safe. We have about one robbery a year."
(When I returned to Tabatinga a few months later during the wet
season, the head inspector of the local civil police confirmed that
Fermina's sunny assessment was technically true, at least on paper, but only because so much violent crime on the border goes
unreported. Perpetrators slip back and forth across borders, dump
victims in the river, or threaten survivors into silence—the kind
of stuff that doesn't end up getting faxed to the capital.)

"What about drug-trafficking cases?" I asked. "I keep reading
tons of stories about cocaine crossing here. I mean, literally, tons
of cocaine."

"Well, yes," Fermina said, making a temple with his fingers as
he chose his words. "The thing is, the traffickers, they are very
smart. On the street, they seem like ordinary people. It's not like
they're driving around with a sign that says 'I'm a trafficker.' They
lead double lives. Triple lives."

"I see," I said. He watched carefully as I jotted notes. "And do
you deal with many cases involving Indians? I've read that cartels
use Indians to help get their product over the border?"

"Well, I'm not the guy to talk to about that," he said. "It's a
little confusing." From his desk he withdrew a sun-bleached legal
pad, turned it toward me, and sketched an elegant flow chart of
Brazil's constitutional structure. "You see, drug trafficking is controlled by the federal police," he said, pointing the tip of his pen
at a box labeled POLÍCIA FEDERAL. Like a coach drawing up a
play, he walked me through the process with strokes of his pen.
"Indian law is different. If some Indian kills someone who's not
an Indian, they go to the Ministry of Justice. If they kill another

Indian, they go to the Ministry of the Interior. Here in this office, we deal with everyday law. Kids getting into fights on their way home from school. Somebody stealing somebody else's cell phone. That sort of stuff."

"Gotcha," I said. "Well, it looks like I'm in the wrong place."

"Sorry," he said. "I'm not sure who you thought I was, ha! But I hope you have a nice visit. We don't get many Americans around here. Don't forget to try the ceviche!"

Drugs and development have upended tribes on all three sides of the border in the Upper Solimões. Where rubber barons once sacrificed Indians as pawns in nearby Putumayo, now cartels and illegal loggers compel tribes to harvest cocoa, manufacture cocaine, cut timber, clear clandestine airstrips, and smuggle payloads through their villages and waterways. During the dry season, the Rio Solimões is the only waterway across the border. At three checkpoints between here and Manaus, federal police agents board and inspect every boat, above and below deck, searching luggage and cargo with K9 units while immigration and customs officials inspect documents. This time of year, when the water runs low, airborne trafficking spikes. Air force patrols and a sophisticated new radar system scan the skies day and night for small planes flitting from country to country like mosquitos.

During the wet season, traffic shifts to the flooded forest. Nobody knows these hidden routes better than the indigenous boatmen who've internalized the watery labyrinth since childhood, a shadow map of the dry season, hills turned to islands, clearings turned to lakes, creeks that can lead you around a federal checkpoint as easily as a thorny catfish ignores a hook. Some of these mules are paid for their expertise, eager to accept cash, food, alcohol, or cans of gas for a quick ride in the night. Others are extorted into service, obeying to keep their wives and children from being tortured, raped, or worse.

Tribes who avoid getting tangled up with smugglers still find their way of life irrevocably changed by the cocaine trade and the insidious cocoa paste it leaves behind. A patchwork of state and federal agencies in Tabatinga provides social services to the thousands of Indians living in the Upper Solimões. Chief among the federal agencies is FUNAI—the same agency charged with protecting the country's isolated tribes—which operates a regional headquarters just up the street from Fermina's office.

At the front gate a few motos were parked askew in a trapezoid of shade. The foyer was wide open and silent. There was a row of blue plastic chairs. An Indian woman sat in one of them, trying to keep her little boy still while they waited to be seen. At the reception desk, a young man swiveled on his seat behind a bare, circular desk. The sterile walls were sparsely decorated with posters of FUNAI's various projects in the Upper Solimões: education, hygiene and suicide prevention campaigns, treatment programs for addiction and depression, fetal alcohol syndrome fact sheets, and census drives to make sure all newborns are registered with a birth certificate.

FUNAI is an institution with a proud but spotty history. One of the few federal organs devoted to indigenous rights, it has earned credibility over the years thanks to monomaniacal leaders like Sydney Possuello, a disciple of the Villas Bôas brothers and founder of FUNAI's General Coordination Unit for Uncontacted Indians, devoted to protecting tribes like the Txapanawa. Yet FUNAI has long been compromised by its subservience to the Ministry of the Interior and, in its formative years, the military government. During the dictatorship, FUNAI was run by a rotating cast of generals who admittedly had never encountered an Indian. The military men shunned anthropologists and outdoorsmen in favor of cronies who supported the federal economic agenda. As a consequence, FUNAI was complicit in the ethnocide of the very people it had sworn to guard. Its attraction teams often arrived in isolated villages just a few miles ahead of the bulldozers, luring tribes out of the way with gifts so the forest could be cleared.

These days, even as it is gradually starved for resources, FUNAI is the keeper of institutional knowledge vital to protecting the country's last tribes, urbanized, isolated, or in between. A member of the regional FUNAI staff invited me into her office to chat—but only briefly—because technically I was only supposed to be speaking with the communications office in Brasilia. On the way back to her office, I passed a stack of enormous reflective metal signs leaning against the wall, still in shrink-wrap, advisories to be posted at key waterways to ward off loggers and traffickers from protected native lands.

The woman I spoke to explained that in an era of dwindling budgets, FUNAI has turned its attention to preserving tribal cultures. Memory is a fundamental human right. No matter how far and wide the Brazilian flag flies, it should never overshadow tribal languages, art, and history. Protecting those tribal memories is easier said than done. A critical task is identifying and monitoring tribes as they migrate, grow, or shrink, mapping their bloodlines and territories if only to bear witness to their destruction.

Many tribes sense doom on the horizon, she explained, which is why so many young people have left their villages for the city. A border town like Tabatinga may as well be a metropolis like Manaus to Indians coming from the headwaters. At first they come here to collect social assistance, but soon they are eager to find work, wear jeans and T-shirts, and borrow money to buy phones and cars like the whites. They bring those totems back to their villages, proof that the tribe has gotten a raw deal. Alcohol and drugs make that raw deal easier to swallow. For tribes on the border, the drug of choice is the paste leftover from cocoa leaves soaked in kerosene, a cheap but potent way to forget where you are—and who you are—even for a few minutes. Despite those federal laws prohibiting the sale of alcohol to Indians, health teams have found pregnant women in villages nursing bottles of liquor.

She shouldn't really say anything more. If I wanted to know about Indian health, I should visit SESAI.

Down Cemetery Road, past the radio tower, sits the regional office of SESAI, the Special Secretariat for Indigenous Health. When I pulled up, staff were unloading pallets of condoms and dental floss while nurses came and went with blood samples. In a corner office with a window to the delivery bay sat Weydson Pereira, the regional director charged with coordinating the mental and physical health of 62,000 Indians in almost 200 villages where a half-dozen languages are spoken. Just thirty-four years old, Pereira was born in a village like the ones he serves. Now he manages hundreds of staff members and volunteers in villages and municipalities across the region, some with as few as nine residents, others with as many as nine thousand.

Seated behind his desk in a SESAI polo shirt, he radiated the exhaustion and determination of a junior bureaucrat in a senior post. "I hear you're writing a book about Amazônia," he said.

"Slowly but surely," I said. "I've been up and down the river. Now I'm trying to get to know the border."

"You could write a whole book just about that," he said.

In this corner of the Amazon, some of the tribes live so far from the main river that they can only be reached by plane. SESAI teams rove from village to village, conducting checkups, collecting data, and administering treatment. Larger communities have a permanent health post. "That's for basic stuff," said Pereira. "If someone breaks a bone or gets bit by a snake, they come to the military hospital here in Tabatinga." If patients need a specialist, they must travel all the way downriver to Manaus. They may be separated from their families and their livelihoods for months, though more often than not, those who go to Manaus come back in a coffin.

"We stay focused on two things: clean water and sanitation," Pereira told me. "Malaria cases are down forty percent, but it hasn't been easy." The most basic infrastructure in remote communities can cost a boatload of money. It's one reason why indigenous politics heat up during times of economic contraction. To complicate matters, enormous government contracts for remote projects are fertile ground for corruption—and the Jet Wash investigation would likely mean that all future contracts would be subject to more red tape.

Two months ago, Pereira inaugurated a $2.4 million chemical water filtration plant in a distant village that will turn the acrid water of the Rio Solimões into potable water for thousands. It is the most sophisticated filtration plant of its kind in Brazil. The opening of the treatment plant was the proudest moment of his career. For the first time, one of the largest and most complex villages in the region would have access to clean drinking water straight from the river they called home. He showed me video of the inauguration day on his cell phone, the men of the village pouring fresh bags of treatment chemicals into their new water supply. Trained to conduct the three-part sanitation process on their own, these leaders will bring pride and independence to the village by earning steady salaries as they secure a safe water supply for their people.

"They will be taking care of their families, earning paychecks right there in the community," Pereira said. "It won't just be collecting benefits from some white man in the city."

For Pereira, the triumph was personal. Prior to this desk job, he spent ten years in the field. Nowadays he spends more and more time at a computer, but he still sees things in the field that won't let him sleep. Pregnant girls on the ground in a stupor, too drunk to stand up. Boys not all that different from him just a few years ago, slitting their wrists before their fifteenth birthday. And why not? When they look at their reflection in the silt waters of the river, they see a boy with no future staring back.

The upper Rio Solimões is the pulmonary artery of the Família do Norte's pounding heart. At least 300 tons of cocaine in various stages of production cross into Brazil from this region each year, floating 700 miles downriver to the Port of Manaus in boats of all shapes and sizes. Traffickers sneak bricks of finished product into shipments of bananas, coconuts, and cheese. They tuck kilos into the bellies of fresh catfish and sew them back up with fishing line. They feed vacuum-sealed product to livestock to be extracted at slaughterhouses over the border. A few kilos are offloaded onto the streets of Manaus, chopped and cut with vitamins, lidocaine, cement mix, Italian baby powder—anything to boost volume on the streets. Tons continue downriver, snowballing in value at each conquered checkpoint. Along the way, some bricks are loaded onto trucks and planes headed for the major cities of Brazil. Others are smuggled on oceangoing vessels at the Port of Belém, destined for Miami, Lisbon, Madrid, London— noses, lungs, and veins around the world, each their own sort of river.

At the federal police headquarters in Tabatinga, I joined the line of locals waiting at the front counter for answers about immigration issues and other grave concerns. Again I was showing up unannounced, but this was the Polícia Federal, where gringos were nuisances instead of curiosities: it would be at least 4:00 p.m.

before I could see the chief. The woman behind the bulletproof reception window noticed my imminent heat stroke and flipped a switch at her desk. Overhead, a rusty ceiling fan ground to life.

On the wall a framed map of Brazil's federal police districts hung next to a dengue fever prevention poster, reminding area residents that it only takes a few minutes a week to clear out any standing water near your house. Beside that notice was a newer, more urgently branded poster showing how the same mosquito prevention tips could help combat a new virus: Zika. When I ran out of posters to read, I eavesdropped on the staff. The clerk's teen-age daughter, released from the school up the street, dropped by to say hello to her mom, who made her daughter sit down and file paperwork. As I waited, the sweat dried on my face in the oven-like breeze of the ceiling fan.

At last, the officer clicked open a security door. "Come on back," she said. The clerk escorted me down a short hallway that opened into a staging area where body armor and other tactical gear hung on racks, ready for the next raid.

Back in Manaus, the communications officer at the federal po-lice had told me twice by email and once by phone that under no circumstances was I allowed to speak to anyone but him without express written permission from central headquarters, so I was sur-prised that the Tabatinga chief had agreed to meet. The recep-tionist knocked on the chief's door and returned to her post. I put my game face on, preparing to meet a battle-scarred Latin Amer-ican strongman in jungle fatigues, sporting a wicked scar or at the very least a green beret. Instead I was greeted by a 6-foot blond woman in a cream and purple flower dress, the whitest person I'd seen in weeks. She invited me to sit, as she settled in her chair on the other side of her desk, stacked with thick blue folders. I intro-duced myself and glanced around the room, looking for whatever

door led to the chief's smoke-filled office. Perhaps he was sizing
me up via closed-circuit camera.

That's when the woman introduced herself as the chief federal
police delegate in Tabatinga. I was momentarily ashamed: of course
women can be ass-kicking Brazilian narco cops.

"I don't usually dress like this," she said, "but everyone's out
for the holidays, so we're only running our regular checkpoints on
the river and at the airport. It's a good time to unwind and get
caught up." She quickly thumbed through her cell phone to share
a photo of a woman who had been caught with 12 kilos of cocaine
shrink-wrapped around her waist. "This was just yesterday."

"Wow, that doesn't seem very smart," I said. "How often does
that happen?"

"Two or three times a week."

"Well, if they keep trying, some of it must be getting through,
right?"

"Unfortunately, yes," she said, "but ninety-five percent of the
traffic in this region is by boat."

To illustrate her point, she guided me through a series of reports and photos on her computer with a spirit of transparency that
would give the communications guy back in Manaus an aneurism.
In the cocaine smuggler's toolbox, sending mules through airport
security was the equivalent of duct tape: cheap, easy, worth a try.
Commercial-scale projects required experience and engineering.
High-volume shipments of white bricks might look badass, but
looking badass is risky, and smart cartels manage their supply
chain carefully. With sweet government fuel subsidies in Brazil, it
can be cheaper to finish the manufacturing process with Brazilian petroproducts. Cartel accountants track currency and commodity exchange rates daily. When rates are favorable on the
Brazil side, the supply chain adjusts so that unprocessed shipments

can be finished across the border with government-subsidized gas. When shipments reach the other side, distributors catalyze those raw materials into potent bricks of blow headed for a port near you. As security and screening measures improved, traffickers and their chemists embraced innovation, discovering ways to cross their product in almost any form: hair gel, clothes, and the pages of books, undetectable by even the most steadfast drug dog. I couldn't help but imagine the man with the Bible I saw on the boat ride up here, heading back downriver for Christmas, reading the tale of the three wise men on gold-embossed pages of cocaine.

"So, yeah," said the chief. "It's impossible to stop everything. They're always changing. We can't keep up. We just have to catch as much as we can."

"It sounds like you really love your job," I said. "You probably have a totally different life out in the field."

"Oh, yeah," she said, opening up another folder on her computer: Cool Photos. "It's not all about drugs up here. There's all kinds of trafficking." She clicked open a picture taken in the middle of an open field. In the center of the frame, she was decked out in tactical gear and shades, hair pulled into a tight bun underneath that badass-looking beret I was expecting earlier. In the background of the photo, a helicopter banked away from her jungle landing zone, frozen in mid takeoff, its wind stirring the underbrush. Over her shoulder, a team of loyal soldiers dashed into the jungle, assault rifles locked and loaded.

She smiled as I processed the photo, mouth agape. "I started back with the civil police in Rio Grande do Sul," she said, "but I went back to school for public administration to get a better salary."

"This is a long way from Rio Grande do Sul."

"I know, huh?" she said. "I'm like the whitest person here! But

I like helping in the villages. And I'm always working with other countries. I just got off the phone with the Czech Republic."

When I returned to the Upper Solimões in the wet season a few months later, I heard the same refrain from an official at the Colombian National Police: the only hope of combating the drug trade was through tight international cooperation. Even when it comes to local operations around Tabatinga, Leticia, and Santa Rosa, traffickers are expert at exploiting loopholes in international law. To ensure national sovereignty, Brazilian, Colombian, and Peruvian enforcement teams working independently are forbidden from firing weapons on foreign soil. In response, traffickers build illegal houses that straddle two countries as waypoints. If a team from any one country arrives without support from their neighbor, the targets simply move to the other side of the house, taunting the police from across an invisible border.

International cooperation has its limitations when international politics are at stake, and what nobody in any country liked to talk about was the origins of the cocaine and weapons on the Peruvian and Colombian side. For more than a year, federal agencies in each country had been cooperating on an INTERPOL investigation to peel back the layers of the FDN. Initial warrants had been issued and arrests had been made in the weeks leading up to my arrival in Tabatinga, but the first details made public painted a staggering picture of narco corruption that touched the highest levels of government. One set of text-message intercepts showed FDN lieutenants cutting deals with the Revolutionary Armed Forces of Colombia (FARC), the recalcitrant communist guerrillas who had been at civil war with the federal government for decades, fueling their revolution with cocaine profits and arms from Russia.

FARC rebels have caused friction between Colombia and Brazil for years. In 1991, FARC rebels attacked a Brazilian army outpost and killed three soldiers. In response, the Brazilian soldiers entered Colombia without permission and killed seven suspected guerrillas. In 1998, the Colombian army made use of a Brazilian air force base without permission during an attack by FARC rebels that killed 150 people along the border.[2] Now the Brazilian federal police had evidence that the FDN had purchased drugs, assault rifles, and even grenade launchers from FARC, but what worried authorities most was the exchange of ideology and strategy. Zé and G had gone beyond cribbing notes from Brazil's criminal organizations—they were learning lessons from one of the most entrenched rebel factions in the world.

It was understandable why the regional delegate of the Polícia Federal seemed to relish small victories. She clicked through to another picture of her releasing a smuggled payload of rare peccaries—adorable wild piglets the size of pugs.

"Aren't they cute?" she said.

I admired the chief's wildlife rescue pictures, wished her Merry Christmas, and thanked her for sharing her expertise. By the time I returned to Tabatinga the following spring to follow up on operations in the wet season, she was gone, transferred to another position in Manaus. Her successor refused to meet with me.

That night a storm rolled across the horizon. The next morning I'd have to turn my moto back in to Roberto and return to Manaus. I took a last ride through the city despite the rain, drops stinging my face in the wind of the impending storm. The central water tower in the town, financed years ago by the World Bank, was adorned with Christmas lights, a nativity scene aglow out front. Turning down a dirt road toward the river, I passed a mother watching her two boys entertain themselves on the stoop of their house, burning plastic bottles for amusement, a pungent blue flame.

All at once the power went out. I heard cheers rise up around town. In the sky over Leticia, the spotlight above the Festival of the Golden Pirarucu went dark. The fate of the competition was now in the hands of the utility company. Within minutes, a repair crew assembled below a transformer on the main strip, climbing a ladder to examine the damage.

At the waterfront, it was as dark as it was a thousand years ago, constellations bright and upside down. In a few months I would return to the Upper Solimões when the hydrologic was at its zenith. The bank where I stood would be submerged under slow, murky water, part of a network of borderless backchannels. For now, bulbs of distant lightning flickered in the clouds, over which country, I couldn't say.

15

OPERATION WOLFPACK

July melted into a hellish August. Throughout the Amazon basin, wildfires burned uncontained, wisps of smoke visible from space. In the northeastern rain forest, German and Brazilian scientists inaugurated a 1,066-foot-tall climate observation tower that pierced the haze, spilling a river of data. Researchers analyzed the flow like doctors monitoring a patient's breathing: carbon, water, wind, cloud formation. They debated what the numbers portended for the hydrologic, the canopy, the human species, distress signals from an ecosystem in flux, storm surges tearing at the canopy of the interior rain forest, while drought on the margins disrupted rainfall patterns as far away as São Paulo.

The security crackdown in the streets of Manaus continued unabated. On the prison road outside the city limits, the FDN took dominion of its new cell blocks, bending their PCC rivals into submission. Memories of the Bloody Weekend weren't so easy to control. A single one of the stories would have been nothing out of the ordinary—a cop caught in the crossfire of a robbery, a murder at IPAT, a turf war in the streets—but the confluence of blood-shed had caught attention nationwide, and even overseas, stories implicating the police, validating the human rights watchdogs who didn't seem to understand that all lives do not have equal value in Brazil, that good citizens have the right to clean streets.

Extermination groups have been a phenomenon in Brazil since the military dictatorship, a "purifying" force not unlike the tor-rential downpours that polish the city overnight during the rainy season. Three decades into the country's democratic experiment, vestiges of the military dictatorship tingle like phantom limbs. Bra-zil still relies on compulsory military service to fill the ranks of its armed forces and paramilitary police—the enforcement branch of its dual police structure. The Polícia Militar, the only police force in the world still operating from barracks, enforce law on the streets. Drawn mostly from the working class who lack the means or connections to avoid serving, PM recruits are trained to fight enemy combatants, not to protect communities. They are ordered to apply force liberally to the threats of a given era: leftist guerril-las in the 1960s and 1970s, gang lords and vagabonds in the 1980s and 1990s, and now the powerful syndicates that have been spawned in the prison-industrial complex. What hasn't changed over time is their biblical sense of justice: an eye for an eye, a tooth for a tooth. As a paramilitary institution, the PMs can operate with almost complete immunity. Misconduct and crimes committed by PMs while they are on duty are investigated and prosecuted under an internal tribunal system that has historically overlooked—and at times condoned—abuse, extortion, torture, and extrajudicial killing.

The Polícia Civil are tasked with detective work, investigation, and prosecution. The bar for entry is higher—most civil police have college educations—but that only means that corruption and abuse take more sophisticated forms, like the extortion of drug traffickers by Colonel Cardoso and his men. "Military police are idiots," according to one detective who preferred to remain anonymous. Like many members of the civil police, he went to college instead of boot camp and earned his badge and gun by passing an aptitude test and completing coursework. "They're always mad at us. They bring suspects into the station, but they never have any evidence. And if they do have evidence, they've screwed around with it. So we have to let people go, and then the PMs get even angrier. It's fucked."

The lack of ballistic evidence at the crime scenes of the Bloody Weekend was one of the first indications that PMs were involved. Eyewitnesses suggested that many of the gunmen were too professional to be thugs from the street. They operated with military precision, wearing identical weapons and masks, sometimes even military-issue boots. Every round from a military police firearm has a serial number, but that number means nothing if an on-duty cleanup crew pulls up after a shooting to collect the spent shells.

In some bureaucracies, the left hand and the right hand don't talk to each other. In the world of Brazilian criminal justice, the left hand and the right hand are arm wrestling, resource-starved investigative units and a corrupt judiciary buckling under the pressure of an entrenched military culture. It can be tough to send violent criminals to prison in Brazil, let alone keep them there for long, and sending a kid away can be like sending him to narco college. The punks often come out more connected than before. Vigilante cops who see repeat offenders on the corner see an opportunity to serve justice where justice has failed.

Among certain well-heeled members of society, vigilante PMs are celebrated as no-nonsense tough guys, straitjacketed by bureaucracy; they operate outside the bounds to preserve law and order. Some Brazilians on the religious right see PMs as warriors of

God, bravely fighting against an evil force that is tearing the country's moral fabric apart. Sometimes that means giving a neighborhood dealer a warning shot in the leg, roughing up street kids known to be a nuisance to tourists and business owners, or giving shoplifters a blast of pepper spray in their mouth or anus. Like a good father, teach them while they're young. Otherwise, the next message might be lethal—a warning for the rest of the neighborhood.

In 2013, the United Nations called on Brazil to demilitarize its police force in the wake of a report that thousands of Brazilians—mostly brown and black young men, including hundreds of children—die at the hands of police each year.[1] And that's just on-duty cops. The military is a brotherhood in Brazil, and brotherhood knows no bounds. For some police, patrolling the streets isn't a job—it's a family, a faith, a way of seeing the world. They form militias, partner with cops and ex-cops, thugs and ex-thugs, improvising laws with righteous badges in their pockets and handguns in their glove compartments.

Before the stains of the Bloody Weekend had been washed away by the rain, the secretary of public security, Sergio Fonte, authorized a task force to investigate the police extermination groups involved in the mayhem. This was more than just a few bad eggs. Internal affairs would need extra manpower precisely when the system was overloaded with fresh bodies. With only three homicide investigation teams covering a thousand murders a year, choices had to be made. Prioritizing rogue cops over traffickers would be choosing to make enemies in city hall, enemies in the media, and enemies in the locker room. If the rank and file knew about the investigation, more evidence and witnesses would disappear. The operation would need to be classified.

Secretary Fonte needed a team that could unscramble this mess and build an airtight case against the killers while working in absolute secrecy—and Inspector General Leandro Almada was the only man who could lead them. A former army lieutenant, Almada had put in ten years as a homicide detective in Minas Gerais and another ten years with the federal police, investigating murders and drug trafficking. He was a pugnacious operator whose years behind a computer screen hadn't dulled his ability to work a case from the street up.

From his office at the Amazonas Secretariat of Public Security, Almada worked long hours at a desk stacked with autopsy reports, surrounded by portraits of his wife and kids and a gallery of commendations, certificates from the Baltimore Police Department, the LA County Sheriff, and even the FBI. His family had put up with a lot over the years. Christmas Eves when he'd be called all the way over to Pará to look at a crime scene, tilting his head to imagine blood splatter while his family waited to open presents. You had to look at this stuff through certain eyes to keep from bringing it home with you.

Almada read the order from Secretary Fonte. *Opa.* Were they serious about cleaning up this time? The brass had given him the authority to draft a nine-person task force: two civil police chiefs, six detectives, a clerk, and a criminal science expert with support from the federal police.[2] Not bad. Not bad at all.

There was just one catch. Aside from Almada and his team, only Fonte and the state judge in charge of approving wiretaps and warrants would know of the investigation; otherwise, it was doomed to fail. There were too many people on the force—old-timers and new recruits alike—who believed that the Ghost Riders were on the right side of justice. Some of those commanders might even condone the killings, if not outright order them.

Even if they let Almada handpick his team, it still might not be enough. They would have 150 days to get to the bottom of thirty-four murders. On the one hand, that wasn't much time. On the other hand, that meant five more months of killers in the ranks, practicing marksmanship at the training range with the same weapons they used for their little parties.

There was a legal framework for this kind of investigation, forged in the wake of an ungodly massacre in Rio de Janeiro years ago.[3] On the night of July 23, 1993, dozens of homeless street children were sleeping in their usual sanctuary outside the Candelaria Cathedral, one of the city's best-known religious landmarks. They woke to the sound of nine gunmen shooting indiscriminately. Sixty children were wounded and eight killed—most under the age of fifteen.

The violence stunned Brazil. Some of the gunmen were off-duty police officers. Witnesses claimed they were seeking revenge for an earlier encounter with some of the children. Others speculated they had been paid by local business owners to clean the streets of urchins that were a constant pest to their clientele.

Only three of the rogue cops were convicted, and though they served only a fraction of their sentences, the incident drew international condemnation, prompting the first formal protocols for investigating and prosecuting extermination groups.

Above all, Inspector Almada and his team would have to prove that the killers were operating as a unit: a common motive, common modus operandi, common weaponry, and common transport.[4] Detectives at the scene had recovered trace ballistic evidence that .38 and .40 caliber police-issue weapons had been used in the killings— but nothing definitive yet. Eyewitnesses seemed to confirm common methods of transport: a red Volkswagen Gol, a black VW Voyager, various motorcycles. Evidence gleaned from social media seemed to reinforce a shared motive—reprisal for the death of their brother in arms, Sergeant Afonso Camacho. The challenge would be piecing these scraps into a definitive list of suspects. Only then could they obtain the warrants they needed to advance the investigation.

First they needed a secure place to work, beyond the prying eyes of other law enforcement. The federal police had just the place: a vacant office within the security perimeter of the international airport on the outskirts of the city. No public access, entry and exit monitored by closed-circuit camera. It was built for long shifts. Seven computer workstations. A kitchen for snacks. A large, hotel-style bathroom for showers. Two beds for catnaps during all-nighters. A large picture window to watch the sun come and go, airfield rumbling with the takeoff and landing of jumbo jets. Day by day, night after night, the task force established a map of the dead, retracing the steps of the killers in hopes of identifying a pattern. Thankfully some of the cases were solving themselves as new testimony and evidence rolled in. Dealers killing other dealers, battles in the war between the Familia do Norte and the Spartan 300s, every confession simplifying the puzzle.

As August wore on, the hunt for the gang that had killed Sergeant Camacho drew to its natural conclusion. Turns out they were small-time bandits. Kids, really, who had divvied up the cash and gone their separate ways on the river. But there was no outrunning the police. Now they were on the nightly news, lined up for the cameras, on display for the press. The leader—a woman named Biti—grimaced at the center of the group. The killers pleaded: they didn't know Camacho was a cop!

Big mistake. Now two dozen unsolved murders stank of police.

Not long after the arrests of his killers, Camacho's hometown honored his memory in the annual parade, his former students, self-proclaimed Camachitas, marching in their red uniforms, holding a banner of tribute. If those bastards hadn't pulled the trigger, how many people would still be alive?

But you couldn't let your thoughts go down that road. There was work to do.

By late August, stories about the Bloody Weekend were finally wiped away by a more sensational death: a baby pitched into the Rio Negro by his father. Now the sun worshippers on Ponta Negra Beach endured the unpleasant sight of a fire boat searching the waters for the body.

With the unsolved murders out of the headlines for now, Inspector Almada and his team had more breathing room to do their job. So far they had segmented the killings into teams of Volkswagens spanning the four quadrants of the city. A red Volkswagen Gol associated with more than fifteen deaths in the Southern and South Central Zones of Manaus. In the Eastern Zone—the FDN's main turf—the picture was more muddled, a variety of Volkswagens, red, black, white, silver, responsible for seventeen shootings. In the northern zone, another death, caught on video, a Black Onyx and a red Volkswagen Gol.

"The red Gol seems to be almost everywhere," said Inspector Almada during a briefing.

"There have to be a thousand red Gols in Manaus," said another. True. The Volkswagen Gol had been the bestselling car in the country since the first model rolled off the assembly line in 1980. Looking for a Gol in Brazil was like looking for a soccer ball.

"We've got multiple witnesses describing custom tires."

"And one of the headlights was dimmer than the other—the left one, I think."

"But the plate doesn't match anything in the system," said the first detective. "They must have switched the plates."

"If they switched plates, there'd still be a match somewhere."

"Guys, guys," said Inspector Almada, jotting the plate number on the board: NOM-0880. "Look." He smudged out the connecting lines of a few of the digits, drew some new ones, changing zeros to eights, eights to zeros. "You can change these numbers any way you want. All it takes is a little electric tape. Every cop knows that trick."

Maybe not every cop.

Time for more coffee. The team sketched out all the possibilities, ran every combination through the system. Bingo: NOM-0390, a red Volkswagen Gol, registered to the mother of Dorval Junior Carneiro de Mattos, patrol leader.

Soon after, just past midnight on August 16, three small-time thugs were minding their corner in Bairro Aleixo when a red Volkswagen Gol crept past. The men inside rolled down their windows and started shooting. The young men scurried down the alleyway, taking fire as the car screeched away. Ambulances were slow to get there, but all three survived, wounded but not critically. They described the gunmen to police as best they could, but all three of the shooters had worn skull masks. The driver? He was chubby. Witnesses in the neighborhood took down the license plate: NOM-0880. They told investigators that the cops in Aleixo had been warning people this was coming: "Watch out for the Ghost Riders."

When internal affairs read the notes from the scene, they wrote up a report for the judge to strengthen their case for wiretaps. NOM-0880 came up cold—a black GM Zafira with no connection to the crime—but it had been altered from NOM-0390, PM Dorval's mom's red Volkswagen Gol.

The plate analysis was dated August 20. At eleven thirty that night, Almada received a tip from an informant: the red Gol was on the move again in Aleixo.

There wasn't much time. Almada scrambled everyone on his team who was on duty—seven officers in total. They loaded weapons and donned bulletproof vests. If they caught the Ghost Riders in the act there would be a shootout. No support from the intel, no backup from the Força Tactica, no explanation in the newspapers if something went wrong.

In two unmarked cars, the team opened the throttle on the way to Aleixo. There they split up, in radio contact as they crept from street to street, checking alleyways. Street dogs scattered in the headlights. Nothing. Midnight came and went, residents eyeing the unfamiliar cars with suspicion. Then the radio hissed: a man had been gunned down just a few blocks away. There would be no showdown tonight, only another body, thirty-eight-year-old Marcos Costa Teixeira, shot in the neck and twice in the gut.

Almada and his team rolled past only minutes too late. A crowd was gathering. The PMs were already on the scene, hands on their belts, making sure everything was under control. They sure got here fast, *né*?

Internal affairs couldn't make their presence known without blowing the investigation. Almada sent two of his guys into the scrum, posing as ordinary homicide investigators. See if anyone caught it on video. Grab pictures of *everyone*—and don't let the PMs see. Now hurry up before the supervisor gets here.

When the civil police supervisor pulled up to the scene, Almada lit a smoke. No choice but to trust this guy. Almada approached discreetly, flashed his ID. "Look, I can't stick around," he said, "but I'm going to need the ballistics."

16

GHOST RIDERS

The evidence was piled on the table: license plate records, autopsy and ballistic reports, eyewitness testimonies, closed-circuit video of the killers from a dozen angles. Inspector General Almada and his team had logged hundreds of hours, long shifts they couldn't talk about with family or friends. There's only so much you can share without spoiling the whole investigation. Only so much you can share without putting your loved ones in danger. The details had to stay in this room. Now and then one of the guys—a barbecue fan—would pass around a hat to collect money for beer and kabobs. They would meet up at his house for *churrasquinho* after quitting time. The son of a *gaucho* father and a mother from Rio Grande do Sul, Almada understood there are some problems that only hot barbecue and cold beer can solve. Standing in a smoky backyard, the team would shoot the shit about old cases they could joke about without jinxing anyone. Jammed rifles. Crashed cars. Miracles on the river. Maybe one day they would trade stories about Operation Wolfpack over the grill, but that day was a long way off. They still didn't have enough evidence on the books.

If the prosecutors were going to go toe to toe with lawyers from the police union, they needed to be able to trace the entire circle of conspirators. The only way to stitch the weekend together would be to access records from the cell phone towers in the neighborhoods where the Ghost Riders were operating. Only then could they prove the killings were coordinated.

Almada had what he needed for a surveillance warrant: screenshots of conversations from the WhatsApp group chats that battalions used to pass the time on patrols, posting jokes, porn, and snapshots from crime scenes. The threads had grown so cozy, the killers barely bothered to code their messages, even if they did disguise their identities. Two officers bragged outright of having killed five people during the cleanup of the Bloody Weekend.[1]

On August 25, Inspector Almada filed a request for a warrant to access data from the Bloody Weekend from all cell towers within proximity of the murders. While he was at it, the judge could approve wiretaps for the suspected military police and their wives. If the judge granted access, they would be allowed to use the surveillance unit, a tiny room filled with hardware in a confidential location in the city. From there, each tower would be a homing beacon, leading the task force down a trail of blood and missing bullet casings.

The same networks that transmitted signals from Zé and G to their men were relaying calls for revenge from cop to cop. Message by message, call by call, the intelligence gleaned from the network intercepts would reveal how the Bloody Weekend unfolded, how it spiraled into chaos. You could tell the bastards thought they would never be caught. One PM had even used a comic book profile pic, the Ghost Rider, when he called his friends out to play: "I'll show you the smile of death."

. . .

Minutes after Sergeant Camacho was pronounced dead at the scene of the robbery at the Banco Bradesco, PMs began posting to their battalion chat groups.[2] A collection would be taken for his wife and kids. The wrestling tournament Camacho was supposed to be coaching on Saturday morning had been canceled. No word yet on the funeral, but there would be an announcement at the school on Monday and some kind of a ceremony. Until then, more pressing matters: A description of the suspects. Cancel your weekend plans.

Sergeant Bruno Cézanne Pereira—Cézanne around the barracks—a twenty-six-year-old member of the Força Tactica—the elite task force that Colonel Cardoso commanded during his extortion scheme in 2013—was the first to circulate the vehicle description on the WhatsApp group chat of the 21st Battalion. A black Volkswagen Gol, license plate JXQ-1866. To light a fire under everyone's asses, he attached the clip of Sergeant Camacho's last moments, culprits running away, faces obscured by the glare of the sun on the windshield. Another old photo of Sergeant Camacho, alive and well, giving a thumbs-up to the camera as if telling his brothers it would all be okay.

Six minutes later, an unidentified sergeant responded: "I think the Ghost Riders are going to haunt the Southern Zone tonight."

Not a minute later, a buzz from Sergeant George McDonald: "I don't think so, I know so."

The chirps of cell messages, like hunters signaling each other through the trees. Thirty minutes later, twenty-eight-year-old Sergeant Dorval Junior Carneiro de Mattos left his wife at home for the night and climbed into his mother's red Volkswagen Gol, one mismatched headlight brighter than the other, as if the car were winking. On his way to the Southern Zone he dialed up a buddy from the police academy, Sergeant Silvio José Silva de Oliveira, a thirty-two-year-old who'd come to Manaus from Belém. Together they swung by to pick up Cézanne and McDonald, the oldest among them, a thirty-three-year-old who worked as a *mototaxista* on the side. Just like their fallen brother Camacho, he needed the extra cash.

From the first day of boot camp, recruits like Mattos and Oliveira are overworked, underpaid, and subject to constant physical and psychological stress. Drill sergeants march them through scorching heat and torrential rains, the sweatiest and bloodiest weeks of their young lives, through simulated ambushes and faux grenade attacks by enemy combatants. Take eighteen-year-old kids from lower-income backgrounds, throw them together in a barracks, hand them firearms, badges, and paramilitary authority, and it's not surprising that what they form resembles the country's most powerful gang.

The Brazilian cop drama *Elite Squad*, an instant classic that became one of the highest-grossing films in South American history, elevated Brazil's fascist police culture to the status of myth, dramatizing the training and indoctrination of a special forces team hell-bent on cleaning up the favelas of Rio de Janeiro by any means necessary. The murder, torture, and cover-ups in the film are closer to documentary than drama—and for some young Brazilian men, they represent the archetype of military authority and cartel power in Brazil, a relentless battle between police and outlaws where men are measured by ferocity and loyalty, no matter which side they're on. Recruits are indoctrinated into a strict rank-and-file hierarchy, codified since the days of the dictatorship. Fresh out of camp, they are assigned to patrols where every cruiser is manned by a commander who reinforces the status quo. Good cops learn quickly that whistleblowing can lead to reprisals against them or their families. Threats can come from any direction in a city like Manaus where the ties between cops and criminal factions run deep. Even in the world of fiction, the line between cops and kingpins is blurry. The leading man who played the tormented police sergeant in *Elite Squad* would go on to star as the notorious Colombian kingpin Pablo Escobar in the worldwide hit TV series *Narcos*.

The Ghost Riders were prepared for a night like tonight: a spark to light their fire. They carried black masks. Extra ammunition. Personal firearms to back up their service weapons. Cézanne packed his submachine gun, a favorite that he liked to show off on Facebook. Were their nerves running high? Did they pass around a bottle of rum? A bag of coke? Perhaps they blasted music, setting the mood, or perhaps they drove in silence to ensure their stealth. At some point they phoned Sergeant Klebert Cruz de Oliveira—simply Klebert around the barracks—twenty-three years old, just a baby in the battalion, to request some cleanup.

Twenty minutes after midnight, the Ghost Riders cruised Bairro Adrianopolis, one of the poshest neighborhoods in Manaus. Mattos hooked into a dim side street. The squad slipped on their masks, glimpsed their reflections in the side-view mirrors to make sure everything was covered but their eyes.

At the Bar do Vasco, soccer fans were chilling with cold beers and highlights on the TV. A young man sat on the sidewalk, probably waiting for his next customer. Mattos slowed the car and rolled down the windows. All at once they opened fire, got him in the stomach, hip, and hand. Mattos punched the gas, the smell of gunpowder filling the car. The kid writhed in the taillights as a friend rushed to his side.[3]

Masks off. Onward to Rua Belo Horizonte. Their first victim

was already headed to the emergency room in a car right behind them.[4]

Bairro Aleixo. Masks on. The Shadai lunch counter. A kid alone at a table, looking like he'd already had one too many. Mattos skidded to a stop. This time the guys stepped out of the car, opened up like a choir harmonizing to the baritone of Cézanne's submachine gun. Before the smoke had cleared, they were back in the car, hearts racing, ears ringing.

Twenty minutes later, still circling Aleixo like hawks. Perhaps more drinks, more blow. A vagabond coming around the corner of Rua Belo Horizonte and 10th Street, up to no good at this hour.

"Hold up, hold up," someone must have said. "This guy."

Mattos touched the brakes, rolled up to the curb. The guys on the passenger side rolled down their windows, called the man over. At the sight of their masks he ran, but they'd already tagged him.

"Turn around, turn around, go go go!" they shouted at Mattos.

The wheelman punched it to the end of the block, flipped a U-turn, the guy running in the uneven beams of the headlights, slipping under a lunch cart, as if he could hide from the Ghost Riders. Dorval pulled to a stop. They stepped out, found the man trembling like a child. Done.[5]

All night Sergeant Klebert trailed behind them like a puppy in uniform, plucking shell casings from cracks in the sidewalk, from witnesses' hands. "I'm going to need that," he might have told them before slipping back into his cruiser. Or maybe he just reached out his glove and let the gun in his holster do the talking. None of the shell casings he gathered were ever reported.

From there the night gets blurrier, the blood of the Ghost Riders' victims smeared with the others across the city, avengers for Sergeant Camacho, avengers for the Giant. Mattos and Cézanne stayed out late, drove to Bairro Japiim to unload on a stoner kid who would die on his way to the hospital.

Silvio had to hit the sack. At seven the next morning, he was back in uniform, driving a cruiser as a shift commander in the 16th Battalion. The 21st Battalion chat group was blowing up. There was no bringing back Sergeant Camacho, but his death would be avenged, his family would have justice, the killers and anyone else who thought they were above the police would be punished.

"I want to hear the news," pinged one sergeant.

"We shined up Aleixo," confirmed Mattos.

The cell records and wiretaps collected by the task force were a web of codes and images that took months to unwind. Inspector Almada and his team sifted through thousands of messages, listened to countless hours of audio, smoked their way through cartons of cigarettes as they cross-checked the cell pings to the times and places where the killings took place. With each piece of the puzzle, they requested more warrants for additional wiretaps, additional puzzle pieces.

By September the picture began to crystallize. Four extermination groups had been operating independently of each other during the Bloody Weekend, each nucleus responsible for murders and attempted murders in all but the wealthiest zones of Manaus. Three of the groups seemed to be one-night outbursts, open-and-shut cases of reprisal killings. It turned out that Sergeants Charles Dos Santos Farias and Magno Azevedo Mafra were also suspected of being responsible for an unsolved triple homicide back in May, revenge for the murder of another PM.

Sergeant Messias do Carmo Leite Junior and his partner Elielton Gama da Silva were responsible for one of the shootings; they hadn't even bothered to take off their uniforms. Brazen enough to seek out their targets from the comfort of their cruisers, they avenged Camacho with righteous confidence in their impunity, a controlled explosion caught on the dash cam.

The outburst of police violence on the Bloody Weekend—and the apparent lack of accountability afterward—emboldened other soldiers. The lone wolfs were bad enough, but it was the so-called Ghost Riders that kept Almada's team watching their backs at night. Mattos, Cézanne, Oliveira, McDonald, and their cleanup man, Klebert. Each wave of killings only seemed to whet their thirst for more. The night that Almada and his team just missed the Ghost Riders in Aleixo, the killers started mixing up their tactics. Maybe they were beginning to suspect someone was on to them.

They started borrowing Klebert's car, a GM Celta, while Klebert drove behind to pick up the pieces in his cruiser. It's hard to say for sure why he was never the trigger man. Maybe he wanted to be part of the mission without getting too much blood on his hands. Being on duty was the perfect alibi, *né*? Maybe the other guys knew Klebert didn't have it in him, that he was too weak to do the job. Maybe he figured if he did get caught, tampering with evidence was the sort of trouble you could hash out with Internal Affairs.

Except Internal Affairs had photos of Klebert on duty in his police cruiser, 25-1843, moments after the latest shooting in Aleixo. Internal Affairs had text messages and phone readouts littered with his name. The other Ghost Riders called him a pussy. He only shot at people to scare them off. Klebert was too scared to kill anyone. Yet Klebert was the string connecting the dots on the map. By September, Almada and the team had identified the core of the Ghost Riders—*Núcleo 1* in their official notes, each with his own troubled background.

Sergeant Silvio José Silva de Oliveira had been involved in a previous off-duty shooting back home in Pará. Months earlier, he'd traveled to Belém with his service weapon in checked baggage, a privilege afforded only to police. One night he got tangled up in an altercation in the street. He pulled his pistol and shot the other man dead on the spot. The authorities in Belém never questioned his claim of self-defense. Now it was clear the guy had acquired a taste for killing, gaining confidence each day as he slipped in and out of his uniform without consequence. For the time being, there was nothing Almada and his team could do but watch, listen, and try to catch them in the act.

It was Mattos and Cézanne who were the main instigators, urging the group on: Mattos was always ready to get behind the wheel, and Cézanne had gone mad with power. One late night in early September, Cézanne settled a score for his new girlfriend Jussara. She wanted one of her rivals shot—a young woman named Carla. Jussara scouted out the corner where Carla was hanging out and sent a signal to Cézanne when the street was clear. Cézanne and Dorval approached in their trusty red Gol, Klebert trailing in a second car. Cézanne rolled down the window and opened fire, nearly killing the young woman. Later that month he went after a mechanic who was taking too long to fix his car, which had been sitting idle in the shop for months. Cézanne threatened the shop owner, summoning a gang of fellow cops on motorcycles to drive by and intimidate him. Arguing with the mechanic, he brazenly warned against crossing him: "Did you see what happened to Carla? What happened to Neto? What happened to Pasta? What happened to Stone?"

Nobody could mess with Cézanne.

By mid-September, the Ghost Riders had drawn their criminal informants into the inner circle. Their most promising seedling was a young dealer named Janilson Monteiro da Frota. Friends on the street called him Little Angel; the Ghost Riders called him

Little Dog. The kid had just turned eighteen and was popular with the girls at school, always hanging on the corner in his Yankees cap. He was a snitch, but a snitch with a nose for stashes of guns, drugs, and cash. One night they took him along for the ride to kidnap an FDN dealer from his own safe house. They drove the target out to a back street. Everyone enjoyed the peaceful night for a few moments. The buzzing insects. The roar of the last international flight descending into Manaus. The guy squirming in the trunk, bound with zip ties.

They popped the trunk and yanked him out. They put him on his knees, facing into the forest. They let the bastard beg for his life. Then his life was over. They even let Little Angel take a shot. All the better in case they needed to pin it on him later. To wrap it up nice and neat, they scribbled the number 300 on a $2 bill and stuffed it in the victim's mouth like a bow, a gift from the Spartan 300s. It was an open-and-shut case. Gang war, what can you do, *poh*?

By the end of September, Little Angel had caught the bug, looping other informants into the game, coming to meet the Ghost Riders with his own ammo and zip ties. He rode along with Cézanne and the others, dumping bodies outside the city. He filled his phone with photos and video, guys pleading for their lives, lives punctuated by headshots, headshots that he showed off to friends along with close-ups of his girlfriend's pussy.

By October, the kid had the Ghost Riders on speed dial. Little Angel knew a guy with two guns—a shotgun and a .38—just begging to be stolen. All they had to do was set a trap. Klebert gave him a call on the afternoon of Tuesday, October 27, to hatch a plan. Almada and the team listened in.

"Are you in class?" Klebert asked.

"Just waiting to go in," Little Angel said, girls chattering in the background.

This would be an easy hit: Little Angel would tell the guy that they had a robbery lined up, but they needed his guns. Once they got him in the car, they'd ice him and jack the weapons.

"You're sure he's a bad guy?" asked Klebert. "A real thug?"

"Yeah, ask Cézanne."

"Who's going to kill him?"

"I'll do it myself," Little Angel said. "We'll be the only ones carrying."

"We need one more guy," Klebert said. "Someone we can trust."

"We'll be fine, just the two of us," Little Angel said. "He's just a brat."

The next afternoon they took Klebert's car out to Tarumã, a neighborhood out by the airport, to pick up the target, Alexandre, a guy Little Angel knew from the juvenile detention center. Alexandre showed up with the guns—and a partner named Leandro. Only one of them would survive to testify.

"You can't burn in this car," Klebert said when they sparked a joint in the backseat. "It's my family's."

They made small talk on the way to the house they were supposedly going to rob. Klebert went inside with Little Angel and Alexandre. Leandro waited behind the wheel, looking up and down the street. It was getting toward sunset when they came back outside a few minutes later. Klebert was carrying a black envelope.

"You know how to drive?" he asked the kid behind the wheel. "Step on it."

They sped back toward the city, Klebert in the backseat with Alexandre, Little Angel up front with Leandro. Near an empty roundabout, Klebert told the kid to pull over—he'd drive now. Leandro rolled to a stop on the shoulder. A white VW Kombi rushed past. When it rounded the bend, Little Angel pointed the pistol at Leandro's head and pulled the trigger.

The gun jammed. Leandro scampered out the car, leaving

Alexandre behind. Klebert yanked Alexandre out of the car and put a bullet in his eye. Little Angel unjammed his pistol and shot Leandro in the thigh as he ran. Before they could finish him off, the kid was out of range, limping aboard the 678 bus back into town, blood pouring from his leg.

So much for Klebert the cleanup man. This was a real shit show. Almada and his team transcribed the phone calls and requested the transit camera footage from the roundabout. There was only one detail from the transit cameras that Almada didn't include in the report, that he didn't tell his team—or his supervisors. One minute before the killing took place, by sheer coincidence, the governor of Amazonas, José Melo, drove through the roundabout in his motorcade, probably on his way to the airport. Had Melo passed by even a moment later, he and his security team would have seen an off-duty PM executing a young man in broad daylight.

The last thing Almada needed was that headline: "Killer Cop Commits Murder Right Under the Governor's Nose." That kind of news could roil the prison system, start riots at IPAT and COM-PAJ, spark another Bloody Weekend, take down the Secretariat of Public Security. Not now. Not when Operation Wolfpack had cornered its prey. Some details have no place in the official report.

By early November, the Ghost Riders had gone off the deep end. They gunned down stoners for smoking weed on the corner. They exchanged smiley-face emojis on WhatsApp, sending pictures of their handfuls of ammunition. When some fellow PMs found out that their mixed martial arts classmate had his motorcycle stolen at knife point, they called Cézanne to help track down and kidnap the robber that night. With help from Little Angel, they tortured the man in his home until he coughed up the name of an accomplice in the neighborhood. They located the accomplice and tortured him until he gave up the name of a third suspect and the location of the chop shop where the bike was taken. When the third interrogation went bad, they shot the final suspect. There was nothing to do with the first two but execute them in the backyard. The next day Cézanne returned to duty and Little Angel returned to school as if it were all in a night's work for the Ghost Riders, a pro bono service for the people of Manaus.

They had no idea that Internal Affairs was dragging and dropping every image into their evidence folders.[6]

The party was about to end. Inspector Almada vowed not to let another execution happen on his watch. At last he had enough evidence to sync up with his colleagues at the federal police, circulating a target sheet of twelve police and two civilians, addresses, pictures of their homes, and two photos each, so there would be no confusion if shots were fired.

The sting took place at dawn on November 27. The streets were quiet until the tactical units kicked down the doors. The Ghost Riders never saw it coming. Their families thought it was some kind of prank. The agents hauled the suspects away in handcuffs. Detectives tossed their homes while their wives, girlfriends, and kids stood by and sobbed. Guns, cocaine, and weed were bagged and tagged, cell phones grabbed, ready to be hacked open by IT.

Inspector Almada had been around the block enough times to know the best evidence comes to those who wait. The idiots had photographed newspaper clippings of their own killings. Little Angel recorded one of the executions on his smartphone, the victim zip-tied and squealing as the shots stung him in the arm, in the ribs.

"Get him in the head man, the head!" yells a voice offscreen before the final shot.

Reading the messages, it was like they thought they were making an action flick. Ghost Riders this, Ghost Riders that. They even referenced the goddamned movie. Nicolas Cage in real life! Mattos texting nonchalantly, "Do you want to go play that game we always play?"

Mattos would have plenty of time to watch movies and read books behind bars.[7] When the search-and-seizure unit tossed his bedroom, they found a dog-eared copy of the sensational autobiography of a big-city PM from Rio de Janeiro telling how he fell from being a cop with good intentions to a killer on the take. Real cliché stuff. The kind of drama kids act out in the alleys. Imagine Mattos just home from his shift, inhaling the pages like porn, heart beating faster, a guy just like him, all the way down in Rio, fighting the same demons, committing the same sins, writing a whole book about it, *Como Nascem Os Monstros*—how monsters are born.

PART III

THE AMAZON CLOCK

17

A LAND WITHOUT MEN

From the bus window the Transamazônica highway looked like it had been abandoned midway through construction: two lanes, unpaved most of the way from Rurópolis to Altamira, etched with petrified tire tracks from perilous rainy season journeys, now baked into the red earth by the sun. The maps call this highway BR-230. It cuts 2,640 miles through the heart of the Amazon basin as if on a dare. During the years it was built, it earned the name Transmiséria.

The road undulates through a checkerboard of untouched forest and clear-cut pasture where ranchers leave a few giant kapok trees standing to shade the cattle. Every few miles our driver grinds the bus into a lower gear to cross one of hundreds of wooden bridges over the creeks, old-growth beams groaning under the weight of the bus. On paved stretches he opens the throttle and for a moment it feels like we're making good time. Along the spine of the main road, hundreds of dirt road offshoots penetrate the remaining forest in fishbone patterns, ribs needling a mile or two before coming to a dead stop wherever it became obvious to the speculators that this was no country for making money.

Rustic as it looks these days, at its genesis the Transamazônica was a marvel of modern engineering, the signature accomplishment of President Emílio Médici, who ruled Brazil from 1969 to 1974 during the height of the military dictatorship, an era remembered as the Bleeding Years. Enemies of the state were imprisoned, electroshocked, tied upside down, forced to swallow what should never be swallowed, and made to watch their loved ones endure the same.[1] Years of betrayal, neighbors compelled to name neighbors disappeared themselves. Years of drought and desperate measures, bulldozers gashing open the interior of Brazil in search of salvation.

Two years after the World Cup, as the country slogged through a deep recession and a Jet Wash investigation that had ensnared President Dilma Rousseff, I was riding twelve hours to see the culmination of another blueprint from the dictatorship era. Back when Dilma and Lula were held captive and tortured by the regime, nobody could have predicted that one day the young radicals would be the ones breaking ground on the Belo Monte Dam, lodestone of the hydroelectric strategy that was to power Brazil into the twenty-first century. Abandoned for decades before being dusted off at the turn of the century, the Belo Monte, the second largest hydroelectric project in the world, was now on the verge of producing commercial energy for the first time. Like the Transamazônica, it was a milestone on the long march to the future, a testament to the will of the Brazilian people, plain as the motto on the flag, *Ordem e Progresso*. A forest must be made orderly. A river must be made to flow in the direction of progress.

The opening of the interior began in the national imagination, long before the Transamazônica or the Belo Monte. At the turn of the twentieth century, Brazil was still pivoting from monarchy to republic, clumsily extending federal power from its cities to the sprawling interior, where millions of its citizens had never seen the flag. In the view of the positivists of the era, creating a Brazilian utopia would require penetrating the frontier where *Indios bravos*— wild Indians—still defended their territories with arrows and clubs.[2]

"Brazil is the country of the future—and it always will be," quipped Charles de Gaulle. It's a burn that still haunts the country like a prophecy. The oligarchs of Brazil sought to follow the development blueprint of the world's great powers, enticing frontiersmen to conquer the Amazon anew, pacifying tribes so they could be strategically relocated. Enough blood had been spilled; for better or worse, Indians were part of the national bloodline. The sooner they could be woven into the national fabric, the sooner the government could clear the way for miners and loggers to unlock the dormant potential of the interior. A new wave of backwoods explorers and missionaries followed in the footsteps of their colonial ancestors, trekking into the rain forest to lure uncontacted tribes from their homes with gifts of machetes, axes, and mirrors.

This seemingly enlightened new attitude toward indigenous Brazilians was inspired by a half-Indian explorer and engineer, Colonel Cândido Rondon. A patriotic idealist, Rondon had witnessed atrocities against indigenous tribes during his formative years. After centuries of abuse, he believed that it was time to integrate tribes into modern society. A strong federal presence would ease the transition, protect their human rights, and prevent more of the massacres and epidemics that had befallen Brazilian Indians since the arrival of Europeans.[3] The expansion of Brazil's telegraph system would provide the perfect occasion to put these new policies to the test. In 1907, the president tapped Rondon to lead a federal commission to establish telegraph lines through thousands of miles of dense jungle, linking the interior to the coast for the first time in history.

In practice the plan was even more audacious than it looked on paper. Thousands of men were recruited from the lower classes—derelicts, prisoners, insubordinate soldiers—and shipped to the Amazon in an effort to straighten them out. Many of the men conscripted to the Rondon Commission considered the assignment a death sentence. Dispatched from southern capitals like Rio de Janeiro, they arrived at distant outposts where mosquitos swarmed and malaria was epidemic.

The day began with taps at 4:00 a.m. Workers bathed in dark rivers, hurrying to wash before they were bitten by snakes. From there it was a two-hour hike to the worksite for a long day driven by the maniacal Rondon, followed by a two-hour hike back on aching legs, looking over their shoulders in fear of ambush by hostile tribes. Some of the men were accompanied by their wives and children, who marched from site to site alongside them, sometimes twenty miles in a day when it was time to move camp. Holidays were the only reprieve, but Rondon did not let a single day go to waste. If the men could not make progress on the line, they would make progress on their souls. Rondon gathered his men for meandering oratories about Brazilian history, as long and nearly as painful as a march.[4]

A seasoned outdoorsman with the endurance of a boulder and a keen sense of sympathy for the Indians, Rondon was seemingly born for the rigor of life in the Amazon. In 1910, he was named leader of the Indian Protection Service (SPI). His motto: "Die if you must, but never kill." The SPI constitution, which he coauthored, was remarkably progressive for its day, forbidding outsiders from forcing Indians into any religious doctrine. Instead, indigenous groups should be left to practice their own beliefs as stewards of the land. In that sense, though Rondon clung to a positivist worldview that flamed out in the mid-twentieth century, his respect for indigenous knowledge, even if only as a step on the path to divinity, anticipated the post-development theory of the twenty-first century. Even as Rondon became "The Father of Brazilian Telecommunications," he embraced the notion that thriving civilizations can exist on many paths outside the capitalist trajectory of resource extraction, production, consumption, and waste.

During encounters with Indians, his men were allowed to fire warning shots in the air but never to shoot back, no matter how many arrows or spears flew their way. If they were struck down, their fellows would attempt to dress the wounds with a blend of tobacco, rock salt, and warm animal fat before maggots threatened to eat the flesh down to the bone. Rot if you must, lose your leg if you must, but never kill.

While some Brazilian historians look back on the Rondon Commission as the first modern offensive against the Amazon ecosystem and its indigenous tribes, there is no denying the hardships the men overcame to bring modern connectivity to the interior. During a fantastic age of global exploration from Antarctica to the Far East, Rondon emerged as a national hero, drumming up funds for his expeditions by appealing to fellow patriots: Brazil must expand and preserve its porous borders. In 1913 President Theodore Roosevelt, having left the White House and thirsty for adventure, joined Rondon on a treacherous expedition along the River of Doubt, suffering a grave leg wound and nearly losing his son to suicide along the way. For Rondon, the company of an international celebrity was a publicity coup. He seized every opportunity for photo ops, indigenous boys and girls wrapped in Brazilian flags, proof that Indians and white settlers could coexist in modern Brazil.

When it was finished, the telegraph line would unite the

country like never before, allowing culture and commerce to thrive in Manaus as easily as in São Paulo. For nearly a decade Rondon's telegraph commission sawed across the country. Station by station, operators expanded the network, living in constant fear of Indian attack. Wet season and dry, they waited like monks for pulses through the sagging cables, timber poles already rotting in the rain. Claude Lévi-Strauss, the French anthropologist who studied Indians in the Amazon in the 1930s, wrote that the work of those early telegraph operators was as lonely as living on the moon. It could take days for a telegram to be relayed from station to station, messages dying alongside operators, dead on the cabin floor with arrows in their back, a feast for army ants.

Within a generation, the advent of radio brought an end to the lonely line. Twenty years after its first telegram, the stations were abandoned and the forest began its reclamation, vines dragging the telegraph poles to the ground.

In 1937, President Getúlio Vargas imposed a new authoritarian constitution in an effort to quell communist and fascist uprisings against his government. Fusing the ideologies of Mussolini's Italy and Salazar's Portugal, Vargas's *Estado Novo*—"New State"— prioritized the national patrimony over individual rights. On New Year's Eve 1937, in a late-night National Radio address, Vargas announced that Brazil would redouble its efforts to explore the interior. Though teeming with plant and animal life, the Amazon was one of the most sparsely populated regions on the planet. Estimates about the scale of its natural resources and arable land were pure speculation. There was only one way to find out: "March to the West."

Chainsaws cleared the way for resource extraction. Cross-country expeditions were supported by a new miracle of the modern world: aviation. Hopping between airstrips, pilots could cross the continent in a day. The Central Brazil Foundation (FBC) was created in 1943 to fulfill Vargas's vision, led by legendary brothers Orlando, Claudio, and Leonardo Villas Bôas. Under the mentorship of Rondon, the brothers would lead a new generation of expeditions, bringing airstrips, weather stations, and radio towers to the interior and encountering new tribes along the way. The Villas Bôas brothers believed contact with Indians was inevitable. The only way to shield the first Brazilians from annihilation was to win their trust so they could be relocated to safe havens beyond the path of progress.

The oldest brother, Orlando, seemed to instinctively know the ways of the tribes. A man of the imagination, Orlando escaped the torments of the jungle by reading crime novels and comic books, delivered monthly to the field outposts. Studious Claudio lost himself in the pages of Marx and other theorists, jotting notes that baffled the Indians. Leonardo would die of disease at the age of forty-three, leaving a stain of grief on the brothers' life's work, but fueling their sense of purpose.[5]

It was the Villas Bôas brothers who first made their way into the headwaters of the Rio Xingu, a remote region of the forest, protected by deadly rapids, where for generations tribes had gone to escape the scourges of slavery and disease. The Xingu was home to an astonishing variety of tribes, coexisting in relative peace, united by their fear of the white man's bondage. Like their forebears, Xinguanos were suspicious of outsiders but fascinated by modern tools. With the benefit of Rondon's years of experience, the Villas Bôas brothers knew to equip their teams with ample gifts to win the favor of tribes they discovered along their path, the same curiosities that had attracted Indians for centuries: mirrors, fishhooks, and metal machetes. Supported by air supply drops, FBC crews carved out airstrips in strategic locations throughout the Amazon, opening the rain forest to the age of aviation.

Today the Villas Bôas legacy lives on in the Rio Xingu Reserve, a place where until recently tribes still lived in near isolation, practicing their beliefs and customs with the support of health teams at Leonardo Station, named for the fallen brother. Yet the enormous reserve came at a terrible cost to the tribes contacted during the era of expansion. Unpredictable epidemics ravaged communities before they could be convinced to relocate. Early contact teams were soon followed by loggers, miners, ranchers, and missionaries, who spread disease, acculturation, and Christianity, destroying ancient ways. As thousands of hectares of virgin forest gave way to cattle operations, indigenous communities abandoned their crops and customs for the ranching life. The intricate biome that blanketed the region, dependent on interconnected systems of water, plant life, and animal migration, deteriorated into a patchwork of fledgling pastures and wilting rain forest, fenced off from the biodiversity it needed to thrive.

By the end of his life in 1958, not long after he had been nominated for the Nobel Peace Prize, Rondon would express regret at having advocated for a march into the interior. By then it was too late.

"Where we Kayabí used to live on the Rio dos Peixes, there were once two thousand Indians in the old village," said Chief Canísio of the forest his people were forced to abandon. "Once there was a big Indian village, now there's only a ranch."

The highly publicized adventures of Rondon and the Villas Bôas brothers disguised corruption festering behind the scenes at the Indian Protection Service, whose agents were mistreating settled tribes under their guardianship and looking the other way while loggers, miners, and rubber tappers razed the frontier and the villages that stood in their way. When the military seized power in a

1964 coup encouraged by the United States, the new leadership accused the SPI of "theft and misapplication of funds, irregular transactions with cattle, and crimes against the national patrimony."[6]

Soon after, the minister of the interior appointed investigator general Jáder de Figueiredo Correia to lead an inquiry into allegations of abuse and misconduct at the agency Rondon founded to protect Brazil's Indians. Completed in 1967, the Figueiredo report drew scorn from the UN Conference on Human Rights. In 1969, the *Sunday Times* of London published a lengthy exposé, "Genocide," situating the findings of the Figueiredo report in the context of centuries of atrocities against Brazilian Indians.[7]

The report found that the majority of SPI officials—500 of the 700-person staff—were guilty of fraud, theft, or worse. In settled villages like Posto Fraternidade Indígena, government inspectors were "famous for the cruelty with which they 'protected' Indians." The stories shamed Brazil on the international stage.

"There was a mill for crushing sugar cane," testified one Indian girl. "To spare the horses they used Indian children to turn the mill."

One government inspector summoned a carpenter to build an oven for his farmhouse. When the worker was finished, he asked for an Indian girl as payment for a job well done. "The agent took him to the school and told him to choose one." Eleven-year-old Rosa was never seen again.

The report also detailed the crimes committed by the men who followed the SPI into the rain forest. In 1957, a party of rubber tappers in the Tapajós baited an isolated tribe with bags of sugar tinged with arsenic and ant killer. "By the following morning, many Indians were dead," read the report, "and the tappers spread the news that a great epidemic was raging in the area."

In 1963, just five years after Rondon's death, in Rondônia, the state named in his honor, the rubber overseer Chico Luis de Brito rented a Cessna to fly over a festival in the villages of the Cinta Longa. "On the first run packets of sugar were dropped to calm the fears of those who had scattered and run for shelter at the sight of the plane," recalled a former SPI inspector. "They had opened the packets and were tasting the sugar ten minutes later when the plane returned to carry out the attack."

The Cessna bombed the village with sticks of dynamite. The bodies were buried in the bank of the river.

Not long after, de Brito led another extermination group by land, telling his men to execute the chief and leave the rest of the killing to him. "Chico gave the chief a burst with his tommy gun to make sure, and after that he let the rest of them have it," one of his henchmen testified. "All the other fellows had to do was finish off anyone who showed signs of life. . . . There was a young Indian girl they didn't shoot, with a kid of about five in one hand, yelling his head off. . . . Chico shot the kid through the head with his .45 and then grabbed hold of the woman—who by the way was very pretty. 'Be reasonable,' I said. 'What's wrong with giving her to the boys? They haven't set eyes on a woman for six weeks?' "

Mad with bloodlust, de Brito strung the Indian mother upside down from a tree and drew his machete. According to the report, the woman was "cut open alive from her pubis to her head."

The gruesome revelations spurred Brazil's recently installed military dictatorship to dismantle the SPI. The most egregious offenders were lightly punished. Two hundred were dismissed. The vast majority were incorporated into the newly formed FUNAI. Brazil's generals had bigger fish to fry in the Amazon, according to their American advisers at the Pentagon. Look at Fidel Castro, Che Guevara, and their band of bearded guerrillas, who had stunned the world with the 1957 Cuban Revolution. They had seeded discontent among the rural poor, thwarted trained military units in the capital, and then retreated to the jungle to consolidate power before overthrowing the U.S.-supported Cuban leadership in Havana for good. Brazil was no island nation, but its military would be foolish to ignore the risk of rebellion in the rain forest.

The Amazon was more than an untapped resource—it was a strategic front where dissent could fester under the cloak of the jungle. Despite its international waterways, economic opportunities were scarce. A faint echo of the rubber boom during World War II had done little to revive the economy of Manaus. Even the great Henry Ford had lost money in the jungle. He imagined that his eponymous settlement Fordlândia, a tract of land twice the size of Delaware, would become a utopia in the middle of the Amazon, complete with all the trappings of American consumer life. In 1928, Ford's explorers cleared the land using 27-horsepower Model N "iron mules," attempting to tame the settlement into an industrial rubber plantation, yet the rain forest proved resistant to the regimen of mass production, and his indigenous laborers resisted his puritanical, all-American work ethic. Fordlândia failed before its founder could pay a visit—although to this day the villagers left behind keep an immaculate bedroom ready for the great industrialist, as if awaiting his second coming.[8]

Poor living conditions and a lack of government presence in the Amazon made the region ripe for a rural guerrilla campaign. As the dictatorship tightened its grip in the 1960s, leaders were already contending with urban guerrillas like Carlos Marighella, the elder statesmen of the Brazilian Communist Party who had defied his comrades by attending a summit in Havana. Unlike Che Guevara, who believed that a successful revolution had to begin in the countryside and advance to the city, Marighella believed the Brazilian revolution would be sparked on the streets of São Paulo.

By the late 1960s, Marighella and his comrades were committing bank robberies around the city to raise money for their rebellion, conducting kidnappings for ransom, and grabbing international attention with the abduction of a U.S. ambassador. By the time government agents assassinated Marighella one evening as he left the theater, it was too late; he had already inspired other guerrillas to take up the revolutionary cause.

If Brazil wanted to keep the interior from rotting, it was time for intervention. The government established a free-trade port in Manaus to restore the city to its glory days. In less than a decade, the Zona Franca helped Manaus bloom into a destination for international manufacturers, which began building appliances, motorcycles, and other "white" goods to be shipped throughout Brazil, subsidized by incentives too good to refuse. The flood of capital saved the city from a potentially fatal bust, drawing a fresh generation of migrants from the northeast, eager to ride the next boom. The move also served as a pretext for an expanded military presence. The Amazon region would soon be home to thousands of army, navy, and air force personnel, commanded by military leaders who studied counterinsurgency tactics at the notorious U.S. Army School of the Americas.[9]

On a breezy morning in 1970, the Brazilian military conducted its first joint military operation for a public audience in Marabá, Pará. The crowd watched an Albatross SA-16 aircraft drop twelve Special Forces paratroopers from 7,000 feet over the Tocantins River. After thirty seconds of daring free fall, they deployed their chutes. Onlookers applauded as the leader unfurled a Brazilian flag, fluttering like a leaf as the squad stuck their landing on a white sandbar. There they delivered the flag to a navy river patrol boat, which rushed the colors to the nearby port where it was relayed to a lieutenant from the jungle infantry battalion. At last it was shuttled to the city square. Amid pomp and circumstance, a public school student raised the colors at the pavilion, to the sound of the national anthem.

On the surface, it was a breathtaking display of military coordination the likes of which had never been seen in the Amazon, but its purpose was sinister: to intimidate a band of guerrillas operating in the nearby jungle. Founded by eighty activists, fifteen of whom had traveled to China during the 1960s to receive Communist Party training, the rebels hoped to establish a Maoist liberated zone in the remote region where the Araguaia and Tocantins rivers meet. The rebels ingratiated themselves in area villages, offering their services as doctors, teachers, and lawyers to recruit locals to their movement.[10] Ordered to crush the rebellion at any cost, the Brazilian military jungle battalion waged a merciless counterinsurgency campaign in the region for three years, from 1972 to 1975.

"The rivers are the blood that irrigate the forest," wrote Colonel Alvaro de Souza Pinheiro in an analysis of Brazil's anti-guerrilla strategy, published by the U.S. Joint Special Operations University in July 1995 as a case study in the art of war in the rain forest.[11] "Before the infantry men can overcome the enemy they must overcome the jungle."

As the Americans had discovered in their disastrous campaigns in Southeast Asia, jungle combat is nearly blind. Aerial observation is limited, neutralizing the advantage of air-to-ground tactics, and visibility on the ground is often less than 50 feet. Humidity and dense vegetation complicate radio communications and the critical logistics of supply and evacuation. A week in the jungle can leave even the most disciplined units in disarray. "If possible, a good supply of vitamins and energizers must be carried as well as a large amount of salt," wrote Pinheiro. Fatigue makes the dense jungle environment even more perplexing, leaving units vulnerable to ambush. A soldier must be capable of detecting traps and creating his own from materials at hand in the forest. "Transform ordinary things into deadly devices that can be used against the enemy," advised the colonel. "With a few feet of cord, wire, and an axe and sharp branches resistant to fire, it is possible to build some creative devices with fatal effect."

More than 10,000 Brazilian soldiers exercised maximum creativity in their three-year campaign. Patrols navigated the jungle with the assistance of native guides, compelled by force to hunt down dozens of rebel men and women and all who would aid and abet them. There would be no trials. Captives were beaten, tortured, and beheaded. Local villagers were caught in the crossfire, expelled from their farms, which were strafed with bombs and bullets and incinerated with napalm. At least one boy lost his life after picking up a live grenade left behind in the forest. Suspected collaborators were flown to Brasilia for sadistic interrogations. "After torturing me with electricity and plunging my head into a water tank until I could no longer breathe, they threw me into a pit of garbage that was filled with snakes and scorpions and held me there for more than a week," recalled Antônio Alves de Souza, who lived near a Brazilian armed forces base. "When they finally pulled me out for questioning, they removed the head of a man from a burlap bag and asked if I knew him."[12]

Aside from the dramatic exercise over the Tocantins River, the military never officially made its presence known in the Araguaia guerrilla war. The conflict was waged as a top-secret operation under the guise of plainclothes federal police. The generals wanted nobody to know that Brazil had needed military force to quell a rebellion within its own borders. The soldiers and police officers responsible for the killings and torture were granted amnesty after the conflict. So were the rebels, but for them it was too late.

In the decades to come, Brazil's generals and elites would look across South America and feel validated. Communist uprisings in the Colombian and Peruvian Amazon proved that malcontents in the jungle could sow the seeds of civil war. The FARC rebels who caused so much trouble for Bogotá would one day supply the Família do Norte and other Brazilian syndicates with cocaine, military-grade hardware, and tactical expertise. Determined not to repeat the mistakes of their neighbors, Brazil's military dictatorship poured resources into fortifying the Amazon. Today it remains the center of gravity for the Brazilian armed forces, with tanks, patrol boats, and Toucan fighter jets ready to contain whatever chaos might emerge from the rain forest.

When President Lula was elected president in 2002, many on the left hoped that the former guerrilla would seek justice for those tortured, killed, or disappeared during the dictatorship. The families deserved to know what happened, where their sons and daughters were buried. Lula demurred. For decades he had been accused of being too radical. Now that he was in power, any hope of building a governing coalition would require cooperation from the right. No use opening old graves. Some skeletons are better left buried.

"We must start up the Amazon clock, which has been losing time for too long," wrote military President Médici in 1971 as if the river, the jaguar, or the sloth were subject to human temporality.[13]

Médici had recently returned from a tour of Recife where tens of thousands of victims of the drought-stricken northeast were fleeing their farms only to find there was no food or housing for them in the coastal cities. The drought had exposed the stunning poverty of the country's rural workers. The elite had reaped the rewards of the military's economic engineering, yet the plutocrats were still unsatisfied. In their eyes, the government had neglected its riverine borders for too long. Now its wealth of timber, gold, and iron ore was at risk of being overtaken by neighbors or foreign imperialists.

For Médici and his advisers, the northeast and the Amazon were twin problems with a common solution: "Brazil has not yet reached the era of a finite world," he told his countrymen. "We have the privilege of incorporating into our economy, step by step, new, immense and practically empty regions."

In the early 1970s the National Integration Program would open the Amazon basin to 70,000 families, Médici proclaimed: "A land without men for men without land."

Transportation was the first step to integration. The audacious Transamazônica was an engineering challenge fit for a country on the verge of world power. Tracing the overgrown path of Rondon's decrepit lonely line, the Transamazônica promised abundant fertile land for the landless poor and access to natural resources for the landed elite. The invisible pulse of telegram signals would be usurped by the rumble of cattle trucks. All who criticized the absurd cost of the plan were silenced by the president's advisers: "Nothing that has altered the face of the world would have ever passed a preliminary test on its rate of return."

As if God were in league with the regime's macroeconomists, the crippling drought fueled a reverse migration back into the interior of Brazil. Families entranced by promises of land deeds, loans, and free seeds followed the grind and growl of bulldozers and chainsaws. Hardscrabble logging crews manned the front lines with little more than axes and machetes, waiting hungrily for the faint drone of the airplanes that dropped supply boxes wherever they saw campfire smoke at dawn. Construction teams and engineers on opposite sides of the forest cut toward each other, devouring acres of forest by the hour, resting only to visit the bars and brothels that sprouted up on their path.

With each new mile of road, the myth of fertile Amazon land grew more vivid. Speculators and prospectors planted tent cities before the dust cleared. They dreamt of a roadway that would one day cross the continent, linking the Pacific to the Atlantic across the world's largest forest. They dreamt of soil as purple as beef flank under a butcher's knife. They dreamt of an endless west of zebu cattle and barbed-wire fences, bananas and mangos and coffee and cocoa, hillside *fazendas* with a view of kingdom come.

The greed fed a vicious feedback loop. As more settlers arrived and cleared forest, property values soared, drawing another wave of settlers who cleared new swaths of forest even as the first-comers' crops began to fail. Then came the rain. Without root systems to hold the soil in place, topsoil was swept away in flash floods. Without the shade of the forest canopy, the intricate creek systems of the floodplain evaporated into muddy pools of standing water. The emaciated cows were so prone to disease that calves were mere food for the vultures.

The military had no use for broken dreams. The Amazon clock would keep ticking, making up for lost years, decades, centuries. Engineers and civil planners drew up a map for the future. The Transamazônica would be populated with *agrovilas*, evenly spaced like the marks on a ruler, clusters of forty-eight to sixty farmsteads, no man more than 3 miles from his fields. Every 25 miles would be an *agropolis*—a slightly larger town with schools, banks, and sawmills. Every 100 miles, a *ruropólis*, a hub of electricity, running water, and industry.[14] The triumph would be broadcast to every television and radio. A drought was no match for a river of heavy machinery. A rebel cell was no match for the army. A disobedient priest was no match for a posse of cattlemen. In a single generation, the population of the Amazon mushroomed from 2 million to 20 million, from the Industrial Revolution to the Information Age.

With the turn of the twenty-first century came communications infrastructure that Rondon and his telegraph operators could never have imagined. SkyNet launched an O3b satellite constellation from the space center in French Guiana, twelve engineering miracles in medium orbit in a fixed point over Ecuador, tracking the planet at the precise speed necessary to reduce latency to 150 milliseconds, boosting link capacities to rival the throughput of long-haul fiber in Rio de Janeiro.

Wi-Fi bulldozers vaporized the high costs of laying cables through the rain forest, signals penetrating deeper than telegraph lines, train tracks, lumber roads, airstrips, and fishbone roads could ever reach. Capital attracted bandwidth and bandwidth attracted capital. Lumber, oil, and ore spilled from the mouth of the Amazon to Europe, Africa, the United States, and Saudi Arabia. Semiconductors, petrochemicals, cocaine, submachine guns, Harley-Davidson Fat Boys, jewels machined from metal and blood, drawn from the veins of South America to the open sea.

"We are bringing the data highways that these communities need to communicate with the rest of the country," wrote one telecommunications executive on the launch of a new satellite.[15]

The bus rumbles on, passengers awake on a nighttime journey across the Transamazônica, the Transmiséria, pale blue faces staring into their phone screens, craving the ping of the next cell tower. The driver double-checking his scheduled maintenance, old bones creaking to the next one hotel town. Rurópolis. Uruará. Médicilândia. Loved ones waiting for loved ones under red neon lights. A country of perpetual waiting. Waiting for a cattle run. Waiting for fire season. Waiting to strike gold. Waiting on a passerby to help push your Kombi from the muck. Waiting for sun. Waiting for rain. Waiting for the soil to admit its mistakes. Waiting for the question. Waiting for the answer. Waiting for Friday night when the only new horizon is straight out of town, gunning your moto, vapor in the gas tank, a phantom in the headlight, the spirit of a chief still awestruck by the white man who commands his rancorous yellow beasts with a wave of the hand.

18

CITY OF VULTURES

At daybreak the bus pulled into Altamira, Pará—gateway to the Belo Monte complex. It was April 2016, and after a generation of controversy, the world's second largest hydroelectric project was on the verge of churning out its first commercial wattage. I wanted to see its turbines firsthand, to witness how five years of excavation and construction had transformed a pit stop on the Transamazônica into a boomtown at the big bend of the Rio Xingu, the largest southern tributary of the Amazon.

The highway splits Altamira in half. Exiting in the semi-dark, the bus transitioned to fresh black pavement, the city's logo and tagline painted on seemingly every flat surface: ALTAMIRA—WORK AND SOCIAL DEVELOPMENT. In less than a decade the population had nearly doubled to more than 150,000 people, warping a rural river town into a planned suburban community, sponsored and built by Norte Energia, the eighteen-company public-private consortium governing the design, construction, and operation of Belo Monte and the social infrastructure intended to lift the surrounding region out of poverty.

Controlled by the state-owned power company Electrobras, Norte Energia is omnipresent in Altamira, an Orwellian force of capital that can create and destroy. Its very mission is godlike: redirect the flow of the Rio Xingu—one of the world's largest rivers—through a series of canals, stop banks, spillways, and reservoirs to generate 5 percent of Brazil's electricity needs, flooding 264 square miles of rain forest—an area the size of Chicago—and a third of the city of Altamira along the way.

In propaganda broadcast on every TV channel and radio station for a hundred miles in every direction, Norte Energia vows to transform Altamira into a clean-energy utopia. On the religious talk radio station, the host and his pious callers are interrupted every few minutes by a sternly benevolent public service announcement reminding listeners of the civic transformation unfolding before their eyes: a new hospital to replace the worn-down infirmary, a sanitation system to make the river clean for swimming again, social services to help even the most despondent citizens of Altamira find new jobs, for there are limitless opportunities in the City of Work.

If you miss the TV or radio spots, you cannot avoid the billboards posted at every corner, as abundant as traffic signs, announcing new and upcoming projects with target budgets and completion dates noted on the immaculate concept art. Other signs remind Altamirans to learn more about the Belo Monte Dam by taking a complimentary shuttle bus out to the construction site to understand why it is not just a hydroelectric project but a project of social transformation. After the floodgates of the Belo Monte complex opened and inundated the lowlands, Altamira became a City of Bridges, providing More Access and Better Quality of Life.

The 20,000 citizens displaced by floodwaters in the new channel have been relocated to higher ground. If anyone has lingering doubts that the Norte Energia neighborhoods are superior, just look at the billboards that compare one of the ramshackle stilt houses with one of the new concrete dwellings, mass-produced like Legos.

The hills overlooking Altamira and the Xingu have been bull-dozed of trees to make way for planned communities, hundreds of houses in each, evenly spaced along fresh roads that have yet to be named. In the heart of the first community the consortium built, Norte Energia supervises the distribution of housing, health, and food benefits from a single-story administrative building sur-rounded by a cluster of antennas and security vehicles, the same brand of SUVs donated to the Altamira police for use as patrol cruisers.

The only thing more transformational than the presence of Norte Energia will be the absence of Norte Energia. Now that the Belo Monte is humming toward full capacity, private support for public infrastructure in Altamira will be phased out over five years. The transition is already underway. Billboards at the newly con-structed bridges around town announce that the city will soon take over road maintenance from Norte Energia, as if the consortium were a proud father boasting about his precocious child. There is no telling what will happen when the city of Altamira is left to its own devices. Even now the men and women at the Norte Energia social assistance building seem to take long lunches while the se-curity guards turn people away at the door.

Which projects will be finished? Which projects will be aban-doned to the care of the city? Even the completed projects are like apparitions, half-empty structures built for a city swelling in pop-ulation but not prosperity. Thousands of the workers who mi-grated here to erect the massive dam complex are returning home or waiting in unemployment lines. Longtime river folk have fled the boom to rebuild their homes elsewhere on the water, to find a life they can afford, a view they recognize. This is a phantom city. Traffic circles without traffic. Schoolhouses without students. Skate parks without skaters. Kids without skateboards, running up and down the half-pipe, performing invisible tricks. Exhausted, they take a seat at the lip of the ramp, legs dangling, staring across the swollen river until they catch their breath. Even the living are ghosts.

At the turn of the twenty-first century, Altamira was hungry for jobs and Brazil was hungry for power. From Manaus to Rio de Janeiro, cities were crippled by blackouts. President Fernando Henrique Cardoso and his party had instituted a decade of inflation control and privatization schemes that stabilized the weak currency but not the lives of millions of Brazilians. The market was supposed to free Brazil from the struggles of being a developing nation, but the country of the future had stalled again, Brazil's young democracy sputtering out of the gate. When President Cardoso announced energy rationing, officials refused to specify the dates and times of rolling blackouts for fear of looting and violence during the outages. In Rio de Janeiro, entire hillsides fell dark, save for spotlights of police helicopters scoping the back streets.

It was a state of emergency, a time to open up old file cabinets from the dictatorship. Gray-bearded advisers recalled a foregone plan for a massive hydroelectric project at the great bend in the Xingu River, the pristine region that the Villas Bôas brothers had devoted their lives to protecting. They had called the dam Kararaô, until someone realized that was the Tupi word for war.

No matter what it was called, the project did seem like war on the river. Six massive dams planned for the Amazon's largest tributary. The mere suggestion of damming the Xingu was sacrilege in environmentalist circles. Lula and the Workers' Party had spent decades fighting against such mega projects, looming ecological disasters that enriched the elite at the expense of workers, who were discarded like demolition waste. Construction had almost gone forward in the 1980s when a woman from the Kayapó tribe, a group aware of the power of public relations, made international news at a town hall event where an energy executive was making the case for the dam. In full tribal dress, clutching a machete, the woman parted the crowd like a sea and confronted the man on stage, touching her blade to his white face. This disciplined display of indigenous resistance ushered in a new era of rain forest activism in the developed world, ultimately forcing the World Bank to suspend funding for the dam system. Pop stars like Sting and Phil Collins stood beside literary luminaries like Gabriel García Márquez, Carlos Fuentes, and Mario Vargas Llosa in calling on the world to defend the Amazon from the incursion of loggers and ranchers. What many outsiders failed to appreciate was how much of the rain forest had already been sold, its trajectory forever altered by highways like the Transamazônica.

In 2002, in the wake of the blackout crisis, the government resurrected a smaller, rebranded effort: the Belo Monte Hydroelectric Project, which would divert the flow of the Xingu River by nearly 70 miles at its biggest bend, inundating more than 150 square miles of rain forest. When Lula and his Workers' Party took the keys from Cardoso in 2003, the situation was clear: to keep his promise of light for everyone, Brazil needed to double down on hydroelectric power. If Lula had learned anything from the Bleeding Years, it was that the state can conjure the authority to do anything. A loophole in the law—and a legacy of the military dictatorship—allowed any project deemed critical to national security to take precedence over environmental and human rights concerns. Now the security of the nation was in his hands. On July 13, 2005, the National Congress authorized construction on the project without any consultation from indigenous groups on the land, as required by the 1988 Constitution.

In 2008, indigenous groups in the area organized widespread demonstrations to draw attention to the potential consequences of the Belo Monte. Lula and his energy minister, future president Dilma Rousseff, sat on opposite sides of the table from the environmental minister and future Green Party presidential candidate, Marina Silva. The former senator from the western state of Acre, home to the Ashaninka of Simpatia, Silva was raised in poverty in a family of rubber tappers. At the age of twelve, when a penetration road reached her community of Bagaço, she lost two younger sisters to the malaria epidemic that followed. "I don't know if I was conscious that the road was bringing all that," she recalled, "but it made me write on my own flesh the consequences of what it meant to mess around with nature without giving the slightest attention to the need to look after it."[1]

Silva would grow up to rally rubber tappers in concert with Chico Mendes, the legendary union organizer who was assassinated by a rancher in 1988 while the police charged with protecting him slapped dominoes at a kitchen table.

"It was like shooting a jaguar," confessed the assassin.[2]

Now it was Silva who carried the torch for this generation as the most credible voice on the environment in Brazilian politics. For thirty years she had known Lula, the rambunctious, smoky-voiced drinker who idolized Che Guevara. Her old friend, enemy of the generals, master of the bullhorn, insisted they move forward with one of the dictatorship's seminal plans for the Amazon.

To make the Belo Monte palatable, the government signed a resolution to reduce the number of dams in the proposal, promising no future hydroelectric projects on the Xingu. Lula guaranteed billions in economic and environmental concessions. There would be a thirty-five-volume environmental impact study and public hearings in 142 villages and rural communities. The workers, the Indians, the rivers and the trees, the silky anteaters, the yellow-rumped cacique, the ocelots and the manatees, every shade of butterfly, the 3 million trees each year that would be "suppressed"—all would be documented down to the last species of beetle.

The catch: this impact study was cosponsored by the National Energy Agency and the construction firms that stood to benefit from the construction. An independent, multidisciplinary scientific report condemned the project as a social, environmental, and human rights calamity in the making, but the environmental ministry succumbed to political pressure, magnified by the World Bank and the Brazilian National Development Bank, which were keen to begin lending. Demoralized by the gutting of the environmental licensing process on the Xingu and elsewhere in the Amazon, Silva tendered her resignation.

Boozy contracts were signed in São Paulo. Breathtaking designs were published in glossy magazines. In 2011, the first blasts of dynamite rocked the Xingu.

Engineers don't know for certain why the Rio Xingu bends wildly here before resuming course due north, why some areas of the riverbed are rock hard, yet elsewhere it crumbles into red clay that generations of brick makers have fired on the banks at dawn. What engineers do know is that the subtle drop in elevation at this latitude, invisible to the untrained eye, is enough to generate monumental amounts of power.

The Belo Monte complex is a system of three dams: the Pimental, the Bela Vista Spillway, and the Belo Monte itself, linked by canals paved with the crushed rock of the riverbed, channeling 3.7 million gallons per second diverted from the main river. The battalion of turbines was manufactured thousands of miles away, each unit shipped in a single 30-ton piece on a six-week journey by boat, then by barge, then along the Transamazônica to its berth carved from the migmatite bedrock of the mighty Xingu. Together they will produce more than 11,000 megawatts of electricity, enough power to light the lives of 18 million Brazilians during peak flow.

The engineers know that the rain forest is a blessing and a curse. Subject to the rise and fall of the Xingu, the Belo Monte will only operate at full capacity from February through May once its final operating license is approved. During the driest months, there will only be 10 percent flow. Although its 11,000-megawatt (MW) potential makes the Belo Monte the world's third largest hydroelectric project by capacity, it will produce half the energy of China's record-holding Three Gorges Dam, despite requiring twice the excavation. These ebbs and flows can be reasonably predicted. Hydrologic models can be recalibrated as the tall tower observatory in the northern Amazon gleans new information about the forest climate, as rainfall levels oscillate, as the clouds inhale and exhale and threaten to withhold rain, yet models are only models, and there is no way to predict with certainty how new manmade tides would influence the river, the forest, and its people.

It is impossible to model the human cost. These consequences the engineers leave to environmentalists, economists, and sociologists. To prevent illicit lumber from being used in the construction, legal timber is tagged with RFIDs and scanned at the worksite entrance. Schools of migratory fish are microchipped and tracked by marine biologists, who monitor how their reproduction patterns will hold up in the face of altered river flows. Riverbanks are measured with laser scope surveys to determine which cattle ranches, cocoa farms, and brick foundries will be submerged, which workers will need to be compensated as their livelihoods disappear underwater.

Norte Energia promised to make those lives whole in accordance with the so-called Basic Plan. The snorkelers who net the coveted zebrafish, the star attraction of home aquariums around the world, will be compensated by German scientists who will save the species from extinction by breeding new batches of eggs in sterile winter laboratories. The brick makers will be compensated with benefit checks and a reprieve from the toxic exhaust of their ovens. The banana farmers will be compensated with superior plots in the highlands, the size of which will be determined by the former market value of their grandfather's homestead, now resting on the muddy river bottom.

Those who remain dissatisfied with the generosity of the basic plan—like the Juruna and neighboring tribes displaced by the Belo Monte floodwaters—would be compensated according to the so-called emergency program, an urgent public assistance supplement to keep protestors from continuing to block the roads to the construction site with burning tires.[3] Qualified mothers are free to join the queue at the FUNAI office in Altamira, armed with their shopping lists and benefit paperwork, while their children squat to relieve themselves in the street. Free to purchase cassava flour in town rather than grind it on their own, free to trade bare feet for sandals, headdresses for Nike ball caps, shirtless backs for wick-away tees. Free to purchase flatbed trucks and truckloads of sugar bags, so many bags of sugar they end up being used as steps stacked at the doors of village huts, crawling with ants.

The gifts of the emergency plan, including a $10,000 monthly payment from Norte Energia for each tribe, ultimately fractured indigenous communities. Some leaders refused to be bribed into silence. Others believed it was their last best chance to extract something from the government. Still others believed they should hold out for more. The asymmetrical negotiation process resembled the Indian attraction strategies of the 1970s more than a real political debate. Norte Energia divided; Norte Energia conquered. Eighteen villages splintered into forty-five villages, smaller, weaker, more dependent on the consortium.[4]

If the chiefs appeared greedy in the eyes of the observers from São Paulo, it was only because they understood the fickle value of the white man's promise. The chiefs were selling their land before it was stolen. Not only the land under their feet but the land from here to their grandchildren. They must take all they can now, for as their grandfathers taught them, the white man will keep taking long after he has exhausted his gifts.

"In the old days, you just gave the Indians a mirror and they were happy," lamented one Norte Energia official. "Now they want iPads and four-wheel drives."

By night the excavation site was bright as day. Towers of construction lamps lit the rain like sparks. Bulldozers grizzled through the mud. Workers came and went by the busload, three shifts a day: truck drivers, climbing welders, trench diggers, crane operators, saw sharpeners, demolition experts, hydraulic mechanics, machinists, surveyors, electricians, a universe of engineers, inspectors, and auditors and a team of medics, ready for action day and night.

Any Brazilian who could lift a shovel could earn more than $500 a month at the Belo Monte, more than twice the national minimum wage. During their off hours, workers retreated to nearby barracks, took meals in a cafeteria where food was served on plastic trays by staff who hailed from the same villages as the crews they served. They all had one thing in common: shitty cell reception. After their meals, workers headed to higher ground at the perimeter fence line, trying to catch a cell signal to call their wives and husbands and ornery kids back home. At night the Belo Monte was visible for miles, a supernatural urban glow drawing more electricity than the entire city of Altamira.

Yet tiny Altamira was straining the grid, bulldozers, backhoes, and cement trucks building a new city so quickly that even the animals were confused. Chickens searched for feed among the hardscape of a luxury hotel, chased away by bellhops. Starving dogs joined packs, hoping to find strength in numbers, leaving paw prints on the uncured concrete as they sniffed their way to the next trash bag. The new hospital that had been promised was forever under construction, and the emergency room at the old military hospital was inundated with trauma cases, mostly victims of a rash of roadway accidents, a 140 percent increase in just one year: pedestrian versus car, car versus bicycle, bicycle versus truck, truck versus horse, the consequence of installing stoplights and traffic circles in a city where boys still whip their mules to market.

Sunday. Payday. Legions of workers shuttled forty miles from the excavation site to the Port of Altamira for hijinks, fighting over the jukebox, bleary country or booming funk, lyrics weighed down by the stink of shit and the clouds of mosquitos, violence before nightfall, men brandishing broken bottles, women pulling hair, addicts smoking crack in the alleys, eyes like knives.

The state of Pará has been a hardscrabble territory since the days of the directorate. When the generals decided to open up the Amazon, these backwoods became a battleground between land speculators banking on the next penetration road and the activists fighting to keep the forest intact. As the country industrialized, millions of migrants followed work to the cities, making Brazil one of the most urbanized countries in the world. Those who remained in the countryside found themselves working land that was rapidly being developed into enormous plantations. Like the directors of the eighteenth and nineteenth century, the owners of these *fazendas* could rely on the illiterate poor for hard labor with almost no accountability, save for the federal mandate to see the land produce.[5] To this day, workers and their families are recruited with the promise of fair wages, rounded up and dispatched to sprawling *fazendas* to harvest crops, work cattle, and slash and burn pastures. Others are sent to remote logging camps, where they cut trees, load timber trucks, and process saplings into bootleg charcoal sold to the pig iron foundries of São Paulo. Trapped in an endless cycle of debt and repayment, these men, women, and children are essentially enslaved in camps where their lives are cut short by malaria, toxic smoke, and abusive masters.

Since the days of the dictatorship, the plight of landless workers in Brazil has inspired missionaries and activists to fight against a feudal system in which wealthy—and often absentee—landlords are free to exploit and dispose of workers with impunity. Landowners maintain private security forces to intimidate and punish families on their territory—and liquidate all who threaten to rise up against them. With decades of bribes and kickbacks, these ranchers have bought their way into nearly every newsroom, police station, and courthouse in the region. Their hit men will torture and execute, and then openly brag at the bar about their latest job.[6]

In 2005, while the environmental impact of the Belo Monte was undergoing a second review, a seventy-three-year-old American-born Brazilian nun became a casualty of this battle. Born in Dayton, Ohio, a child of the Great Depression, Sister Dorothy Stang had lived in Brazil since the 1970s, mobilizing indigenous communities against the loggers and cattlemen riding the bull of the Transamazônica. On the morning of February 12, Sister Dorothy was walking to a town hall meeting in the rural community of Anapu, about fifty miles from Altamira. For years she had received death threats from the timber and cattle barons in the region, who accused her of trying to wrest control of the area by brainwashing the poor. Their dominion was under siege, not only by Sister Dorothy and her unholy peasant army but from the politicians she had awoken to the plight of the Xingu.

That very day, environmental minister Marina Silva was set to sign sweeping new forest restrictions that would shield unprecedented tracts of the Amazon from development. The cabal of speculators who control land in Pará had warned Silva: blood will spill if you go through with this.

Crossing a bridge along the path, Sister Dorothy was stopped by two unfamiliar ranch hands.

"Do you have any weapons?" the ranchers asked Sister Dorothy. She had been accused of smuggling guns into small farming communities to help peasants defend themselves from exploitation.

"This is the only weapon I carry," Sister Dorothy answered. Opening her Bible, she read aloud to them a passage from the Beatitudes, "Blessed are the poor in spirit."[7]

"What the hell are we supposed to do now?" one of the ranchers asked his partner.

The second man drew his pistol and emptied it, two shots to Sister Dorothy's abdomen, four to her head.

A local farmer who'd been hiding in the bushes ran to alert the authorities. Word spread like wildfire. When the news reached Brasilia, Lula swore revenge. He dispatched 2,000 soldiers to regain control of the region, beginning with a manhunt for the wealthy cattle rancher who had allegedly ordered the killing before fleeing the region in a small plane.

Days later, to prove that his administration would not be intimidated, President Lula signed into law the sweeping forest reserves. The accused rancher was eventually apprehended and sentenced to jail despite multiple mistrials in the notoriously corrupt Pará judiciary. Yet the pattern of violence against activists would not cease. Since 1986, more than a thousand organizers and activists have been killed.[8] In 2010, on the day another forest protection law was being debated in congress, another activist and his wife were ambushed and murdered while crossing a bridge. They were shot fifteen times, the man's ear cut off as a message to legislators.[9]

On and off its federal reserves, the Amazon frontier remains a Wild West dominated by wealthy ranchers and loggers.[10] Hours before I arrived in Altamira, federal highway police at a checkpoint between the city and the Belo Monte worksite had stopped a tractor trailer for inspection when they heard murmurs from inside the trailer. Officers ordered the driver to unlock the door. The man stepped down from his rig and rustled through his keys as if he couldn't find the right one. At last he relented. When the officers opened the door, they had to hold their noses to keep from gagging on the odor of shit and piss. One of the officers shined his flashlight inside: fifteen faces peered back, men packed like cattle without ventilation, swinging in hammocks on a suffocating ride to the next worksite.[11]

The next morning I drove out to the checkpoint to speak with the officers who'd intercepted the truck. Dusty under the sun, muddy in the rain, the highway station was where broken-down buses and impounded cars went to rust. Deputies sat smoking on a patio outside, radiating a casual sense of authority as a daisy chain of cement trucks lumbered on to the Belo Monte.

"Excuse me," I asked. "Can I talk to you about that truck that came through here last night?"

One of the men whistled over to the stationhouse where their commander was wrapping up a phone call. I told them I'd wait, lit a cigarette, paced around the auto yard littered with crashed cars, seats covered in broken glass and bloodstains. The commander came out sooner than I expected. I stamped out my smoke in a show of respect. He looked at my sweat-caked mop of hair and my rented Volkswagen Gol, no doubt wondering what the hell I was doing out here.

"Where are you from?" he asked.

"The United States," I said.

"United States, huh?"

"But I was born in Brazil. Belo Horizonte."

"Ah, I see," he said. "They say you're doing some kind of research?"

"Yeah, I was just curious about that truck you stopped last night. The paper said it was carrying slaves."

"Ah, no, you must have misunderstood the report," he said, clarifying. "That's not what we said. We said 'conditions akin to slavery.'"

"I see," I said. "And the difference is . . . ?"

"Those men had jobs! It's just dangerous for them to be riding around like that. No ventilation. No bathroom. Very unsafe. You see?"

"Gotcha," I said. "And how often do you stop a truck like that?"

"Not that often," he said. "Once or twice every few months. Not like before."

"I see," I said, thinking back to the bus ride to Altamira the night before, the college kids beside me, trying to charge their MacBooks and iPhones, the trailer trucks roaring past us on the road, kicking up dust on our headlights. How many of those trucks carried livestock? How many carried workers struggling to breathe in the dark?

A lumber truck approached the checkpoint, slowed down for the rumble strip, blew right past. "Well, I'm glad I checked," I said. "I know you're busy, so I guess just one more question. How much of the timber that passes through here would you say is illegal?"

He looked up and down the highway, squinting as if counting some invisible trucks. "If I had to say, I'd say ninety percent?"

"Ninety percent?" I said. The heat must have been getting to me. Surely I'd misheard.

"Give or take some percent."

"Wow, uh, okay. And what happens to the timber?"

"We confiscate it."

"And the drivers?"

"There's not much we can do with the drivers," he said. "They're just driving."

To date, more than half a million square miles of the Amazon have been deforested—most of it in the last three decades. While Brazil's forest controls temporarily helped stem the crisis, logging is on the rise again, and illegal operators in the eastern Amazon have proved every bit as creative as the drug smugglers who dominate the western borders. A 2015 Greenpeace operation exposed a pattern of abuse by which illegal logging trucks shuttle timber from remote worksites to the riverside port town of Santarém, where the payload is "laundered" into legal timber before being shipped worldwide, including to leading timber companies in the United States and the European Union.[12]

Since 1995, when Brazil officially recognized the active use of slave labor in its economy, more than 50,000 people have been freed from "conditions akin to slavery."[13]

No landowner has gone to jail for these crimes.

• • •

Altamira, City of Social Transformation. Before Norte Energia, Altamira was known as the City of Vultures, a sleepy former missionary village that was startled awake when the Transamazônica crossed the Xingu, bringing thousands of migrants eager to flee their drought-stricken lives in the northeast and pursue their dreams of rubber fortunes, cattle ranches, and an endless river of fish. Soon cows in the municipality of greater Altamira outnumbered people until more than 400,000 head of cattle grazed across pastures that were once várzea forest. Public services in the area expanded to serve livestock, not people. Hospitals and schools remained relics of the dictatorship. Altamira was never deemed worthy of proper sanitation or waste management infrastructure— the river provided that for free. The river provided everything for the thousands of Altamirans in homes on stilts on the banks of the Xingu, living off fish, manioc flour ground by the local Indians, and the good luck of their fathers who'd brought them here. Overhead, vultures circled like war planes, visible for miles in every direction. On the streets the birds strutted among the carcasses of stray dogs, impervious to the heat, feathers of obsidian sheen.

By 2012 Norte Energia boasted to reporters from the *Folha de S. Paulo* that the sky was free of vultures for the first time in decades.[14] The consortium had cleaned the streets, buried the trash, and double-buried the landfills. Behold the new Altamira: highlands bulldozed into subdivisions, fields of dark red earth where utility poles and sewer pipes would soon be connected like toys, a new forest of streetlights planted on the hillsides, visible for miles up and down the river. Crews installed European-style traffic circles with yellow-and-black-striped curbs surrounding art deco monuments as if the city were awaiting a grand prix. Modern commerce ensued, video billboards blaring advertising to a revitalized city center, 3-D superhero blockbusters saving the day in a new cinema, a strip of posh hotels along the waterfront where contractors could safely ask for ice cubes in their cocktails, a basketball court, a food court, a volleyball court, an empty courtyard where parents rent Power Wheels for their kids to race around as if practicing for their future middle-class lives. A prodigious cover band playing Bryan Adams and R.E.M. for an audience stuffed with cheeseburgers and Budweiser. An artificial beach where children toe their way into clean water. Not like before. Not like the old neighborhoods, underwater now, thousands of shacks on stilts, home to more than 40,000 displaced by the floodwaters.

Norte Energia wanted reporters to know that those people loved their homes because they knew nothing better. Even if the river sparkled at sunset, it sparkled with particulate matter. The river folk had grown so accustomed to traces of shit in the water that they barely smelled it anymore, not until their children got sick leaping from old-growth trees into old swimming holes. The new sanitation system would remedy all of that, but the new sanitation system was still under construction, and for now the waste of the new Altamira would continue to pour into the open drain of the Xingu. The rising and falling tides of the reservoir systems might periodically and unpredictably rush through neighborhoods with enough force to sweep structures and children off the bank, the manmade channel might wipe out the breeding grounds of the pacu, the pião, the curimatá, the matrinchá, fish that people relied on to fill their bellies and coin jars, but Norte Energia would bring that under control, as it brought everything under control, and if need be those stilt houses would be demolished, inundated along with every other memory, the shallow graves of dogs and first-born, the suicide notes, the murder weapons, the hand-carved canoes, the old box of love letters, erased by the new waterline, the

Xingu Novo, where—look now!—a man on a jet ski zips from bank to bank like a water skipper.

In late 2015, Norte Energia released the waters being held back by the Belo Monte complex, flooding the area and forcing a third of Altamira's residents to higher ground. They took their valuables and keepsakes, left the rest of their old lives to the rising water, and moved into their assigned homes in a patchwork of five housing projects with market-tested names like São Joaquim, Jatobá, Laranjeira, and Agua Azul, each with their own unnamed, alphabetized streets: Rua A, Rua B, Rua C . . .

Residents approved for new housing could choose from three floor plans of three-room homes with a bathroom and an American-style kitchen, walls poured from specialized concrete injected with air bubbles that keep the interior 5 degrees Celsius cooler than ordinary housing materials, a specification above and beyond the Basic Plan, mind you, courtesy of Norte Energia. Distinguished only by varying paint jobs and a temporary number spray-painted near the door, each home has its own modest driveway, a sapling tree planted in a wooden frame, and a power meter conspicuously fixed to the front of the house as if to remind folks this is no favela, this is the grid, this is your new electricity bill, fivefold more than the cost of lighting your old stilt house, payable to Norte Energia.

In the subdivision of Bairro São Joaquim, a few miles from downtown, loyal bureaucrats of Norte Energia share a hillside with displaced river folk, a barbed-wire fence separating the two neighborhoods. On the Norte Energia side of the fence, traffic enters through a security gate, Ford trucks gleaming in the driveways, joggers with ear buds grabbing some quick cardio after dinner. On the *ribeirinho* side, empty driveways, a dormant social assistance office, a four-square church, and an unfinished school where neighborhood kids gather for pickup soccer games.

The neighborhood of Agua Azul features identical homes in an identical layout, but in a world apart from the city, plotted on a hillside across the Transamazônica. Without the waterside breeze, afternoons are intolerably hot, streets vacant, sleeping dogs not bothering to open their eyes at the sporadic traffic. Vultures stare brazenly at passing cars, defending their new territory, barely bothering to flap out of the way of a passing car.

Only when the sun begins to set does the neighborhood stir to life. On a Wednesday night, I cruised Agua Azul for an empty bar stool. There was only one option, a little bar beside the construction site of a half-finished public dance hall. The *barzinho* was owned and operated by a shirtless, fifty-something barkeeper with the gray hair and black melanoma spots of a man who'd spent his life on the water.

"I wondered when you'd drop in," he said. "We've seen you driving around."

I ordered a cold beer and took a seat by the empty pool table. A neighbor passed by to pick up a bottle of Cachaça 51 to take home, looking surprised to see a stool occupied.

"So how long have you been here?" I asked the bartender, lighting a cigarette.

"Just a few months, he said. "I'm a fisherman. Was a fisherman. Now I have this little bar."

Another neighbor who looked like he'd already been drinking stumbled by, overcome by a second wave of thirst. He sat on the stool next to me, withdrew a pouch of tobacco, and began rolling a cigarette. When I introduced myself as a writer he seemed to sense an opportunity to unload burdensome thoughts.

"These neighborhoods were supposed to be finished by now," he said. "But everything's broken. The school's not finished. We don't have water. We lose power." He turned to the bartender: "How often would you say the water goes out?"

"A few days each month," the bartender said, pouring the man another drink.

"You see?" the patron said. "No water. No power. Nothing works. It's all corrupt. Can I have a smoke?"

I held out my pack to save him the trouble of rolling another. He plucked a cigarette; I gave him a light. "They give us money, but it's not about money, it's about work. You've got to have work. But there's no jobs now that the dam is finished. I've done all kinds of work, but there's nothing to do up here away from the river. It's expensive just to take a bus down to town. Buy me a drink?"

I glanced at the bartender as if to ask whether this dude really needed another one. The bartender was already reaching for the bottle. I bought us a round. The man tipped back his rum. I already regretted buying him the drink, as if I'd inserted a coin into a machine that dispensed anguish.

"The school's not finished," he said. "My kids have to go all the way down the hill for school. Now that the dam is finished, they don't want to finish any of the projects they promised. And even when the school is finished, what kind of future are my kids supposed to have around here?"

"If you want to hear all about it," the bartender said, "you should go to the community meeting. It's tonight."

"Where?" I asked.

"At the community center," the other man said, staring into his empty cup. "It's just down the street. I'll take you there."

We paid our tabs and slipped out the door. After a long hot day, I was still sweating, but at least the sun was down. The community center was just another unit among the hundreds, a model home repurposed as a gathering space for the residents of Agua Azul. The event was already underway when we arrived, a dozen or so citizens in a semicircle of plastic chairs. Stepping in with booze on our breath, I felt as if we were unwelcome guests at an AA meeting.

A team of three Norte Energia bureaucrats was facilitating. They asked us to sign in on a Norte Energia–branded sign-in sheet. The lead facilitator was a white woman in her fifties with reading glasses and whitened teeth, clearly not from around these parts. She identified me immediately as another outsider. Other than the Belo Monte, there was no reason for us to visit this place. Earlier that day at a lunch counter down the street, the owner's kid had pegged me as a gringo as soon as I walked in the door: "Are you from Norte Energia?"

The facilitator invited us to sit. There was only one empty seat. My drinking buddy invited me to take it, choosing to stand in the center of the circle where he proceeded to hijack the meeting with a reprisal of the same laments he'd shared with me at the bar, only at higher volume this time, as if he were in the throes of an upstart political campaign.

The group entertained his screed politely for a few minutes longer than I expected. Then, as the man ran out of steam and circled back to his first talking point, one of the Norte Energia facilitators invited him outside for a smoke. My buddy nodded his head at me as if I should join him in solidarity, but I signaled that I wanted to stay a while longer and listen. I'd meet him back up at the bar afterward.

On with the meeting. The residents of Agua Azul were in the process of drafting a constitution that would govern all five new neighborhoods in Altamira, specifying what kinds of modifications could be made to their homes, what goods could be sold on the street on what days, and so forth, a master Home Owner's Association of sorts to ensure the developments didn't fall into disrepair or disarray.

The river folk of Altamira are like folks everywhere, which is to say, creative people who like to customize their homes whether they own the land beneath their feet or not. While the public works projects of Norte Energia plodded along, its construction workers napping through the hottest parts of the day, the new homeowners of Agua Azul were busy expanding their houses, waiting for deliveries of bricks that would become new walls, bedrooms, and storefronts. There is a time for *saudade* and a time for setting up shop: a pizzeria, a clothing boutique, a salon, a real estate office offering referral bonuses if you convince your friend to be your neighbor. If you can't find a job, make a job. A freelance traffic director waves cars through the crowded intersection of the Transamazônica and Bom Jesus. A woman and her son sell fresh açai fruit and fish and religious books from a table in their driveway. Nannies and housecleaners galore. Slowly but surely, the Norte Energia concept art would become a neighborhood. It wouldn't be long before Ruas A, B, and C were rechristened after beloved grandparents, legendary fishermen, and soccer heroes. On the hillside above the neat grid of Agua Azul and its carefully plotted bus stops, settlers were already building homes of wood in the old style of the river.

Regardless of how Norte Energia wanted to develop Altamira, Altamira was developing itself. The facilitators struggled to conform the community meeting to its neat agenda. The conversation flitted from the preordained minutes to the urgency of the crisis at hand: the buggy water system, the blackouts, the fumigation squads aggressively losing the war against Zika. The chief facilitator did her best to stick to the agenda. *"Meninos, meninos, fica tranquilo!"* Calm down, little ones.

When the meeting was over, she discovered I was a writer from the United States, and to my astonishment, she did not recite a list of talking points. Instead she opened a side room and invited every attendee at the meeting, in turn, to sit down and air their grievances. I opened my notebook and turned on my audio recorder. One by one they came inside, closing the door behind them for privacy. The major issue was transportation. Folks had been relocated too far from their old lives, beloved friends scattered like seeds among the five Norte Energia neighborhoods. Now they had to take expensive buses or mototaxis everywhere. The school down the street from the community center was supposed to be finished a year ago. Now the kids had to go all the way to the *centro* to attend a school where most of the teachers had left for better salaries driving dump trucks at the Belo Monte.

I listened, took notes, sobered up. Below the logistical concerns was a deeper sense of loss, a longing for the river, its rhythm as primal as their mother's heartbeat in the womb.

"How often do you make it down to the water?" I asked one man, a lifelong fisherman who looked at his hands as he spoke.

"Just once or twice a month now," he said. A memory crested over his face. "I used to wake up there every morning."

19

SOUL COUNTS

In the air-conditioned activity room of a retirement home in Lakeland, Florida, a flock of white-haired Christians pass the afternoon watching *Judge Judy* as they stuff sandwich baggies with
floss, toothbrushes, and sample-sized tubes of toothpaste, donated
from a local dental office, now tucked carefully alongside a condom-
sized pamphlet about the promise of eternal life. Soon these DIY
hygiene packs will make the long flight from the sweltering Pan-
handle to the sweltering port city of Santarém, Pará, where the
Amazon meets the Rio Tapajós, arriving in the checked luggage
of Pastor Dave McClamma, president of Hope for Brazil Ministries,
Inc., a 501(c)(3) nonprofit organization devoted to spreading the
Good News throughout the rain forest.

On a bright Thursday morning in April 2015, I waited for Pastor Dave on the main tourist dock in Santarém. A few fishermen
cast their strings into the water, a patient crane perched at their
side. At the end of the wood-plank dock, a freshly painted white
and turquoise riverboat bobbed on the river, *Ha Esperança*—There's

Hope—the fruits of a four-year fund-raising drive that would allow the ministry to tap deeper into this frontier market of souls.

God is everywhere in the Amazon, from song-filled evangelical churches, to Pentecostal services where true believers spasm in tongues, to the spiritualist clinics where insomniacs, recovering addicts, and trauma victims can discover the past lives that haunt their present ones. Despite its strong Catholic tradition, Brazil hosts an all-you-can-eat buffet of Protestant churches, the spawn of generations of missionaries who have found fortunes and lost lives on the continent. If anyone knows the rain forest better than Indians, anthropologists, and resource engineers, it's missionaries. In the twenty-first century, it's not easy to find an honest-to-God pagan, but if you have the faith enough to journey to one of the most remote corners of Earth, it's still possible to find tribes who've never heard the words Jesus Christ.

But it's not easy. Even these days, missionaries reach villages years ahead of the utility crews, planting churches like flags. The real spiritual battleground remains on the tributaries, where roads have yet to penetrate—and may never. On these rivers, *Ha Esperança* is a spiritual battleship.

Pastor Dave's wife, Robin, a petite grandmother with a kind smile, saw me on the dock and called out from the boat: "Dave is still out picking up supplies! Come on up and take a look around!"

I stepped up the gangplank on the port side. *Ha Esperança* was a beauty, 65 feet long, with a 16-foot beam, a traditional three-level riverboat with a main deck, a cargo hold below, and an open-air top deck, upgraded to meet the needs of the modern missionary. In the pilot house, a brand-new GPS system was posted near the wheel, loaded with nautical maps of the entire region. A nearby cot was positioned to absorb the blast of a factory-fresh air-conditioning unit. Robin and a small cadre of volunteers from back home were hard at work on the main deck, preparing the ship for its maiden voyage tomorrow. There was Jake, an OSHA inspector and Florida Gator alum on his second mission trip to the Amazon. There was Beth, Jake's wife, a strawberry-blond middle-school teacher, wisely lathered in sunscreen for her first mission trip to the Amazon. There was Mr. Cornell, a white-haired southern gentleman and ministry board member, looking a tad fatigued in this weather but also like a tough old bugger who keeps spry in retirement by pushing himself to the edge of his physical limits from time to time.

Together they were busy with the finishing touches. Robin, Beth, and Mr. Cornell set out a load of the white plastic chairs, removing the unsightly price stickers one by one.

"Does anyone want some Goo Gone?" asked Beth in a southern drawl as thick as the humidity. "I got some Goo Gone somewhere around here."

Jake was installing new safety lights with the help of two Brazilians who spoke the universal language of hot wires and ground wires but not much English. Jake's big on safety but also on health care. "I'm studying for my EMT license," he told me as he worked. "That way when I'm down here I can give medicine and even vaccines."

It felt awkward watching these folks work while I took notes, so I climbed upstairs for a peek at the top deck. At the bow, they had installed a new set of radio antennas and an AC compressor with ample tonnage to send the wheelhouse to the ice age. From there I could see the entire Port of Santarém, a charming crescent of pastel colonial buildings that disguised the fact that the city was a central distribution hub for the timber and soybean shipments that were decimating the rain forest. The tourist port was conveniently devoid of commercial vessels. Instead, the docks were crowded with traditional riverboats just like this one, except without a crew of white folks.

When I returned to the main deck, Mr. Cornell was sipping from a water bottle. He could tell I was impressed with the boat.

"She's nice, ain't she?" he said. "We got her for fifty thousand dollars. She's worth at least eighty thousand"

"Holy cow," I said. "It must help that the dollar is so strong right now."

"You bet it does," he said. "The best part is she's sturdy enough we can expand up."

Robin noticed me glance at a futuristic contraption near the portside railing, which looked like a folded-up robot at rest before a mission. "That's our dental chair!" she said. "It's solar-powered. It weighs fifteen pounds, so our dentist can hike it in anywhere."

"A thousand dollars apiece," said Mr. Cornell.

"You'd be amazed what a difference it makes," said Robin. "And the kids on the river are so brave. When they get a tooth pulled, they don't cry or anything. They just want it out! Our dentists have pulled a lot of teeth over the years."

Ha Esperança is new, but Robin and Pastor Dave have been visiting the Amazon for almost twenty years. When they first came to Brazil, they were so terrified of bacteria that they packed their own straws and wiped down the rim of every Coke can before touching it to their lips. Over time, they've learned which foods to eat, which foods to avoid, how to keep from getting sick. "Santarém is our second home," Robin said. "We love it here. And we're so blessed to have this boat—God's boat, really. But I'll let Dave tell you all about that. You should be talking to him, not me!"

In Robin's universe, Jesus is working through Pastor Dave and Pastor Dave is working through *Ha Esperança*, and everyone onboard is bound for God's glory.

In the world of contemporary Brazilian missionaries, there are 501(c)(3) nonprofits with advisory boards, riverboats, and solar-powered dental chairs, and then there are startups fueled by

ecstatic dreams. In 2001, back when I was still a godless undergraduate at the University of Oregon, hiking high on mushrooms
on Easter Sunday to commune with the spirit of Ken Kesey, a young
Christian named Brad Miller was rising up the corporate ladder
in Topeka, Kansas. A sales and service vendor for Kodak, 3M, and
Xerox equipment, Brad spent his days driving endless stretches
of midwestern highways, cornfields like white noise outside his
window. Nights he returned home to a castle full of blessings, a
beautiful wife and two children tucked in a five-bedroom home,
replete with two brand-new Hondas, a 4 × 4 pickup, and a boat
he could tow anywhere he liked.

One afternoon, on an otherwise unremarkable drive to the next
Xerox machine, Brad was overcome by what he can only describe
as a vision. The highway melted away. There he was, in the middle
of a jungle, preaching to a flock of Indians.

"Five minutes later, I was back on the road," he told me. "That
night, I got home and told Melissa: 'God had spoken to me.' I told
her we have to sell everything."

Selling everything seemed a bit rash, even for his supportive
wife. "God needs to speak to me, too," Melissa said. When Brad
shared the story with members of his church in Topeka, they worried he'd gone Pentecostal. But true believers are undeterred. It
was only a matter of decoding the vision. At the time, the Millers
were sponsoring a community of Laotians. It could only mean they
had to go to Laos.

By the end of the year, Brad, Melissa, and the kids were off to
California to finish Bible college and start a new job. They sold
half their belongings, the trappings of a materialistic life, keeping
only the essentials. That first year on the West Coast, the Millers
lived in the middle of an Asian neighborhood near Anaheim. Their
landlord was the only one who would rent to them without proof
of a new income. The only trouble was, after six months of work-

ing in an Asian community, Brad realized maybe Laos wouldn't
be a good fit. "I just couldn't get along with the culture," he said.
What could it all mean? Half of their remaining possessions lan-
guished in a storage unit, evidence they were still on the wrong
path.

Soon after, during a Friday night Bible study, Brad and Melissa were introduced to a Brazilian couple who had recently moved
to the United States from Rio de Janeiro. The woman came up to
him immediately, an astonished look on her face.

"When I walked in the room," she told Brad, "I had a vision of
you in the middle of a jungle. You had a shepherd's staff. And there
was a glow around you."

"The thing is," Brad recalled. "We hadn't told a soul about the
vision in two years. After what happened in Topeka, we just didn't
know how people would react. But now we knew. It was real. And
that's when Melissa knew it was real. I told the Brazilian woman
what I'd seen. I knew I was supposed to be preaching in the jungle.
I just didn't know where."

"What about the Amazon?" the woman asked.

Years later in Manaus, where Brad and Melissa relocated the
family in 2012, Brad recalled the moment to me over coffee, chuck-
ling: "Brazil? I thought the Amazon was in Africa."

It was getting toward noon when I finally met Pastor Dave, a fit
man in his sixties sporting a Hope for Brazil polo short and baseball cap, wire-rimmed glasses, and a neatly trimmed white beard.
A man with the keen posture of an NFL coach, he speaks with a
loose, folksy drawl, often likening people's moods to those of an
alligator. An upset person is an angry gator. A sad person is an un-
happy gator. Hungry? You're one hungry gator. And so forth.

After a long morning of haggling for supplies downtown,

Pastor Dave was a thirsty gator. He flipped open a blue cooler, plucked a bottle of water from the pool of ice inside, and offered me one.

"No, thanks," I said. He cracked his open and pulled up two white plastic chairs for us on the portside railing. The rest of the crew took it as a signal that they could take a break, too. By and by they arranged their own circle of chairs on the starboard side.

"So you're just in from Altamira, huh?" he asked.

"Yup," I said. "My bus just got in at sunrise. Twelve hours on the Transamazônica. Rough road."

"That's one of the few places in this part of Brazil I haven't been," he said. "Did you pass through Bela Vista?"

"Sounds familiar," I said. "We drove through the night. Passed through a lot of towns."

"They just got electricity there a few years ago," he said. "We built a church back before they even had a road. Next year it'll be twenty years since I came to Brazil. I think I might do a little anniversary tour."

Turns out Pastor Dave had been one busy gator, turning over every stone in Brazil looking for places in need of an evangelical church, honing his ministerial philosophy along the way. Modern missionaries of all stripes have been sowing seeds in the Amazon with renewed fervor since the 1960s when the Catholic church changed its approach to working in indigenous communities. Liberation theology took hold. No longer should missionaries approach tribes as spiritually bankrupt. Their spiritual practices, primitive as they may have seemed, were seeds of faith to be cultivated. Clergy trained in the basics of anthropology could steer tribes toward Christ.[1] In the worst years of the military dictatorship, missionary unions were among the fiercest advocates for indigenous rights, urging tribal leaders to form their own unions, enter politics, and raise their voices against the federal government. Inspired by lib-

eration theology, rain forest activist Chico Mendes brought together tappers and tribes who had been at war with each other for
years, forming the Alliance of the People of the Forest before his
assassination in 1988. Over the years, priests and nuns like Sister
Dorothy Stang have been threatened or assassinated for defending
the rights of the poor in the Amazon. Pastor Dave might not live in
the Amazon full-time, but he fund-raises for people who do. He
might not embrace liberal doctrines, but he embraces the challenges
facing tribal communities—and he has an unflinching conviction
that Christ is their way out of the darkness.

"It's all about building relationships," he said. "Let me give you
an example: we were the first ministry in Brazil to work in a prison.
This was right here in Santarém. Years ago. I mean, you know how
the prisons are down here. It was murder, it was rape. We started
prayer groups and played worship music. They wouldn't let us build
a church inside, but we put up a cross right over the fence where
everyone could see. And guess what?"

We floated a moment in the amniotic fluid of his pregnant
pause.

"What?" I asked.

"Everything dropped. Murder. Rape. Assault. Nothing. That's
the power of the word of the Lord."

"Wow."

"Of course, then the warden changed and now it's bad as ever."

A Brazilian man briefly interrupted to inform Pastor Dave, in
English, how much he needed for food. Pastor Dave reached into
his khaki shorts and counted out R$1,000 in cash, a month's min-
imum wage for three workers these days, enough to buy a week of
basic food supplies for a hundred people. The man pocketed the
cash and headed back downtown.

"That's Joaquim," said Pastor Dave. "He's like our adopted son.
We've known him for years. Eight years ago, actually, I was here

in Santarém, attending a service, and the pastor asked me to deliver a sermon. Well, I've been here twenty years, but I still only speak the basics of Portuguese. Joaquim stood right up and said, 'I'll translate.' We've been side by side ever since."

"That's great," I said. "So, *Ha Esperança*. Congratulations. Tell me what you're up to." Notebook in hand, I listened to Pastor Dave tell me about why having a boat is a critical step toward fulfilling Hope for Brazil Ministries' 2020 Vision for Hope. As he spoke, I couldn't help but overhear the crew on the starboard side, leaning back in their chairs with bottles of water, engaged, it seemed, in a heated debate. A law had recently been passed in North Carolina dictating who is allowed to use which bathroom. Pastor Dave carried on about his twenty years of work, planting churches in Manaus, watching neighborhoods thrive around those churches, the Lord working through him, through Robin, through their local Brazilian partners, but even as I jotted down the details, I couldn't shake the conversation on the starboard side. I wanted to close my notebook, excuse myself a moment, and hush them: Here you are overlooking one of the most gorgeous natural wonders in the world, the almighty Amazon River, mother nature abound like you may never see again in this lifetime, so why are you talking in friendly, mystified tones about who gets to use which bathrooms in North Carolina?

Perhaps sensing that my attention was divided, Pastor Dave leaned forward in his chair. "We used to have to rent a riverboat," he said. "And believe me, that gets expensive." With a hired pilot and the guidance of Joaquim, the Hope for Brazil crew would coast along the banks of the Amazon and the Tapajós, looking for fishing villages ripe for their message. Anchored offshore, they would fire up a PA system and read scripture and warm spiritual greetings in English and Portuguese, gospel floating across the water until at last they were invited ashore. There they would lavish the tribe with gifts and amusements. Classic attraction team stuff, straight out of the Villas Bôas brothers playbook. Ice cream. Magic tricks. Toothbrushes.

From his backpack, Pastor Dave pulled out one of the hygiene packs filled and sealed by someone's great-grandparent back in Lakeland. "Let me tell you about the power of a toothbrush," he said, holding the hygiene pack in his palms like a holy scepter. "On the river, if people have toothbrushes at all, it's one they share with the entire family. One time, I gave a man a toothbrush, and the man tells me, he says, 'You mean it's just for me? I don't have to share it?'"

Another pause for that to sink in.

"A toothbrush," said Pastor Dave. "One of these dinky little things—a dentist back home gives us hundreds of 'em for free—and this man, he had tears in his eyes. That's how much it means to him. I tell them: it is a gift, just for you. But it's not the greatest gift. The greatest gift is the gift of Jesus Christ. The gift of eternal life."

And now Pastor Dave was welling up. And for a moment I felt rotten inside. I grew up in a secular family in Oregon. My mom and dad dropped my brother and me off at Sunday school once or twice when they needed mom-and-dad time. Once in middle school, when I was in Boy Scouts, the scoutmaster pulled me aside to help me select a religion patch to sew on my uniform alongside my fishing and astronomy and archery merit badges. I told him I didn't go to church; he gave me a look of wonder and pity. I recognized that look in Pastor Dave now as he wiped his eyes.

Early August, rivers running high. Tomorrow Brad Miller will say good-bye to Melissa and the kids and go to work. Once he drove his air-conditioned Honda across the great plains of America; now he boards a slow boat at the Port of Manaus for a forty-hour journey to the interior, east down the Amazon, then southwest at Santarém up the Rio Tapajós, the channel growing narrower as it snakes toward the state of Acre, past a FUNAI sign at the border of the reserve, past a FUNAI checkpoint that guards the home of some of the most isolated tribes on the continent. Technically, outsiders are not supposed to enter indigenous lands without the express written consent of FUNAI, but Brad is already here, these boats don't turn around, and he explains that he is only going to visit friends. Lately FUNAI is too overwhelmed with trafficking and violence to worry much about gringo ministers.

Around midnight on the second day, a member of the crew stirs Brad from his hammock: *O Pastor, estamos aqui.* The riverboat moors at the mouth of an inlet so narrow that in the dry season it can only be accessed by pontoon. Brad gathers his bags and cargo and slips into a motorboat on the dark water. The motorista pulls away from the riverboat, which continues on upriver, floodlights vanishing around the next bend. The jungle is so loud you can hear it over the stroke of the motor. The motorista shuttles him to a floating boat house in the middle of the lake, where an Indian watchman greets him by torchlight, *Bemvenidos, Pastor.*

It's always hard to sleep the first night. Dawn comes slowly. The Indian gasses up and yanks the engine cord, ready to ferry Brad another three hours inland from the main river. There he will arrive at a village where for the past two years he has carried on the mission of two women who practiced their ministry in this reserve for thirty-five years until they turned it over to the disciple from Topeka, Kansas, who saw this work in a vision.

In the village, Brad meets the chief and distributes provisions, purchased with donations from evangelical congregations in Manaus. He visits every two months, sometimes with his eldest son, to deliver two sermons a week from texts translated into the indigenous language by his two predecessors. Drawing electricity from a gas-powered generator, Brad projects PowerPoint presentations about the book of Genesis onto a white bedsheet, drawing upward of sixty members of the tribe to hear the story of creation.

"A hundred years ago, these people practiced cannibalism," he told me. Tribes in these areas practice a mix of animism and spiritualism, mixed at times with missionary doctrine delivered over the years. According to Brad, some tribes still cling to rituals of human sacrifice. For example, when twins are born, one of the infants is taken to the edge of the village to die because two spirits cannot be born into the world at the same time.

Yet in just two years, Brad has seen a world of changes in the village. Their homes used to be open huts with thatch roofs. Now they have walls, doors, and zinc roofs. There are seven generators, a satellite dish, and a cell phone for every man, woman, and child, all purchased by the chief with government funds. Even though the nearest cell tower is hundreds of miles away, the devices are breathtakingly powerful.

"A lot of people blame missionaries for things," Brad said. "But I didn't bring these changes here." He worries that the modern world brings material distractions, and competition for souls, from other missionaries eager to plant their own names on the church established here by the sisters years ago.

By firelight he shares homemade beef jerky with the elders, catching up on village news and reinforcing the lessons of Jesus Christ. His work is bearing fruit. On a recent visit, he was overjoyed to hear that ten of the villagers wanted to become disciples themselves. They knew of a village upriver that had yet to hear the Good News.

"*O Pastor,*" they asked. "Come with us."

• • •

"Satanism, spiritualism, devil worship, witchcraft, that sort of thing," said Pastor Dave, listing the kinds of religious practices he encounters in the villages of the Amazon. "Once, we went to the island across the way from Santarém. A church had been built there years ago, but it had fallen into disrepair. Cracks in the walls, holes in the ceiling. When we arrived, one of their shamans came out casting spells. As a true believer, I can be *impressed* but not *possessed*. But, man, I tell you, that place is wicked."

In a region where Catholicism, Christianity, native practices, and new-age spiritualism have been cross-pollinating for generations, Pastor Dave has seen many places too far gone for his work.

"I don't know if you're familiar with the Lider Hotel in downtown Manaus?"

"Sure," I said. In fact, I'd spent a week there just a few months earlier. Cheap rooms, clean beds, AC, close to the port. Done deal.

"We used to stay there, but that entire area of downtown is now, I don't know how to explain it, but you can feel it, a heaviness, an evil presence in the air. Have you felt it?"

"Uh . . ."

"Not far from there, in the market, you'll see people selling idols, worshipping the devil."

"Hmm," I said. "So what do you make of the fact that, you know, in this region, people have a, um, complicated history with missionaries?"

"How do you mean?"

"How do I put this? For all the good you and your ministry are doing down here, religious zealots have caused a lot of harm all over the Amazon. For centuries."

"Look," said Pastor Dave, pivoting to one of his talking points.

"I've seen a lot of work down here I wouldn't agree with. This work is about more than just planting churches. I'll try to work with anyone, but one thing I can't compromise on is doctrine. We want to empower, not enable. It's all about building relationships."

There's an example right here on the boat. Today they will load up a freezer full of delicious Mexican-style ice-cream bars, manufactured in Santarém. Until recently, these particular ice-cream bars would have been thrown away as defects, too misshapen to sell, but for the relationship Pastor Dave built with the woman who owns the company.

"Here's what I told her," he said. "I told her, 'Do you know, there are children on the river who have never tasted ice cream before?' She couldn't believe it." Now the woman sets those defective ice-cream bars aside for the children on the river. Relationships, relationships, relationships. Pastor Dave and his team build relationships through motorcycle washes, sometimes washing 300 motorcycles in a day while their owners cool off with some air-conditioning, a cold bottle of water, and the Good News of the Lord. He builds relationships with the fledgling American-style football clubs in Manaus, printing scripture on gridiron-themed pamphlets that liken eternal life to scoring a touchdown. He builds relationships with local optometrists, giving them eyeglass manufacturing kits, showing them how they can restore sight to the blind. He builds relationships by offering that $1,000 solar-powered dental chair to the local dentist for free if he pledges to go out and use it himself. "Get out there, man," Pastor Dave told the dentist. "Help your people." Back in Lakeland, the ministry will raise money for another.

Mr. Cornell chimed in: "We're already on our third chair."

"I mean, you know how the politicians work around here," said Pastor Dave. "They may come in around election season, they may put up a satellite dish, make all kinds of promises, but they never come back. Once they get that vote, they never come back. These people have been left behind by their own government."

Pastor Dave does not want to leave anyone behind. The name *Ha Esperança* came to him through prayer. Months later, back home in California, I check the mailbox one grumpy morning. Tucked in a stack of bills and grocery inserts, I find the latest quarterly newsletter from Hope for Brazil Ministries. Pastor Dave wants us to know that God is working through them, through Robin and Jake and Beth and Mr. Cornell, through Joaquim and the ice-cream bars and the food bags, through the World War II vets stuffing hygiene packs with their arthritic hands at the retirement center. Together they are saving souls, each one counted in the newsletter, alongside a callout box about the upcoming spirit night at Chick-Fil-A. They are crushing their fund-raising goals. Another callout box: *Ha Esperança* on the river, a recap of the maiden voyage. If money can buy a resource that can help the families on this river, Pastor Dave will raise that money. If money cannot buy it, he will come down here and find it himself, with Robin and Joaquim at his side, as long as their bodies are able. Vision 2020. They will plant a church somewhere that only *Ha Esperança* can take them. Already Pastor Dave has conducted flyovers in a prop plane, binoculars in hand, counting the population of villages unseen from the main waterways, listening for Jesus to tell him who is ready to hear his word.

Before I left the boat, Pastor Dave asked that we pray together. I closed my eyes, folded my hands, and bowed out of respect, as I would at a funeral. It was a good long prayer—for the ministry, for the villages here and our villages at home, for the book you are holding in your hand.

I listened politely while the ship bobbed like a cradle. Though we were sitting in the shade, I felt a sensation of warmth. Of course it's warm, I told myself, we're in the Amazon. It's probably just sunlight refracted off the river. We finished. I thanked him and said my farewells.

"One more question," I asked before I stepped down the gangplank. "Out on the river, is there one piece of scripture that seems to resonate most with people?"

Without a moment's hesitation, Pastor Dave recited John 3:16 as if he'd been waiting an eternity for someone like me to ask: "For God so loved the world that he gave his one and only Son, that whoever believes in him shall not perish but have eternal life."

Brad Miller and his new disciples floated fourteen hours deeper into the forest, farther than he had ever been before. His companions seemed to know exactly where they were going, turning down creeks as easily as he would have taken an exit in Topeka, though to his eyes they were surrounded by an impenetrable wall of jungle.

It was clear when they arrived at the village that its people had little contact with the outside world. Some of the Indians wanted to touch him; others kept a safe distance. But at least one outsider had been here before him. The chief led him to a statue of Saint Joseph perched in a place of honor below a tree outside the village. How long the statue had been there, nobody could say for sure, but it was to Saint Joseph the villagers prayed and to Saint Joseph they made their animal sacrifices.

"My heart was cut," Brad said. "They had the right idea. They knew. They understood the need to pray. But they were praying to a false god."

With the help of his new disciples, Brad convinced the chief to cleanse the area of decomposing remains and pitch the idol into the river. They would need to start over. From here on out, the new disciples would have to keep on with the Good Lord's work. There was no telling when Brad and his family would be called to other pastures. His flock would need to keep making this journey on their own, saving money for gasoline and gifts. They were the true missionaries now. For Brad, a father who uprooted his wife and children from a life of suburban comfort, these disciples were the fruit of his sacrifice.

"A Christian cannot worry about the past," Brad told me.

I asked if he was afraid in that distant village, staring into the eyes of an idol-worshipping tribe, a world away from his storage units, his photo albums, his artifacts of American life.

"I don't get afraid," he said. "If they wanted to sacrifice me to the idol, I'm sure I'd be afraid a little bit right there at the end, but I know that in the end game, I know where I'm going, and I know that I'm there in the name of God."

There has been only one night in my life I was sure of God. Ten years ago, here in Brazil, a summer alone in the country, Rio de Janeiro, Manaus, that long, slow boat to Belém, on to Salvador, and finally to Belo Horizonte, the city where I was born in 1981.

For weeks I'd been lugging around an anthology of Brazilian poetry, adding new words to my handwritten phrasebook, *uma imprevista verdade*. Deep in my pack, where I was sure it would never be stolen, I kept a collection of my birth documents, given to me tearfully by my mother before I departed.

"This is everything we have," Mom said.

Dad, arms folded across his chest: "Just remember, some doors, once you open them, they can't be closed."

I tucked the papers in a folder: my original birth registry from the state hospital, my adoption certificate, the infant passport my parents used to cross me through customs in Miami, my face like a squished potato, eyes still adjusting to the light of the world. The only trace of my birth mother was her name, Tania Feliciano. My middle name is Feliciano, a gift from my mom and dad, a keepsake, a link to the past like the tiny Brazilian flag they bought for my nightstand after I was naturalized so that I didn't forget where I came from.

My first night in Belo Horizonte, I found a cheap hotel near the bus station. Later I would learn it was not the kind of area where a gringo should be walking alone. The city was hot and noisy, the third largest metropolis in Brazil, a blue-collar industrial capital in the shadow of São Paulo and Rio de Janeiro. After a lifetime of wondering where I'd come from, years of writing maudlin poems about an imagined city and the imagined mother who'd carried me, I was back in my birthplace, looking for her. As it turned out, the search required no detective work: her name was in the phone book, the only Tania Feliciano in a city of 2 million people.

I needed to cool down. A beer at the café downstairs. Time to turn the idea over. A second beer. Time to consider the possibilities from all sides. *Mais uma cerveja.* It was now or never. I went back up to my room, splashed some water on my face, and picked up the common phone in the hallway. Holding my breath, I dialed.

A woman answered: *"Alô?"*

Despite all my hours of Portuguese lessons, I had no words.

"Alô?"

I started with a question: "Did you have a son on January 22, 1981?"

The woman hung up.

I dialed again, asked the same question, "Did you have a son on January 22, 1981?"

Again she hung up.

I found a housekeeper in the next room, humming as she unfurled sheets over a bed.

I knocked gently on the door and explained my dilemma. I asked if she would call once more on my behalf. She did me that favor, standing at the phone with a hand on her hip, waiting for a stranger to answer. The woman hung up on her, too.

"She thinks it's a prank," the housekeeper said with a smile of exhaustion and pity. "She said never call again."

Back downstairs, dejected, a fourth beer. I had an address. I could visit her house. Would that be crossing a line, opening one door too many?

Uma imprevista verdade. An unforeseen truth. A man at the next table noticed me. I must've carried a certain weight in my eyes. He invited himself to sit at my table. His name was Sebastian. We ordered another beer. He asked if I was Spanish, I said no, Brazilian, but I'm still learning Portuguese. I explained my dilemma, showed him the phone number I'd jotted in my notebook. He didn't seem to think it was a dilemma at all. It was the most natural call to make.

Without warning, Sebastian plucked the number from my hands. Before I could think to stop him, he was at the corner, tucked inside an egg-shaped phone booth, talking with great animation to someone on the other line. He returned to the table.

"She's on her way," he said. "Another beer while we wait?"

Panicked, I felt an urge to step away from the table and run back to the airport, away from this city, back to the United States, back to the farmhouse that I never should have left. No traffic, no chaos, only the familiar sound of frogs and sprinklers outside my window.

Sebastian poured us both a fresh glass as if to keep me in my seat. Before we could finish, a Volkswagen Gol pulled up to the corner. An entire family stepped out. A guy about my age, twenty-something. Two teenagers. An older gentleman. And a woman I recognized immediately as my mother, my face in her face, the first family resemblance I had glimpsed in my life. I could not speak. They spoke for me. Sebastian told me to go pack my things. I was going with them. He would wait downstairs. I stuffed my pack through blurred vision, my notebooks, my gringo clothes, my sunscreen, and my bug repellant. I was trapped now. Dad was right. Some doors, once you open them, they can't be closed.

There was no choice. Back downstairs, the Felicianos were waiting in tears. I checked out of the hotel. We squeezed into the car, shoulder to shoulder as we rushed uphill to their good Catholic home. I'd forgotten to say good-bye to Sebastian, to say thank you or what's next or why did you take this into your hands? Weeks later, back in Oregon, telling the story to my mother at the kitchen table, we wondered, half-chuckling, if maybe he was an angel. How else to explain an encounter like that in a world like this. Even now I wonder if he was an angel.

20

GUARDIANS

I n July 2016, two years after the Txapanawa village massacre forced survivors to emerge from isolation, tribes in the eastern Amazon were going to war against the loggers encroaching on their territory. For years, lumberjacks had been crossing the borders of the Arariboia indigenous reserve in far eastern Maranhão state, razing the forest, then loading trucks with precious hardwood while the Guajajara Indians struggled to meet their basic needs. Now some tribal leaders were determined to push the loggers off their land. Today they had the help of a gringo, Dr. Robert Walker of the University of Missouri, who arrived in the village with a new tool to help the Guajajara patrol their reserve from the sky.

Dr. Walker was experimenting with a new kind of flyover: using small, unmanned drones to conduct aerial surveys of the interior Amazon. With a 6-foot wingspan and a range of more than 16 miles, the drone resembles a miniature spaceship. To the tribes living on this reserve, it is exactly that, a UFO whirring 50 to 200 meters above their villages, capturing images that Dr. Walker hopes will be the next evolution in tracing the movements of isolated tribes and the invaders who threaten their survival.

Conducted properly, drone surveys have the potential to be a less invasive alternative to the old-school Piper Cub flyovers pioneered by the Villas Bôas brothers. Dr. Walker had been practicing back home in Missouri, but he was still a rookie pilot; if he crashed the drone, it would be a magnet for attention—and a potential vector for infectious disease. Before takeoff, he wiped down the drone with disinfectant tissues, polishing its wings to a high, sterile shine. Then with the touch of a button, the bird whirred to life. The tribe watched the strange machine rise and glide away, Dr. Walker steering with a joystick not that different from an Xbox controller.

The leaders of this village of 20,000 were eager to see their reserve from the perspective of a white-winged swallow: the thick canopy interrupted by cattle pastures, the rivers where the Guajajara children played tag, the charred remains of the wildfire that roared through the forest last year, an act of arson, retaliation from the loggers.

To the Indians land is never guaranteed. The leaders of the Guajajara know this, for they know the story of the Yanomami of the northern Amazon. Few tribes in Brazil have had to guard their land more vigilantly. Protected for centuries by the hills and rapids on the borderland between Brazil and Venezuela, the Yanomami were the largest indigenous nation to survive into the twentieth century in isolation, their 68,000 square miles of territory dotted by hundreds of *yanos*—enormous thatch roundhouses that accommodate as many as 400 people living in commune with the surrounding rain forest.[1]

Bruce Albert, a French anthropologist who began studying the Yanomami in 1975, has spent decades interpreting their lore as it evolved to explain the confounding white visitors who would change their way of life forever. In their creation myth, another world before their time was crushed by the collapse of the sky, dooming its people to the underworld. The Yanomami emerged on the back side of those fallen heavens, and to this day, they call their forest "the old sky." Chaotic spirits relentlessly attack the new sky, which Yanomami shamans defend with the help of their ancestral spirits, the *xapiri*, to avoid another collapse, which would usher in a third sky.

Yanomami shamans believe that white men did not come to the forest from a faraway land; they were returning to the river of their origins. The story of their creation begins with a brawl among the ancestors of the Yanomami, which disturbed the seclusion of a young married couple during the girl's first menses. When the boy heard his brother outside battling other warriors, he abandoned his wife to join the fight. Without warning, the sky turned black with clouds. From the ground rose a deadly wave, flooding the *yano* with rushing water. The villagers ran for their lives. Those who fled into the forest turned into deer. Those who climbed trees turned into termite nests. Those who tried to swim drowned and were torn apart by giant otters and caiman, bloodying the flood-waters. The deity Omama—father of the first shaman—filled his palms in the current, molding the bloody foam into human forms and placing them in a distant land on the other side of the waters. The bee spirit Remori taught the creatures to speak the garbled language they speak today, a separate tongue intended to keep the peace between the forest people and outsiders. "You will not hear the words of others," Omama and Remori warned their new creations. "You will only understand your own and that way you will only quarrel among yourselves. The same will be true of them."[2]

Omama's creations began returning to the forest in the 1950s and 1960s, prospecting for gold in the nearby hills and rivers. With them came the epidemics. The Yanomami legend evolved to explain why so many of their people were dying: the evil spirits arrived in the crates the white men brought to the *yanos*, a lethal, greasy odor: "The whites say to us, 'Come here, *compadre*,' and we breathe in this smell," one man explained to Albert. "It is in fact the vapor of metal tools. . . . The smoke gets into us. This odiferous metal smoke that was shut into the boxes of machetes . . . once released, makes us die. We had fever. Our living skin started to peel."[3]

To fight the spirits, some Yanomami men would force themselves to vomit after receiving tools from the strangers. Others soaked the tools in the cleansing waters of the stream until they were safe to use. Yet still the spirits kept killing warriors, women, and children without mercy.

The Brazilian army arrived, surveying for a road through the region, dishonoring the women on the path. Missionaries arrived to deliver angry sermons, to ask villagers to build *yanos* in the name of the white man's god. Anthropologists arrived with shotguns and notebooks, taking notes while warriors battled over the gifts, taking notes during sacred fireside rituals, taking notes when gangs of men dragged unmarried girls into the forest, taking notes during their own marriage ceremonies, taking nine-year-old wives, leaving those wives behind when they returned downriver with their notes.[4] One of the visitors used only boys as guides, preferred to walk with them alone in the forest, though they knew less than half as much as their fathers. The visitor gave the boys shotguns, gifts suitable for a man of honor, yet when he invited them into his hammock, he asked them to do what no man of honor in the village would do.[5]

Albert earned the trust of the Yanomami through years of living in their communities, studying their language, way of life, and shamanistic practices to comprehend the forest, the world, and the cosmos from their perspective. In doing so, he struck a friendship with one of the Yanomamis' most respected young shamans, Davi Kopenawa, known among his people as "Angry Hornet."

Over nearly one hundred hours of interviews spanning more than a decade, Albert recorded the oral history of Kopenawa's life and people in the shaman's own words.[6] Born around 1956 on the upper Rio Tootoobi, Kopenawa first saw white people as a young child, back when the elders in his village lived long enough to have white hair and lose their sight. In 1967, his mother died in a measles epidemic brought to his village by an American missionary. Repulsed by Yanomami funeral practices, the Christians buried the dead in secret, defying the tribal belief that doing so would keep their spirits from being released. "I was never able to learn where my mother was buried," Kopenawa recalls of the missionaries who never revealed the location of the graves. "Because of them, I was never able to mourn my mother the way our people usually do."[7]

In his youth, Kopenawa worked as a FUNAI interpreter and worked with government agencies to combat the poaching of caiman, giant otters, and jaguars, but he continued to refuse Christian teaching and the white man's ways, instead choosing the path of the shaman. Yanomami allies sent him to a school to learn Brazilian ways and property law, but when he returned, the government tried to keep him in his village. "FUNAI wants to keep me hidden," he said. "It wants me to keep quiet, not to protest, not to talk to others, not to speak to the white supporters, but I am not willing to sit still and keep quiet while my people are dying. I need to go out into the world . . . to cry out, to protest what is happening."[8]

In 1975, a radar imaging survey of the Brazilian Amazon located radioactive minerals on Yanomami land. Without delay, the

Ministry of Mines declared the area open to extraction. The governor of the territory of Roraima announced that the Surucucu Hills were brimming with "wealth waiting to be mined . . . not only uranium, but gold and diamonds and who knew what else besides." Lying about the size of the Yanomami nation, he urged his countrymen to seize the opportunity: "An area such as that cannot afford the luxury of a half-a-dozen Indian villages holding up development."

Anthropologists persuaded FUNAI to establish a sprawling reservation for the Yanomami where the government could provide health and aid, but a powerful general dismantled the plan, citing the work of American anthropologist Napoleon Chagnon, whose controversial bestseller about the Yanomami cemented their reputation as "The Fierce People."[9] In the generals' view, the tribe was an inbred population unworthy of a large national park. The military conceded several "islands" of reserved areas around major *yanos*, but no more. Several aid workers and missionaries were expelled.

By the 1980s, miners were digging into the unprotected forests between the archipelago of protected areas. In 1984, the dictatorship declared it was in the national interest to open the entire reserve to national mining companies. While the federal government mapped out its boundary lines, José Altino Machado, a rugged and opportunistic prospector who believed it was best for the industry to dig first and ask questions later, organized dozens of *garimpeiros*—prospectors—to raid the area, using clandestine airstrips to hack open the jungle for their camps.[10]

Machodo's men were just the beginning. By the mid-1980s, more than 200 *garimpeiros* a day were crossing the border into Roraima, swarming airstrips and grinding deeper into the jungle on BR-174, the penetration road that cut from Manaus to the boomtown of Boa Vista. "These fierce men appeared in the forest suddenly, coming from all over the place, and quickly encircled our houses in large numbers," recalls Kopenawa. "They were frenetically searching for an evil thing that we had never heard about and whose name they repeated unceasingly: *oru*, gold. They started digging into the ground in every direction like herds of peccaries."[11]

Planes filled the sky like mosquitos, bush pilots accepting payments in gold dust to shuttle prospectors to remote riverside camps. "They had dug vast ditches bordered with huge gravel heaps all over the place to find the shiny dust they were relentlessly searching the streams for," Kopenawa remembers. "All the watercourses were flooded with yellowish mud, soiled by motor oils, and covered in dead fish. Machines rumbled in a deafening roar on their cleared banks and their smoke stank up the entire surrounding forest."

At first the outsiders were amused by the peculiar Indians who would do anything for the most basic tools. The Yanomami would dig for hours, paddle anywhere in their canoes, wash silt with mercury, anything for an axe or a shotgun. Yet honorable or wicked, all of the white men carried evil spirits to the *yano*. The evil spirits must haunt the white man's lands just as they haunt the lands of the Yanomami. The spirits were multiplying, spreading four maladies: measles, malaria, diarrhea, and whooping cough. The spirits fed on the fumes of outboard motors, trucks, and airplanes now growling through the forest every hour of every day.

"They approach our houses during the night and set up their hammocks inside but we are unable to see them," Kopenawa says. "Then they look for the most beautiful and chubbiest of our children. . . . If our *xapiri* do not act to rescue these children very quickly, they die instantly. After this, the *xawarari* epidemic beings tie up the elders and the women who have the weakest breath of life."[12]

With support from advocates like the Commission for the Creation of the Yanomami Park and the National Conference of Brazilian Bishops, tribesmen wrote to the government for help preserving their borderlines: "During the past two years, *garimpeiros* have been invading our Yanomami lands, removing our gold, bringing diseases, desiring and taking our women, and stealing from our gardens," they wrote. "Our lands are not demarcated, and we Yanomami Indians want demarcation immediately. Otherwise, all our lands will soon be invaded by *garimpeiros* and ranchers."

Their pleas went unheard. In 1986, when Brazil emerged from two decades of dictatorship, the Constitutional Assembly recognized Indian property rights, but with caveats: any lands should first and foremost be utilized for the national interest. Among Brazil's elites, the suspicious campaign for a Yanomami Park reeked of an international conspiracy to strip Brazil of its most valuable land. The new government doubled down on its military presence in the Amazon borderlands, constructing new barracks and expelling more missionaries and aid workers.[13]

Over the next four years, the rush for gold in Yanomami territory accelerated into a frenzy, penetrating the rain forest right up to the *yano* clearings. The landscape the tribe depended on was ravaged by mining, overhunting, and overfishing. Starving villagers could only rely on miners for survival. The Yanomami worked, begged, and sold themselves for food, wandering their villages in a daze, lost in their own homes, tormented by the din of pickaxes and high-pressure pumps, their rivers tainted by mercury and mosquito eggs. Alcohol, drugs, and prostitution were plentiful. The miners no longer found the Yanomami amusing. They had become a nuisance, endlessly begging, endlessly stealing rice or rum. Competing for veins of gold, the *garimpeiros* were unafraid to kill anyone in their way. Anyone could go missing in the forest. The soldiers out here were as bad as the miners. The police wouldn't come this far out into the forest. And if they did, the evidence of violence was already gone. The Yanomami were quick to cremate their loved ones to keep their spirits from wandering between worlds—and they were forbidden to speak the names of the dead.

The Yanomami needed a leader to help them unify their voice—but few spoke Portuguese. Kopenawa heard the call. He coordinated the first Yanomami Indigenous Assembly near his *yano* in 1986, gathering a hundred of his tribesmen to call for an end to the invasions. Some of the representatives from deep in Yanomami territory were unaware of the threats at their door, but now they understood: if the whites weren't there yet, they were coming—for their forest, for their rivers, for their wives and daughters.

In 1988, Kopenawa took his voice to Brasilia. The UN Environment Program gave him its prestigious Global 500 Award. In 1989, at a Survival International meeting in London, Kopenawa declared to the world: "We are people, just like you. People with blood and mouths to speak."

In 1991, he spoke at the United Nations in New York City. His visit was chronicled in a profile in the metro pages of the *New York Times*. Like many visitors to New York, he arrived frustrated that the airline had lost his luggage—a gift of bows and arrows that he'd been forced to check at the gate. That is where his kinship with the "The People of Merchandise" ended. "Man has become crazy," he said on an excursion to Times Square. "They are like the ant. They start one way and turn around and go the other way. They look all the time at the ground and never see the sky. Why do they do that?"[14]

During the Rio de Janeiro Earth Summit of 1992, Brazil's president, eager to be seen as an environmental crusader, approved the creation of Yanomami Park, a single, monumental reserve. When the president was impeached for corruption the following year, it was the first of a decade of setbacks. The lines of the reserve had been drawn, but a raid by FUNAI, the air force, and the police managed to expel only a fraction of the *garimpeiros*. Those who did abandon their stakes left an estimated 600 tons of refuse behind, littering the forest with broken machinery and crashed planes.[15]

Kopenawa warned that the situation could worsen. The prospectors who stayed behind were competing for thinner veins of gold. In 1993, his prophecy came true. A French nun working for the government health agency sent a note to headquarters: a massacre had taken place in the village of Xidéia.

According to the testimony of survivors and perpetrators, it all began with a dispute over hammocks and clothes.[16] When a camp of miners refused to give a group of Yanomami men the gifts they were promised, the Indians ransacked their camp and stole their cooking pots. Fed up, the *garimpeiros* resolved to make an example of any Indians who crossed them again. When six Yanomami returned a few days later to ask for food, they found a group of miners playing dominoes. The cook sent the Indians to another camp with a note they could not read: "Have fun with these idiots!"

The *garimpeiros* at the second camp read the note and invited the Yanomami into the forest to hunt tapir. Hiking single file on the trail, the miners seized the Indians' shotgun and executed four of the Yanomami at point-blank range. The two survivors only escaped by throwing themselves in the nearby river. One recalled his friend's final plea, the only Portuguese he knew, spoken as he stared down the barrel of the gun: "*Garimpeiro* friend."

The Yanomami recovered and cremated their dead before plotting their revenge. After a two-day hike, they surrounded the prospecting camp in the sizzle of a tropical rain. Only two men were present around the fire. The Indians shot one man, filled his remains with arrows, and split his skull with an axe. The other man was wounded but managed to escape.

Garimpeiros from all the nearby camps held meetings to

organize their reprisal. Fifteen prospectors, supplied with weapons and ammunition from their bosses, staked out a Yanomami village. When they arrived, it was nearly empty. Anticipating an attack, the able-bodied men in the tribe had left to join allies in a feast, confident that the whites would adhere to the same traditions of combat and spare the women, children, and elderly left behind.

The Yanomami underestimated the savagery of their enemies. "Children were playing, women cutting firewood, and the rest lying in hammocks," survivors recalled. The *garimpeiros* emerged from hiding and opened fire on the garden, advancing in unison. When they exhausted their ammunition, they entered the *yano* to finish off the survivors with machetes and knives. A blind woman was kicked to death. The killers knew they had missed the men of the village, so they left a message by mutilating and quartering the victims: an elderly man, two elderly women, a woman visiting from a nearby village, three adolescent girls, three boys between six and eight, a three-year-old girl, a one-year-old girl, and a sleeping infant, pulled from a hammock, smothered with a scrap of cotton, and stabbed to death.

When word of the massacre reached the outside world, the international media searched for words to describe what had happened. The Yanomami and their white allies provided one: genocide. Kopenawa's voice had not been enough to stop the violence, but now he roused the conscience of the world. Brazil was shamed into action. In November 1993, a paramilitary commission declared that there had been "a crime of genocide committed by Brazilian *garimpeiros* on Venezuelan territory."

Justice takes its time in the Amazon. In December 1996, after an agonizing legal process, five miners were sentenced—in absentia—one of the few times in history of anyone being charged with genocide. Two were finally apprehended. Three had vanished, never to be prosecuted, yet investigators hoped the verdict sent a powerful message: violence against Indians would not be ignored.

Kopenawa knows the white men will continue to return—next time without gifts. He has seen the world beyond the forest. Great blue seas, snow-capped peaks, steel buildings that touch the sky. In his travels and during his visions, he has arrived at a third interpretation of the white men and their epidemics. The evil spirits rose during the white man's search for gold. Omama had buried the *xawara* deep in the earth. Avenging the shamans who had died from the epidemics, the spirits were multiplying, their smoke threatening the entire world. The white men must be warned.

"They only pay attention to their own speeches, and it never crosses their mind that the same epidemic smoke poison devours their own children," he says. "The sky, which is as sick from the white people's fumes as we are, will start moaning and begin to break apart. . . . The back of the sky bears a forest as vast as ours, and its enormous weight will crush us all."[17]

Today tribes like the Guajajara have decided to take matters into their own hands, forming a militia they call the Guardians to fend off the invaders.[18] Wearing uniforms and face paint, armed with shotguns, they patrol the forest for the illegal loggers who cut down trees by the truckload. Unlike their forebears who fired arrows at intruders, the Guardians do not shoot to kill, but they have no qualms burning logging trucks, stripping lumberjacks of their chainsaws and clothes, and sending them naked off the reserve, equipment smoldering behind them.

To bolster its own poorly funded forest protection efforts, FUNAI has begun supporting the Guardians, supplying guns, ammunition, uniforms, and boots. According to one local chief and FUNAI staffer, a year ago as many as 130 logging trucks used to leave this reserve each day. Some villages, desperate for resources, allow loggers to cross into their territory for as little as $25 per load. Since the Guardians have begun their patrols, that number has dropped to 15 trucks per day.

The loggers have begun to retaliate. During the drought of 2015, they allegedly set fire to the dried-out forest. With little help from the government, thirty indigenous firefighters tried to contain the blaze, but the fire line soon extended more than 60 miles, growing into one of the largest wildfires in Brazilian history. By the time it was contained, more than 45 percent of the reserve had been scorched.[19]

Dr. Walker hopes the drones will help the Guardians protect their land and hold the government accountable. "It's kind of applied anthropology," he said. "Some people have a problem with us using drones, but if we know that loggers are the top threat, and the drones help the Guardians see where these loggers are working, then I have no problem with it."

Dr. Walker's applied anthropology opens another front in the battle between advocates for "controlled-contact" and stalwart "no-contact" groups like Survival International,[20] which also supports the Guardians, providing them with communications equipment and a worldwide platform to amplify their story. One of the first messages they helped the group record was an indictment of Dr. Walker and his colleague Dr. Hill.

"We are aware that some anthropologists have been calling for 'controlled contact' with the uncontacted Indians," said one of the Guardians' leaders, Olimpio, looking directly into a Survival International camera. "We will not allow this to happen, because it would be another genocide."

Preventing extinction is Dr. Walker's goal, too. He considers the 2014 contact with the Txapanawa to be evidence of what's possible with a carefully controlled contact. According to Fiona Watson of Survival International, the Txapanawa incident wasn't controlled contact—it was controlled chaos. FUNAI and the federal police should have never abandoned the Xinane River base when it was attacked in 2011. The contact team was late and unprepared in its response to the Txapanawa in 2014. Despite the skillful response of Dr. Rodrigues, only blind luck prevented more deaths—and we still only know the government's version of events. Anything could have happened once the Txapanawa returned to their village. Watson witnessed the horrors of the gold rush in Roraima firsthand from 1987 to 1988. After joining Survival International in 1990, she worked tirelessly on the Yanomami campaign and now serves as director of research and field work.

"They are playing God," Watson said of Dr. Walker and his colleagues. "It's very paternalistic. What they're doing is a rather colonial approach, saying we will contact the natives, because we know what's best for them, and they need the benefits of our wonderful society." Watson is even more troubled by the policies that may be enacted based on their conclusions. "They are doing the dirty work of governments and multinational corporations that want nothing more than for these tribes to be contacted, and out of the way, so they can go about their business."

For no-contact advocates like Survival International, technology and data have a role in protecting tribes, but Indians themselves should determine how those tools are used. "What data doesn't address is the issue of self-determination," Watson said. "Nobody can really know what these people think or want, but there are quite good indications. Survival isn't saying 'Keep them in some sort of zoological pristine wilderness.' Far from it. We're saying they have the right to decide whether they want to make contact or not. It's not up to Survival or anthropologists or FUNAI to make that decision."

In the face of illegal trafficking and rampant corruption, the situation for isolated tribes can look hopeless, but controlled-contact and no-contact advocates agree on at least one solution: nothing will be achieved without tribes getting organized and fighting for their rights—with international support to pressure their home governments. All is not lost. Despite centuries of challenges, FUNAI is raising its estimates of the number of isolated tribes in the rain forest.

"These people have survived the most tumultuous century," Watson said. "The massive opening up of the Amazon. The rubber boom. And they are still here. The onus is on all of us to make the state protect these areas. They have the money to do it. They may lack the political willpower, but they have done it and they can do it."

When the Txapanawa emerged from isolation, Site X was taken off Dr. Walker's roster. For better or worse, the Txapanawa are now considered contacted, even if they haven't been seen since the summer of the World Cup. The fate of Site Y, the abandoned Yanomami village, remained a mystery. Dr. Walker and his team feared they had been decimated by the *garimpeiros* who continued to work a vein near the overgrown *yano*. For almost a year, he and his team parsed satellite imagery for evidence that the tribe had avoided a massacre.

Then in May 2015, the quiet hallways of the anthropology department at the University of Missouri erupted in cheers. The team had located a few pixels of open ground, a patch of forest cleared by hand, a lifeboat in a sea of jungle. Site Y had resurfaced. The *yano*, previously just sixteen structures, had expanded to seventeen. Against all odds, a delicate tree, sprouting new roots.

21

LAST DANCE

By spring of 2016, the Ghost Riders were awaiting trial, nine military police and two criminal informants accused of orchestrating nineteen homicides and attempted murders, beginning on the Bloody Weekend of July 17, 2015. Família do Norte strongman João Branco was back in prison after being apprehended on the Venezuelan border, looking a little different around the eyes, cheeks, and chin, his face altered by plastic surgery while he was on the run. Manaus was absorbed in Brazil's national political drama: the impeachment proceedings of President Dilma Rousseff. After months of investigation into the Jet Wash scandal at Petrobras, federal police had exposed a graft scheme that spanned continents, involving politicians at every level, including Luiz Inácio Lula da Silva. On a Wednesday morning in April, the former guerrilla, labor leader, and president was pulled from his home in São Paulo to be questioned about money laundering and identity fraud related to a luxury condominium he owned in the beachfront town of Guarujá.[1]

In the streets of Manaus and cities across the country, demonstrators were calling for the impeachment of Lula's protégé, President Rousseff. While investigators had yet to uncover any evidence directly linking her to the scandal, her rivals were content with guilt by association. She had been minister of energy and chairman of Petrobras for more than a decade, for God's sake. How could she not know that Petrobras contractors were systematically overcharging the company for contracts and using the proceeds to line their own pockets and fill their campaign coffers?

Until evidence of a Jet Wash connection came to light, Dilma's opponents would pounce on her dwindling approval ratings, attacking her on the basis of accounting irregularities in the federal books. Her own vice president, Michel Temer, next in line to become president, was already building his new coalition. Workers' Party loyalists held their own counterdemonstrations, accusing Dilma's enemies of plotting a soft coup, aided by the GloboNews conglomerate that had been a tool of the hard right since the days of the military regime. The entire spectacle was turning into an international farce. Late-night hosts in the United States were mocking Brazil at a time when the world was supposed to be turning its gaze to the Summer Olympics in Rio de Janeiro. A nationwide survey of Brazilians showed that the majority of people believed that the imminent games, the culmination of a decade-long vision, would bring more shame than pride to the country.

The sensational drama surrounding Brazil's leadership pushed investigations into local corruption off the front pages. I spent the hottest part of every day in front of the air-conditioning unit at the Hotel Express in Manaus, sifting through documents about the Bloody Weekend. Hundreds of pages of police reports, eyewitness accounts, and autopsies. Hours of grainy surveillance video, murders captured from a dozen angles. Endless wiretaps and cell phone screen captures, the story of how monsters are born.

It was far more difficult to find details about the victims' lives. Out of fear or loyalty, few people in the neighborhoods where the murders occurred would talk to me about the Bloody Weekend. Even local reporters struggled to get sources to say anything on the record. The authorities were eager to dismiss the dead as gang members who had it coming. As for the innocent, they were classic cases of wrong place, wrong time.

The police listed the thirty-eight victims in minimalist fashion: name, occupation, time, date, and location of death. Among the fry cooks, night watchmen, freelancers, and restaurant workers, there was one case I couldn't shake. I kept going back to Bairro Aleixo. To Anderson Sales Soares. Thirty-four years old. Dancer.

Sergeant Camacho was shot dead at 3:00 p.m. at the Banco Bradesco in Educandos. The Giant was beheaded at 4:30 p.m. at the Instituto Penal Antonio Trinidad. Now the sun was finally down, but the heat wouldn't quit. At closing time in Bairro Aleixo, a working-class neighborhood in the South Central Zone of Manaus, workers from the Municipal Secretariat of Infrastructure punched off the clock, blue uniforms slung over their bare shoulders as they left headquarters. They lit cigarettes at the corner, stood around waiting for a bus to Terminal 1 or Terminal 2, where they could transfer to one of the outer zones: an hour home on a good day. Tonight residents lingered at the crest of the hill for a touch of a cool breeze on their cheeks. Stray dogs stopped in their tracks to sniff at the air, barbecue smoke tinged with waste from the creeks at the bottom of the hill.

Friday night brings out all the regulars. Across the street from the taxi stand, old-timers faced off across chessboards, protecting their queens and grumbling about lunatic drivers who treated Aleixo like a Formula 1 track. Over the years the neighborhood had turned into a shortcut between chic Adrianopolis and chic Vieiralves, attracting assholes with fast American cars and no regard for the boys and girls still learning how to thread a pass in street soccer.

Dark hours passed but the temperature held steady. Even the jukebox seemed heat-struck, oozing popular Brazilian music while listeners poured little glasses of beer from liter bottles sweating in insulated holders on their plastic tables. You could already tell it would be a late night. Dancing, yelling at old lovers, staring ruefully up the street while a song from a past life made you thirsty for another taste of rum.

It was around 11:00 p.m. when Anderson Sales Soares came by the Shadai for a beer.[2] It had been three years since he'd lived in Aleixo, but the kid still hung around a dance club up the street that played traditional Brazilian music. Thirty-four years old, he'd split from the mother of his four children, but the kids still brought a smile to his face whenever he talked about them with his grandmother down the hill while she gave him a haircut in her kitchen.

Anderson wasn't supposed to be drinking these days, not after that scuffle with his ex and her new boyfriend a while back, but Friday night lends itself to contemplation. Across the street at the 24-hour liquor store, the owner held court over an ever-expanding circle of folding chairs where he and his daughters brought out fresh beers for the customers who chatted numbly, peeling the foil tops off can after can of Itaipava.

Later, despite the commotion, the neighbors would agree on a few of the details. The vehicle came out of nowhere, a red Volkswagen Gol, one of its headlights brighter than the other. When it skidded to a stop, three men stepped out with a supreme sense of purpose, faces concealed behind black balaclavas. Two carried pistols and one brandished a submachine gun.

Rosiemarie da Silva, owner of the place, had already gone to bed upstairs, but shots ricocheting off her stucco walls tore her awake.[3] "They just kept shooting and shooting," she recalled. "I don't know why. We've never experienced anything like that around here before."

Before Rosiemarie could register that it wasn't a nightmare, the shooters sped away. She came downstairs to the reek of burning rubber and gun smoke, customers huddled over the body of Anderson, gone already, six shots, dozens of shells glinting on the sidewalk.

Neighbors stepped out from under cover, but not too close. Witnesses called ambulances, murmured prayers, tried to close Anderson's eyes.

A police cruiser appeared. The PMs cordoned the scene, telling everyone to back off while they picked through the evidence. Reporters arrived, crowding the slack yellow tape, photographing bullet holes and bloodstains, trying to wrangle testimony from the stunned observers. The police radio hissed with dispatches from other zones. Moments later, the reporters' phones buzzed with fresh assignments. This was no ordinary night.

Anderson was pronounced dead on the scene at around 11:30 p.m. on Rua Gabriel da Gonçalves, not far from my hotel. I went there in December 2015, a few days after the Ghost Riders were arrested in Operation Wolfpack. Now that the offenders were behind bars, I hoped I could get someone to talk to me. I started by looking for Rosiemarie da Silva, the thirty-seven-year-old proprietor of the *lanchonete* where Anderson was killed. Maybe he was a regular. Maybe she could tell me more about him, or what she saw and heard after the shooting. At the very least she could point me to an eyewitness or someone who knew Anderson.

I made my first visit on a Sunday afternoon before sundown. The holiday spirit had touched Manaus and good Samaritans were planting Christmas trees in potholes. Neighbors in Aleixo were hanging lights. Just up the street was a strip of lunch counters, corner bars, liquor stores, salons, and churches where folks from the bottoms hiked up to do business, gossip, and catch the breeze. Cats tiptoed on corrugated roofs, waiting for the rats to come out.

There was no telling which lunch counter belonged to Rosiemarie. I found a place that seemed like a likely candidate and took a seat at a plastic table. On the TV, local mixed martial arts hero José Aldo squared off against Conor McGregor while Madonna sang on the jukebox. Cabdrivers huddled at the taxi stand. At a table nearby, two men played chess. The Pentecostal church down the street began blasting worship music from a PA system while two girls handed out pamphlets on the sidewalk outside, trying to draw people in.

A lady wiped down the counter, her curls tucked into a hairnet.

"Excuse me," I asked. "Is this Rosiemarie's place?"

"Rosiemarie?"

"Rosiemarie da Silva? She owns a lunch counter around here? I think she's about my age?"

"No, this isn't her place," she said. "Why?"

"I was just hoping to chat with her," I said. "Thanks."

I finished my beer, tried the next place, and the next, trying not to seem too nosey, but it was no use. Over the next several days, I returned to Aleixo every afternoon at quitting time, trying every hamburger on the block, talking to anyone who would listen, dredging up a memory they wanted to forget. One night, I talked to the owner of a 24-hour beer store who sat on a plastic chair on the curb, drinking beer with his daughter.

"Oh, yeah, I remember," he said after we'd had a couple. "That was right over there." He pointed across the street.

"Why Anderson?" I asked. "Was he in trouble? I heard he was a dancer."

"I don't know," he said. "Nothing like that's ever happened around here. He lived just down the hill, I think."

There were a thousand homes along the creek down the hill. The economy was scraping along the bottom of the worst recession in Brazil's history. The president was under threat of impeachment. In a country that was falling apart, these neighbors wanted to leave the whole business of killings behind them, to turn their attention to a new year, 2016.

On a Monday night in mid-December, I finally came across a woman who knew Rosiemarie. She'd seen me around before. A middle-aged woman with bottle-blond hair, she entertained a few questions as she counted up the wrinkled bills in her cash register.

"You're the writer," she said.

"Yup," I said. "So you know Rosiemarie, huh?"

"She's a friend of mine."

"Do you know when she'll be around?"

"She knows you've been asking about her," she said. "She doesn't want to talk."

"I understand," I said. "I don't want to bother her. I just want to know more about Anderson. The newspapers don't say much."

"That's because it's not a good thing to talk about," she said, eyeing the men over at the cab stand.

"I understand," I said. "Do you think you could talk to Rosiemarie for me? Maybe I could come back and see her later?"

"He was a good kid," she said. "This isn't that kind of neighborhood, you know."

The woman picked up my bottle and wiped the counter. A police SUV whipped around the corner, down toward the creeks. From the look in her eye I could tell she didn't want to see me again.

. . .

For months I kept searching for the ghost of Anderson every time I passed through Manaus, asking around Aleixo, asking detectives in the civil police for details about his case. On a Tuesday night, I stopped in at Bar do Manguiera, an open-air pool hall at the bottom of the hill in the shadow of art deco condos. It was a neighborhood hub, kittens and kids running around, women walking past selling homemade cupcakes, shirtless men shooting billiards while a teenage girl replenished their beers. When I asked after Anderson, people shrugged. When I alluded to the murders of the year before, they turned their shoulders as if telling me to just let them forget.

A group of women chatting in the shade of a tree read the frustration on my face.

"Hey," said one of the women. "Come over here a second." I sat down beside them. In a low voice, she went on: "I didn't know Anderson, but I know his grandmother." She pulled out her phone, called someone briefly, then sent me around the corner. "First house on the right."

I thanked her and crossed a wooden bridge over a gray-water creek. The path ended at a T. It was the kind of neighborhood where you always know who's coming or going, one way in, one way out, each house with an open window to the alleyway. At the first house on the right, a woman leaned outside her window, waiting for the gringo.

Dona Maria Teixeira Sales, grandmother of Anderson, had been living in this house for twenty years. It was impossible to guess her age, and I wasn't about to ask. She spoke to me, as children ran up and down the alleyway asking for her attention. In the room behind her, a teenage boy was getting his hair buzzed.

"All I can tell you is he was always dancing," Dona Maria said, "ever since he was a boy. He spent all his time at the studio."

"Do you know anyone else I can talk to? Family, friends? Anyone who knew him?"

"Everyone on this street knew him," she said. "But you have to know, you're a stranger here."

"I just want to find out more about him," I said. "People should know his story, not the killers."

"I've said all I can say," she said. "You need to talk to his foster mother, Cileste. She's working tonight, but maybe you can meet tomorrow."

I was leaving the next day for Altamira. Dona Maria borrowed her son's cell phone and called Cileste. We spoke on the phone briefly. I could hear her cry at the mention of Anderson's name. I told her I didn't want to talk about his death, only his life. Of all the cases of wrong place, wrong time, his death seemed the most wrong. A dancer cut down by bullets. Maybe I was just telling myself what I wanted to believe about him, but Cileste must have believed it, too. She agreed to speak to me. We would meet at her house the following Saturday.

At the funeral, Anderson's dance mentor had told reporters under condition of anonymity that his pupil was a good father, a good man, and a beautiful dancer. Inspector Almada had told me that Anderson was a recovering alcoholic, sober for a good year or so, but that he'd slid back into drinking again. No matter who he was or wasn't, I just wanted to know more than his name, age, and occupation. In a country where homicide victims are reduced to pixelated bodies on the front page, I wanted to share what Anderson was like when he was alive.

Friday night I called Cileste's phone to confirm our meeting, but nobody answered. I called again Saturday morning with no luck. All day I tried, but no answer. At sunset I parked up the hill from Dona Maria's. A woman was preaching into a PA system on the second floor of her family restaurant, delivering a sermon about the power of Jesus to give love, clarity, and truth.

"A thousand pardons, Dona Maria, but I need your help," I said. Her grandchildren or great-grandchildren or maybe just kids from the neighborhood sat on the wooden bench outside her window, enjoying the cool sunset, waiting for a haircut. "I can't get a hold of Cileste. We were supposed to meet this morning." A little boy in a diaper looked up at me from the doorway. *"Oi, filho,"* I said. *"Tudo bem?"*

"I'm afraid you missed her," Dona Maria said. "She's gone off to work. She's a teacher in the interior. She'll be gone the whole month of May. When I see her I'll let her know you came. Maybe the next time you return?"

"Is there a number where I can reach her?"

"Not where she's going."

"Okay. Well, is there anyone else you think I could talk to? I know I'm a stranger, and I'm sorry, but I don't mean to cause anyone pain. It's just that I've already talked to the investigators—"

"You have to understand," she said. "It's dangerous to talk about these things. People are afraid."

All she could do was point me in the direction of the studio where he used to practice, up the hill not far from here on Avenida Belo Horizonte. The night he was killed, Anderson had just finished a performance and was stopping in for a beer near his bus stop.

I drove up and down the street, found three gyms side by side, not far from Adrianopolis, one of the nicest neighborhoods in the city. The dance teacher who'd spoken to the press was a fifty-five-year-old retiree, but maybe he still gave lessons in one of these studios. I asked about Anderson at each one to no avail.

"Sorry," said one of the coaches. "My oldest student is twenty-seven years old. There used to be another dance studio up the street, but it's been closed for a while."

I found the shutdown studio, a second-story unit with faded silhouettes of dancers on the stucco exterior. How much longer could I pick this wound? The more I looked for details, the more it seemed the details of his life had been devoured. The Ghost Riders had not only taken his life; they'd taken his story. His survivors would barely speak his name.

I stood on the corner of Rua Belo Horizonte, a street named after the city where I was born, imagining Anderson standing on the same corner after practice, still sweating, the melody, the rhythm still in his head, in his feet. Maybe he saw a sunset like the one I was seeing now, but instead of feeling lost, he felt home.

Almost two years after I learned of his death, I still can't say why I became so obsessed with Anderson. Maybe it had something to do with the sheer chance of his murder, a life swallowed in a storm of violence. In a way it was the opposite of my own, delivered from the tumult of dictatorship to a quiet farm at the foot of the Cascade Mountains. Being in the wrong place at the wrong time cost Anderson his life. Being in the right place at the right time gave me mine.

I spent the rest of the day writing in my tiny room, trying to capture everything I'd seen and heard. I was just back from two weeks crisscrossing the jungle: boat, plane, bus, car, motorcycle. I was tired of swatting away mosquitos and chasing leads. Soon I would cram myself into a coach seat back to Panama, then another jet back to my California suburb. Back to my house with its failing tomato garden. To my wife, who would ask about my latest exploits in Brazil. It would be months before I'd be back in Manaus.

I was ready to leave the chaos of this city behind, but I wanted to feel its pulse one more time before I left.

It was past midnight when I stepped out into the street. For the first time in ten years of traveling in the Amazon, I felt what could be described as a cold breeze, an uncanny shiver that almost drove me back to my room for the sweatshirt I always packed but never used except on the long, frigid flights between hemispheres. I was going out for a last night out with a friend. He'd lost his driver's license last time we went out months earlier, and he still hadn't replaced it, so we took my rental car, a Volkswagen Gol, the people's car of Brazil. My friend sat in the passenger seat, the navigator, the person I trusted most in Manaus, the one who knew the map of the city by heart.

We were ready to stay up until sunrise, but a moment later it started pouring. The crowds that had gathered at the open-air bars began to seek shelter. The only people safe and dry were the evangelical churchgoers downtown, singing late-night gospels. The sky seemed to open up as if answering their prayers.

Throughout the city, *azevinhos,* little planes, the boys who carry grams of cocaine and weed from corner to corner, had retreated to their safe houses. "Turn here," my friend said, directing me to go the wrong way down a one-way street, an empty three-lane road. At a certain hour in Manaus, street lights and signs don't matter anymore. You draw even more suspicion by following the rules of the road.

Blowing red lights, we raced downhill through the acrid smell of sewage. Up ahead a pair of military police trucks lurched across the intersection, sirens blaring. I wondered who they were chasing, how it would end.

I gripped the steering wheel and checked my rearview mirror. My friend could tell the police cruisers had rattled me.

"No worries," he said. "This is a nice car." We were safe in this new rental car with its rental car plates, no wrong place for us, no wrong time.

The rain quit as quickly as it began, leaving streets empty and glittering. We turned toward the bottoms, toward neighborhoods haunted by Ghost Riders. Parque 10. Parque 14. Bairro Union. We sped from corner to corner, *igarapé* by *igarapé*. Anyone left on the street after the storm was hard up for money or drugs.

My friend spotted a corner house in the yellow wash of a sodium light, three sentinels posted at each door, watching traffic, whistling like birds at passing cars. He signaled out the window. A boy signaled back.

I pulled up to the corner and left the engine running. The *azevinho* met us at the window, just a kid. A kid with a fluorescent fanny pack, the kind American tourists loved in the 1990s. A kid like the one I could have been if I'd never left Belo Horizonte, standing on the street with a gun tucked in my shorts. What was I doing in this neighborhood, in this city? Why did I keep returning to the north country instead of to my birth family down south? I'd traveled more than 3,000 miles in Brazil in less than two years, crisscrossing the Amazon, but I hadn't been back to Belo Horizonte since the World Cup, hadn't seen my Brazilian brother Ramon since the day his first daughter, Luana, was born, since I'd held her in my arms, wondering what kind of country she would inherit. "When are you coming back?" Ramon asked whenever we spoke on the phone. Our mother was worried that I'd vanished again. I assured him: I'll get back down there soon. When Mom called from Oregon, I said one day I'd take her down there, too. At last we would close the circle, but there was no circle, only a door, a door only I had the power to open or close. Now I looked at the kid through the open window as if looking into a mirror; the kid looked back as if he knew I had no rightful business on his corner.

Quick as a low-five we were on our way, that cold breeze again through the window as I cranked the radio dial, stomped on the gas, and rushed us back to higher ground.

"There was no reason he should have been killed," Dona Maria had said the first night I met her in Bairro Aleixo. She leaned out the window while I stood in the alley, listening. "He drank a little like anyone else. But he never used drugs."

Before I left, she wanted to show me something. She called her eldest son who lived a few doors down. A moment later he appeared with a flip phone, dialed up the video he knew she was looking for, and passed it to Dona Maria. She cradled the phone in her hands while the video rolled.

"He used to dance with me," she said, squinting at the screen. There was Anderson in the middle of an empty dance floor, watching another man and woman dance to an American song, the kind I used to roll my eyes at when I heard it in the Amazon, as if pop music could spoil the rain forest.

Anderson waited politely for his opportunity to cut in. Maybe this was the end of a class. Or the last lonely hours of a wedding. He was smaller than I expected, boyish in his red shirt. Finally he stepped in, took his partner by the hands. You could see grace in every step, the care he took with the girl as he dipped her.

As quickly as the video began, it cut off. Dona Maria sighed as if debating whether to play it again for me.

A rooster crowed. She played it again, holding her breath, waiting for the moment when Anderson cut in.

22

THE TORCH AND THE JAGUAR

The 2016 impeachment day protests in Manaus were held in the same public spaces where, less than two years ago, crowds had gathered to watch the World Cup. At the pro-impeachment event in Ponta Negra Park, families descended from their luxury condos to watch the congressional vote projected on a big screen near the amphitheater. A year of anti-government demonstrations had spurred a cottage industry, vendors selling inflatable Lula and Dilma dolls in prison uniform, inflatable Minions for the children, Brazilian flag bandanas the perfect size for toy dogs.

The bridge that spanned the Rio Negro seemed to glow as a thunderstorm lumbered toward the city, a single flash of lightning over the distant forest. Yachts and jet skis bobbed on the water, passengers taking in the sunset. Ten years earlier none of these marvels were here, but Lula's development projects had turned on him like a golem. Now his people were glued to a giant screen broadcasting live from Brasilia, cheers erupting every time a senator cast a vote in favor of impeaching his protégé, Dilma, putting an end to a decade of Workers' Party rule.

At the anti-coup demonstration at the Teatro Amazonas, the Workers' Party and its allies agonized in front of a smaller screen. The organizers had shown up early to erect a stage and light show, but no amount of decorations could turn the tide of the vote. A few police milled about in the crowd, but after weeks of marches, the left wing in Manaus was too tired to make trouble. There were better ways to waste energy. That night there was a match at the Arena da Amazônia, a faceoff between two Carioca teams, a marvelous distraction from politics. For the first time since the World Cup, the stadium would be full.

The impeachment proceedings began four hours late. Outside the congressional building in Brasilia, the police had erected corrugated tin walls between the pro-impeachment and anti-coup demonstrators in hopes of keeping the yellow and red from colliding. Protestors had been camping in tents for days; the Workers' Party faithful received a pep talk from Lula himself, his voice hoarse from days of speeches, from shuttling back and forth from the federal building to the Tulip Hotel where he was desperately trying to trade favors for votes in hopes of keeping Dilma in office. Their nemesis, Vice President Temer, had already leaked a tape of the speech he planned to give once he assumed the presidency.

In the hours before the vote, deputies took to the dais and gave their last pleas, wearing anti-Dilma T-shirts over their suits, waving protest flags, leading the chamber in victory song before the voting had even begun. The votes were delivered state by state in alphabetical order, ambition crackling in the politicians' voices as they addressed their colleagues, their constituents, and the cameras.

"There will be no coup!" said one Workers' Party senator, met by cheers at the Teatro Amazonas.

"In the name of my sons and daughters and their grandchildren and future generations of Brazilians, I vote yes for impeachment!" said a senator on the right. Cheers at Ponta Negra Park.

The senior congressional leadership tried to withhold their glee, banging their gavels to keep the proceedings moving. By rule the members were limited to just ten seconds to announce their decision, but this was precious national exposure, so congress members took their sweet time, dedicating votes to their families and friends, to doctors and entrepreneurs, to those with land or without land, to the black man, to the Indians, to every constituency in every state who might turn out with a critical vote. At one point there was confetti and glitter. At one point there was spitting that led to a skirmish. Right-wing presidential hopeful Jair Bolsonaro dedicated his impeachment vote to the military men of 1964—the same ones who had tortured Dilma during the Bleeding Years. At last the president of the Senate cast his own vote with no fanfare: "God help us all."

While the votes were cast in a glittering modernist hall some 1,300 miles away, the stakes for the Amazon were higher than for any other region of Brazil. The wheels of development in the rain forest had been set in motion decades ago, but whether the machine veered right or left would determine the pace of progress for the next generation. Would the new administration open the coffers for more infrastructure and public services, or would it do the bidding of the treasury analysts pleading for austerity? Would stewardship of the forest be granted to more tribal leaders, or would the indigenous reserves be opened back up for mining and oil concessions? Which roads would be paved and which would remain muddy backwaters? Which new promises would be made, and which old promises would be broken? Only one thing was certain: it was easier to impeach a president than it was to reform a country.

One by one the votes mounted up, odds stacking higher against the Workers' Party. At the Ponta Negra Park demonstration, giant flags fluttered over the ebullient crowd, but soon the storm clouds were spitting rain. The assembly dispersed, demonstrators covering their heads with protest banners. The scales had already been tipped, the final result a foregone conclusion. Across the sea in Japan, the Brazilian stock market leapt 4.5 percent in defiance of the unemployment figures. The time had come to rid the government of waste and corruption, to slash the sprawling safety net and restore Brazil to meritocracy. The families of Ponta Negra went to sleep with full bellies, portfolios fattened.

By then the signs at the Teatro Amazonas had been discarded, a few hardliners asleep in the flicker of the enormous screen as if they would soon wake to discover that the coup had only been a nightmare. There would be six more months of investigation and deliberation, almost certain to end in Dilma's removal from office, but for now the debate was over: left or right, at least Brazil would be moving on, even if it was from one group of bandits to another.

Even in a place as corrupt as the Amazon, there would be no escape from the heat. Governor José Melo was on the brink of being removed from office, accused of voter fraud during his 2014 reelection campaign. Working with evangelical church leaders, he allegedly promised special favors if they could deliver their congregations in exchange for computers and tablets in their neighborhood schools. Where the carrot didn't work, Melo relied on the stick. Investigators had turned up evidence that he ordered military police to intimidate residents of the poorest neighborhoods into voting for him. If they made the wrong choice, whatever small protection they had from trafficking violence would vanish.[1]

There was evidence that Governor Melo's deputies were playing the other side. The same federal investigation into the FDN that revealed the Amazonas state government negotiating for peace in the prisons also accused state officials of trading favors for votes. A 2014 recording allegedly captured Major Carliomar Barros Brandão, the state subsecretary of justice and human rights, promising Zé legal protection in exchange for votes from FDN loyalists.

"Nobody will touch you," he assured Zé in a secret meeting.[2]

"He will have more than 100,000 votes," Zé said, flexing the FDN's political muscle in his old neighborhood. "You imagine every prisoner who has family there. If we give an order, they will comply."

Soon it was clear that officials at every level of Brazilian government and industry were entwined with criminal organizations. The very politicians who had taken down Dilma were under investigation for every felony under the sun: bribery, sexual deviancy, homicide, drug trafficking, the entire pyramid crumbling under the pressure of the Jet Wash scandal. The country had been torn asunder by one snitch—a money launderer quietly keeping his accounts from behind the counter of a Petrobras station, a ledger he was willing to hand over to save his own ass.

No amount of money could stop the prosecutors from turning the pages. The richest man in Brazil, Marcelo Odebrecht, king of the country's largest construction company, was in jail, opening his own books to earn a house arrest in one of his mansions. At least there he could delight in watching the Summer Olympics in Rio, where his namesake firm had been awarded billions in contracts in the lead-up to the games, even if the city itself was now so bankrupt it made Manaus look fiscally sound. The disasters in the marvelous city were piling up. Athletes dropped out of the games for fear of contracting the Zika virus. A bicycle bridge collapsed into the sea, killing seven citizens. The waters of Guanabara Bay failed tests for fecal matter at levels guaranteed to sicken athletes, a sanitation crisis that local activists had been complaining about for years. Yet the city would look marvelous on camera, Cristo Redentor opening his arms to the world, thousands of soldiers dispatched to pacify the hillside favelas while the richest international visitors stayed in yachts off the coast of Ipanema.

Few Brazilians were surprised by the chain of corruption, but as the games approached, there was also a sense of relief. After years of buildup, the Olympics had arrived. It was time to focus on the here and now. In Tabatinga, indigenous health coordinator Weydson Pereira focused on the falling malaria numbers, on the rising Zika numbers, on the new water treatment center running low on chemicals. In the Tururukari-Uka village, Francisco Uruma focused on the tribe's new water tower, its new one-room schoolhouse, decorated with a poster about the benefits of coaching that Professor Guedes had presented at Harvard. In Altamira, the community council of Agua Azul focused on the unfinished sanitation works, in the hope that Norte Energia would finish the system before it fired up more turbines on the Belo Monte. In the office of the Secretariat of Public Security, Inspector Almada focused on a job well done, on the text message he received from a mother of one of the victims: "Thank you. We did not believe, but you helped us find justice." There would be other Ghost Riders, but maybe it would be a slow summer, a chance to barbecue and watch football with his son and catch up on the history books he liked to read after his family had gone to bed.

Tomorrow would always be an unforeseen truth. *Uma imprevista verdade.* Soon, the interim president, Michel Temer, would be embroiled in his own corruption scandal. The economy would get worse before it got better, unemployment rising like a river spilling over its banks. Venezuela would get worse and worse again, refugees pouring across the border, pitching tent cities in the shade of the underpasses of Manaus. Colombia would find peace, but war would migrate to Brazil, FARC hardliners refusing to lay down their arms, crossing the border to join the Familia do Norte and the Principal Capital Command. Not even a new year could stem the chaos, not when the FDN was still seeking revenge, not when 2017 would begin with a New Year's massacre on the prison road, fifty-six rivals of the FDN butchered, heads thrown over the perimeter fence, a warning for the PCC, for Governor Melo, for all who dared defy the family.

For now the country of the future could only worry about 2016. The Olympics in Manaus would strike quick and bright as lightning. The Arena da Amazônia would host a handful of soccer games, and for a few brief nights the basket of the stadium would light up the city once more. The health inspectors were already working double duty to make sure that every restaurant in the city, even the floating bars in the middle of the river, were ready to serve food that was gringo-clean. Entrepreneurs refreshed their inventories, sushi bars, poker rooms, burger and brew joints, and every variety of food truck bracing for a tide of business that would lift all boats. At Mirage Park, families would line up for popcorn and Ferris wheel rides, fathers emptying their wallets to win their daughters stuffed Minions. The amphitheater at Ponta Negra would fill with spectators who could watch the games on a dozen screens. Teenagers would bumble through the festivities with their eyes glued to their cell phones, hunting virtual creatures across the promenade in a brand-new Pokémon game while kids elsewhere in the city hid from monsters on their streets.

Moeses Martins and his wife and children, the family I first met on my visit to the World Cup, would skip the Ponta Negra festivities this time.

"It's complicated," Moeses told me the afternoon that the U.S. and Brazilian teams were in town.

For months he had been out of work, and it might be months again before there was money for such extravagancies. At least his children were healthy. At least this year there had been no flooding. At least this year the city had finished the noisy utility project in the neighborhood, new steel utility towers dwarfing the rickety poles on the banks of the *igarapé*. In Bairro São Jorge, the power still cut out some evenings around five thirty, but the gleaming transformers outside their windows channeled energy uptown like a dream.

After I left Moeses I walked the bank of the *igarapé*. I climbed into an abandoned home that threatened to slide into the water during the next flood. Out the broken window, I watched a man nudge his canoe up the creek, his boat cutting a path through the refuse. With a net he fished out empty cans and slipped them into a garbage bag. From this vantage my birth country seemed plagued with nearly insurmountable challenges, but perhaps no more than my home country with its endless wars, its Abu Ghraibs, its mortgage-backed securities, its Deepwater Horizons, its Sandy Hooks, its Fergusons, its Flints, its Standing Rocks, its cycles of horror and hope as ceaseless as the Amazon clock.

By May the Olympic torch was on its way to Manaus, traveling through three hundred Brazilian cities in one hundred days in a relay from the northeastern coast to the banks of the Amazon, across the Pantanal to the colonial gems of Minas Gerais, through the last patches of the Atlantic rain forest and finally to the Estadio de Maracanã in Rio de Janeiro where the cauldron would be lit to open the games.

At nearly every stop on its 2,000-mile journey, the torch was delayed by protests, but even if it arrived late, the torch kept burning. The relay had been planned years ago, long before the Jet Wash scandal, long before the Txapanawa massacre or the Bloody Weekend or the inauguration of the Belo Monte dam. Thousands of Brazilians would carry the torch. Even animals would be involved—sea turtles and river dolphins and jaguars—trained to demonstrate Brazil's natural wonders, the harmony between man, animal, and the jungle.

On June 20 in Manaus, fifty days before the start of the Summer Olympic Games, Francisco Uruma's nephew Tashira and his fellow indigenous archers had the great honor of carrying the torch through the capital. For three years the young athletes had fired thousands of arrows, pacing the 70-meter range at the Olympic Village, stepping over the concrete sewage pipe that drained in the nearby *igarapé*. A dozen quivers each morning, a dozen quivers each afternoon, penciling their scores on the corner of their targets, 51, 51, 52, 51, 54, another day, another two hundred arrows. Month by month, Tashira watched video of his practice sessions, witnessed his own body changing in the weight room mirror, a new manner of breath, a new sharpness in his eyes. At night he would call home, hear the familiar ambience of the village on the lonely line. On weekends he would return to visit his mother or his uncle and demonstrate his new bow for the children, children just like he used to be, stubbornly fashioning their own bows to impress their fathers. When his grandfather, Waldomiro Cruz, passed into the next world, Tashira was at his side at the Indian hospital in Manaus, a boy again, waiting for a blessing, waiting for the next story.

Eight times out of ten, Tashira's arrows found the bull's-eye that from 70 meters is no larger than the eye of a fish. Before long he was peering at his score in lights at international tournaments. First in São Paulo and Rio de Janeiro, then in Guatemala City and

Costa Rica, even a tournament in the United States, in Phoenix, a barren red landscape devoid of trees or rivers, as foreign as the surface of another planet.

When it came time to qualify for the Olympic Games in Rio de Janeiro, Tashira and his indigenous teammates fell just short, missing the final cut for the national team. Coach Anibal Forte was not surprised or disappointed. The archers on the national team had been training in São Paulo for years. Some had been training with carbon fiber equipment since before Tashira and his teammates had mastered the native bow. Others were second- and third-generation archers from Japanese-Brazilian and Chinese-Brazilian families. Tashira and the others had gotten closer than anyone had imagined, and they were closer to the beginning of their careers than the end. Four more years, forty thousand more arrows, and Tokyo 2020 would be theirs.

The Sustainable Amazon Foundation was busy marketing the results of its indigenous archery initiative, generating international media for the young archers and their Olympic ambitions. Tashira had been profiled as an Olympic story on the Banco Bradesco's web page, his journey from the village to the city raising awareness of the less fortunate among his people, the lack of opportunity, the systemic oppression, the epidemics of suicide and addiction. Now the young archers would take turns carrying the Olympic torch through the streets of the capital, not as a consolation prize but as proof of how completely they had been integrated into the Olympic vision, into Brazil's vision of itself, as beautiful as the tribal dancers who would perform at the opening ceremony in Rio, dramatizing the genocide of their ancestors while cameras broadcast the spectacle to the world.

The sky over Manaus was hot and hazy on this June morning. On the river, the torch was symbolically passed to a river dolphin, bribed with a fish to rise from the water. News reporters covered the menagerie of local celebrities, politicians, and athletes carrying the flaming white torch through a barricaded path flanked by fans and protestors, cheering for what would be won, for what was already lost.

Tashira's Olympic Village roommate, Gilbert, carried the torch past the Teatro Amazonas. For years he and Tashira and the others had compared their best scores on the range, joking about who among their tribes were the best archers. Together they had learned to fall asleep in the strange din of Manaus, sirens, jets, and helicopters blaring outside their windows, so far from their home villages where the night air was filled by the roaring of howler monkeys in the understory.

Tashira carried the torch on one of the city's main throughways, Avenida Djalma Batista, past the new malls, past the new hotels, tracing the route of the silver transmission lines powering the Arena da Amazônia.

The torch was on its way to the capstone event of its stop in Manaus, a ceremony at the Jungle Warfare Training Center, pride of the Brazilian military, a blanket of forest within the city where soldiers lived and trained, maintaining a small zoo where citizens could come to admire the animals of the Amazon. Tortoises and coatimundis, sloths and caimans, all manner of snake, lizard, and fish. When the soldiers were not undertaking exercises, they were maintaining the zoo habitats, repairing monkey houses while the monkeys looked on, pitching fruit pits at their masters. Military units from around the world came here to master the art of surviving and killing in this harshest of terrains: how to find food where none could be seen, how to fashion spike pits that could spear the enemy like a pig, how to set a trap that could catch a live jaguar.

For jungle warfare units in Brazil, the jaguar is the symbol of all that is holy and unholy about Amazonia. The statue at the entrance of every jungle battalion in the country is the same: a soldier and a jaguar, fighting in tandem, power, ferocity, unity. Every battalion raises a jaguar mascot, an orphaned, sick, or injured cub intercepted during animal trafficking operations, bottle-fed and bathed by soldiers who worship them.

For the soldiers, the jaguars are reminders of the dark heart of man, of the smugglers at war with the forest they are sworn to protect. Expert trainers work the jaguars through obstacle courses and discipline exercises. Over time they become playful as kittens, taken on excursions to bathe in the Rio Negro, pouncing after soccer balls and water wrestling with the fresh-faced recruits.

The torch ceremony today would dramatize this harmony. Several hundred guests were in attendance for the grand photo opportunity: an eight-year-old jaguar, Juma, pride of the battalion, sitting nobly alongside the Olympic torch.[3]

In the courtyard at the Jungle Warfare Center, the final relay runner knelt with the torch. Juma the jaguar had been fed and tranquilized in advance. Now she yawned in her chains, held patiently by her trainers. Later investigators found that she had not been authorized to participate in the event.

Experts speculated that the sensory overload of the ceremony was too much for Juma to process. The applause. The hundreds of strangers. The crackle and odor of the torch. A jaguar, born for isolation, freedom, invisibility, its camouflage perfect from the jungle to the Pantanal, forced to sit prone on hot concrete under the incessant clicks of cameras, hundreds of Manaus elites recording the moment on their smartphones.

The scheduled speeches were rousing. At the conclusion of the program, as attendees filed out from their seats, the handlers urged Juma from her resting place. On the way back to the cage, she must have seen, heard, or smelled something. Danger. Opportunity.

With a twist of her neck, Juma slipped her leash. Before the handlers could believe their eyes she was loose. The veterinarian fired a tranquilizer gun. No effect. Another dart. Still nothing.

Perhaps it was the adrenaline jolt of freedom. The scent of open river over the razor wire. Juma seemed not to recognize her men.

The soldiers said she pounced. They said there was no choice. It was us or the jaguar.

A pistol shot. Commanders shouting blame. The torch floating to the next village, flickering in this perpetual water between the long shores, down the river, lost in the river, inside the river . . . the river.

Acknowledgments

Many people made this book possible. Richard Florest, my agent at Rob Weisbach Creative Management, is a bottomless well of faith in my work. Brilliant editor Anna deVries helped me find a way into the Amazon and back home. Elizabeth Bruce appeared magically at several crucial turns to point me in the right direction. Bri Scharfenberg and Shannon Donnelly found readers who care. To everyone at Picador, thank you for making a dream come true, especially P. J. Horoszko, whose correspondence in the early days of this project fueled my fire.

Though I was born in Brazil, I will forever be a visitor in that bighearted country. If this book focuses on problems there, it is only because I want to see those problems solved. If this book captures even a hint of the verve and complexity of life in Brazil, it is thanks to the Brazilians who always made me feel like I was coming home. In Manaus: Leco, Sid, Rodrigo, Marcelo, and Natan. Among the Tururukuri-Uka: Francisco Uruma and Coach Guedes. At the Olympic village: Tashira and Gilbert. (Tokyo

2020!) In BH: the Santos family. In São Paulo: Ligia Castro, tutor, translator, friend.

Foreign correspondents come and go. The best reporters in Brazil spend decades on their beats in one of the world's most dangerous countries for journalists. I want to thank the staff of *A Critica, The Jornal do Commercio, Diário do Amazonas,* and *Rádio Nacional do Alto Solimões* for their daily coverage of crime and heroism, corruption and hope. In Pará, Lúcio Flávio Pinto has been publishing the one-man newspaper *Jornal Pessoal* since 1987 despite threats against his life and livelihood. Many of the most courageous Brazilian storytellers of my generation are women. Bia Ferro Gomes, Rosana Villar de Souza, and Carla Albuqurque, thank you for your generosity and insight.

It's hard to talk Brazilian politics without talking about corruption, but everywhere I traveled, I met public servants doing everything they can for their country within a Kafkaesque bureaucracy. Not all those people can be named here, but special thanks to Kamila Lira in Manaus, Thaís Santi in Altamira, Weydson Pereira in Tabatinga, and Dr. Douglas Rodrigues of the Federal University of São Paulo. Dave and Robin McClamma showed me how faith can fill voids left by the state. Thank you to Hope for Brazil Ministries for praying for me.

When I wasn't in Brazil, I was reading about Brazil, and it's impossible to comprehend a region as vast as the Amazon without standing on the shoulders of giants. In the English language, nobody looms larger than John Hemming. Anyone looking to dig deeper into a scholarly history of the Amazon and its people should start with him.

Jon Lee Anderson was reporting from South America before I was born and his writing on Latin America is indispensable. Scott Wallace wrote the riveting book *The Unconquered,* the story of his search for the isolated "People of the Arrow" with legendary FU-NAI leader and activist Sydney Possuelo. I urge you to follow their work if you aren't already.

Dr. Robert Walker of the University of Missouri and Fiona Watson of Survival International helped me understand the gravity of what's at stake in the rain forest.

Several editors took a chance on my pitches from Brazil: Eleanor Barkhorn, Spencer Kornhaber, Jeremy Kheen, Erin Berger, Boris Muñoz, Isvette Verde, Alexandra Le Tellier, Vincent Bevins, Wilbert Cooper, Benjamin Soloway, and Dan Treadway.

Many institutions supported my writing over the years with scholarships, fellowships, prizes, community, or a place to work: Central Oregon Community College, The University of Oregon, The University of Texas—Brownsville, The National Writing Project, The Sirs, Rudy's BBQ, Betty's Tortas, Purdue University (its English Department and its Summer Intramural Softball program), Spurlock's Pub, The National Society of Arts and Letters, The Key West Literary Seminars, *The Atlantic Monthly*, *Playboy*, *Zoetrope-All Story*, St. Albans School, the Bread Loaf Writers' Conference, and the National Endowment for the Arts.

I've been fortunate to have great teachers who became friends after I left their classrooms. John Russial, Julianne Newton, Dylan Nelson, Jamie Passaro, Porter Shreve, Bich Minh Nguyen, Patricia Henley, and Lyon Rathbun, I hear your voices in my head when I revise. Most importantly, I want to tip my hat to my English teacher at Redmond High School, Mr. Windom, who nudged me down this crazy path.

Mom, Dad, Josh, I love you. To the Arnolds, the Elmers, the Borlens, and the Meyers, the stories we tell around the campfire are the ones I will never forget. To the Wilsons, the Hickmanns, the VanSooys, and the Larsons, thank you for letting me loiter in your homes throughout my childhood. To the Tenorios: thank you for letting me into your family and for teaching me to love California.

The Felicianos of Belo Horizonte are always with me.

Finally, Reyna. For your patience, for your impatience, and for everything in between, my heart is yours.

Notes

1. Fan Fest

1 "Blatter diz que, no início, Brasil queria ter 17 estádios na Copa," *O Globo*, May 24, 2014.

2 "Brazil's Lula: The Most Popular Politician on Earth," *Newsweek*, September 21, 2009.

3 Nicholas Lemann, "The Anointed," *The New Yorker*, December 5, 2011.

4 "Brazil: The First Financial Crisis of 1999," *Southwest Economy*, March–April 1999.

5 "Leia íntegra da carta de Lula para acalmar o mercado financeiro," *Folha d. São Paulo*, June 24, 2002.

6 "Lula's Legacy," *The Economist*, September 30, 2010.

7 Elaíze Farias, "Garbage Is Choking the Amazon's Biggest City," *Americans Quarterly*, Fall 2015.

8 John Hemming, *Amazon Frontier: The Defeat of the Brazilian Indians* (London: Papermac, 1995), 265.

9 Richard Collier, *The River That God Forgot: The Story of the Amazon Rubber Boom* (New York: E.P. Dutton, 1968), 20.

2. Isolation

1. Survival International, "The Ashaninka," http://www.survivalinternational .org/galleries/ashaninka.

2. Alan Taylor, "The Ashaninka, A Threatened Way of Life," *The Atlantic,* December 14, 2011.

3. Lunae Parracho, "Struggles to Survive in the Amazon," *Reuters,* April 3, 2014.

4. Felipe Milanez, "Traficantes invadem área de índios isolados no Acre," *Carta Capital,* August 8, 2011.

5. Scott Wallace, "Concern for Uncontacted Tribes as Armed Gang Invades Brazilian Forest," *National Geographic Voices,* August 8, 2011.

6. Survival International, "Brazilian Officials Warn of 'Imminent' Death of Uncontacted Indians," June 26, 2014, http://www.survivalinternational .org/news/10308.

7. John Hemming, *Tree of Rivers: The Story of the Amazon* (New York: Thames and Hudson, 2008), 291.

8. Scott Wallace, *The Unconquered: In Search of the Amazon's Last Uncontacted Tribes* (New York: Broadway, 2012), 227.

9. Tom Phillips, "Brazil Uses Radar to Protect Isolated Tribes," *The Guardian,* November 19, 2008.

10. Rory Carroll, "Rumble in the Jungle," *The Guardian,* July 3, 2009.

11. BBC, "Uncontacted Tribe," *Human Planet,* February 3, 2011, https://www .youtube.com/watch?v=5lWVVFHzuLE.

3. A Way Back from Oblivion

1. Damian Carrington, "First Amazon Bridge to Open World's Greatest Rainforest to Development," *The Guardian,* August 5, 2010.

2. John Hemming, *Red Gold: The Conquest of the Brazilian Indians* (London: Papermac, 1995), 234.

3. Hemming, *Amazon Frontier,* 261.

4. Site X

1. Heather Pringle, "Uncontacted Tribe in Brazil Emerges from Isolation," *Science,* July 11, 2014.

2. Department of Anthropology, University of Missouri, *Protecting Isolated Tribes,* https://isolatedtribes.missouri.edu/.

3. Survival International, "The Uncontacted Indians of Brazil," http://www .survivalinternational.org/tribes/uncontacted-brazil.

4 R. S. Walker, D. C. Kesler, and K. R. Hill, "Are Isolated Indigenous Populations Headed toward Extinction?" PLoS ONE 11(3): 2016, doi:10.1371/journal.pone.0150987.

5 Survival International, "Defending Tribes' Right to Remain Uncontacted," July 16, 2015, http://www.survivalinternational.org/news/10839.

5. The Real Jungle

1 NASA Earth Observatory, "The Meeting of the Waters," September 7, 2012, https://earthobservatory.nasa.gov/IOTD/view.php?id=79111.

6. The Brazil Reader

1 Rodrigo L. Moura et al., "An Extensive Reef System at the Amazon River Mouth," *Science Advances,* April 22, 2016, doi: 10.1126/sciadv.1501252.

7. Wolves Among Sheep

1 Hemming, *Tree of Rivers,* 54.

2 Ibid., 55.

3 Hemming, *Red Gold,* 98.

4 Ibid., 29.

5 Ibid., 33.

6 Ibid., 434.

7 Ibid., 434.

8 Hemming, *Tree of Rivers,* 64.

9 Ibid., 65.

10 Hemming, *Red Gold,* 324.

11 Ibid., 250.

12 Ibid., 287.

13 Ibid., 334.

14 Ibid., 64.

15 Hemming, *Amazon Frontier,* 13.

16 Ibid., 98.

17 Ibid., 14.

18 Ibid., 53.

19 Hemming, *Red Gold,* 39.

20 Ibid., 417.

21 Hemming, *Tree of Rivers,* 81.

22 Jon Lee Anderson, "An Isolated Tribe Emerges from the Rain Forest," *The New Yorker,* August 8, 2016.

8. The Devil's Paradise

1 K. David Jackson, ed., *The Oxford Anthology of the Brazilian Short Story* (Oxford: Oxford University Press, 2006), 101.

2 Hemming, *Tree of Rivers*, 178.

3 Ibid., 202.

4 Ibid., 175.

5 Ibid., 178.

6 Ibid., 179.

7 Ibid., 183.

8 Ibid., 180.

9 Ibid., 181.

10 Hemming, *Amazon Frontier*, 264.

11 Ibid., 182.

12 "Rubber Scandals," *Sydney Morning Herald*, July 23, 1912.

13 Hemming, *Amazon Frontier*, 298.

14 Jordan Goodman, *The Devil and Mr. Casement: One Man's Battle for Human Rights in South America's Heart of Darkness* (New York: Farrar, Straus and Giroux, 2009), 140.

15 Hemming, *Tree of Rivers*, 197.

9. Quarantine

1 Douglas Rodrigues, "Ações de saúde no contato com os 'Isolados do Xinane,'" Universidade Federal de São Paulo, July 17, 2014.

2 Survival International, "Uncontacted Tribes: The Threats," http://www.survivalinternational.org/articles/3106-uncontacted-tribes-the-threats.

3 Andrew Lawler, "Do the Amazon's Last Isolated Tribes Have a Future?" *New York Times*, August 8, 2015.

10. Biti's Gang

1 Gisele Rodriguez, "Em Manaus, temperatura chega a até 44°C no ônibus do transporte público," *Diário do Amazonas*, August 16, 2015.

2 Vinicius Leal and Náferson Cruz, "Suspeitos na morte do sargento Camacho, morto em 'saidinha de banco,' o vigiavam há 2 semanas," *A Crítica*, August 7, 2015.

3 Alexandre Pequeno, "Sargento Afonso Camacho é homenageado em desfile cívico," *A Crítica*, September 5, 2015.

4 Kamyla Gomes, "Assaltantes em fuga matam PM em estacionamento de agência bancária da Zona Sul," *A Crítica*, July 17, 2015.

5 "Sargento da PM é morto após reagir a assalto em estacionamento de banco, no Educandos," *D24AM*, July 17, 2015.

6 Jamile Alves, "PM é morto a tiros após ser assaltado em saída de banco, diz polícia do AM," *G1 Amazonas,* July 17, 2015.

11. Maximum Power

1 Umanizzare, "Unidades," http://www.umanizzarebrasil.com.br/unidades/.

2 Secretaria de Estado de Administração Penitenciária, "Complexo Prisional Anísio Jobim," http://www.seap.am.gov.br/complexo-penitenciario-anisio -jobim/.

3 Chris Feliciano Arnold. "Brazil Has Become a Gangland," *Foreign Policy,* June 6, 2017.

4 Flávio Costa e Paula Bianchi, "Chefe da FDN pegou 120 anos por chacina em 2002 no mesmo presídio de Manaus," *UOL*, January 10, 2017.

5 "Os Donos do Crime," *ISTOÉ,* January 6, 2017, https://istoe.com.br/os -donos-do-crime/.

6 Polícia Federal, Superintendência Regional do Amazonas, *Relatório Final de Operaçao La Muralla,* January 19, 2016, 20, http://politica.estadao.com .br/blogs/fausto-macedo/wp-content/uploads/sites/41/2017/01 /Relat%C3%B3rio-final-IPL-222-de-2014-DRE-OPERA%C3%87% C3%83O-LA-MURALLA.pdf.

7 Paula Miraglia, "Drugs and Drug Trafficking in Brazil: Trends and Policies," Brookings Institution, July 2016.

8 Joana Queiroz and Monica Prestes, "FDN: Conheça os pilares da 'família do crime' no Amazonas," *A Critica,* November 28, 2015.

9 Polícia Federal, Superintendência Regional do Amazonas, *Relatório Final de Operaçao La Muralla*, 529.

10 Ibid., 37–45.

11 Bruna Souza "Delgado Oscar Cardoso é executado com mais de vinte tiros em Manaus neste domingo," *A Critica,* March 10, 2014.

12 "Policiais prometem 'fazer justiça' pela morte do delegado Oscar Cardoso," *A Critica,* March 11, 2014.

13 Bruna Souza, "Ainda desaparecido, 'João Branco' tinha rádio comunicador da polícia e cela especial," *A Critica,* March 19, 2014.

14 "Traficante mais procurado do AM pode estar fora do país, diz polícia," *G1 Amazonas*, February 7, 2015.

15 Joana Queiroz, "Líderes da facção FDN ordenaram mortes de adversários no fim de semana que registrou 38 mortes," *A Critica*, November 25, 2015.

16 "Detento decapitado no Ipat é o terceiro morto nos presídios de Manaus em julho," *D24AM,* July 17, 2015.

12. The Bloody Weekend

1 Secretaria de Segurança Pública do Estado do Amazonas, "Série do homicídios," *Relatorio Final de Operaçao Alcateia,* November 27, 2015.

2 Secretaria de Segurança Pública do Estado do Amazonas, "Relatório de Diligência Policial: Erick Soares da Silva," *Relatorio Final de Operaçao Alcateia,* November 27, 2015, 3.

13. A Sense of Security

1 "Em Manaus, ajudante de pedreiro é o 35º morto a tiros desde noite de sexta," *G1 Amazonas,* July 20, 2015.

2 Fábio Oliveira, "Após mortes em série, boatos espalham medo nas redes sociais," July 21, 2015.

3 Polícia Federal, Superintendência Regional do Amazonas, *Relatório Final de Operaçao La Muralla,* January 19, 2016, 145.

4 "Sérgio Fontes e Orlando Amaral tomam posse na SSP-AM e na Delegacia Geral, respectivamente," *A Critica,* January 21, 2015.

5 Adneison Severiano, "PM-AM anuncia pacote de ações para 90 dias e combate a desvio de conduta," *G1 Amazonas,* January 30, 2015.

6 Vinicius Leal, "Justiça Militar decreta e PM prende policiais que agrediram e torturaram jovens em Manaus," *A Critica,* May 9, 2015.

7 "Cúpula da Segurança Pública trata série de homicídios como 'evento fora da curva,'" *D24AM,* July 18, 2015.

8 Sérgio Rodrigues, "Ciops vai integrar câmeras privadas a sistema de segurança, diz SSP-AM," *G1 Amazonas,* July 24, 2017.

9 "Em Manaus, ajudante de pedreiro é o 35º morto a tiros desde noite de sexta," *G1 Amazonas,* July 20, 2015.

10 Ibid.

11 Ibid.

12 Kamyla Gomes, "Polícia Militar seguirá com buscas para localizar envolvidos em assassinato do sargento," *A Critica,* July 17, 2015.

13 Cristina Serra, "Fantástico exibe reportagem sobre assassinatos em série, em Manaus," *D24AM,* July 27, 2015.

14 Vinicius Leal, "Após três dias com 36 mortes, Manaus fica 24 horas sem registro de homicídios no IML," *A Critica,* July 21, 2015.

15 Sérgio Rodrigues, "Após série de mortes, polícia realiza operação contra crimes em Manaus," *G1 Amazonas,* July 21, 2015.

16 "Polícia Militar monta operação de segurança em todas zonas de Manaus," *G1 Amazonas,* July 31, 2015.

17 "CMM: mortes do fim semana transformam homenagem a Sérgio Fontes em 'audiência,'" *A Critica,* July 20, 2015.

18 Joana Queiroz, "Líderes da facção FDN ordenaram mortes de adversários no fim de semana que registrou 38 mortes," *A Critica*, November 25, 2015.

14. Três Fronteiras

1 Leo Johnson, *Tres Fronteiras: One Square Mile of Brazil*, BBC World Radio and TV, September 21, 2012.

2 "Fear of Trouble Upstream," *The Economist,* September 28, 2000.

15. Operation Wolfpack

1 Amnesty International, "Brazil 2016/2017," https://www.amnesty.org/en /countries/americas/brazil/report-brazil/.

2 Secretaria de Segurança Pública do Estado do Amazonas, *CRIA Força Tarefa*, August 15, 2015.

3 Donna Bowater, "Brazil Marks 20 Years Since Candelaria Child Massacre," *BBC News,* July 24, 2013.

4 Secretaria de Segurança Pública do Estado do Amazonas, "Relatório Final de Operaçao Alçateia," November 27, 2015.

16. Ghost Riders

1 Secretaria de Segurança Pública do Estado do Amazonas, "Inquirito Policial de Operaçao Alcateia," Apenso 1, vol. 1, 2015, 20.

2 The events described in the remainder of this chapter are derived from evidence gathered during the internal affairs investigation, which included cell phone triangulations, mobile voice, photo and message data, as well as eyewitness accounts, surveillance video, autopsy reports, and ballistic and forensic evidence.

3 Secretaria de Segurança Pública do Estado do Amazonas, "Relatório Final de Operaçao Alçateia: Inquérito Policial," November 27, 2015.

4 Secretaria de Segurança Pública do Estado do Amazonas, "Relatório de Diligência Policial: Bruno Silva Oliveira," "Relatório Final de Operaçao Alçateia," November 27, 2015.

5 Secretaria de Segurança Pública do Estado do Amazonas, "Relatório Final de Operaçao Alçateia: Inquérito Policial," November 27, 2015, 32.

6 Secretaria de Segurança Pública do Estado do Amazonas, "Relatório Final de Operaçao Alçateia," November 27, 2015.

7 At the time of this writing, Mattos and the other Ghost Riders have been in custody awaiting trial since November 2015.

17. A Land Without Men

1 Thomas E. Skidmore, *The Politics of Military Rule in Brazil, 1964–85* (New York: Oxford University Press, 1988), 120.

2 Todd A. Diacon, *Stringing Together a Country: Cândido Mariano da Silva Condon and the Construction of a Modern Brazil, 1906–1930* (Durham, NC: Duke University Press, 2004), 5.

3 Ibid., 4.

4 Ibid., 55–61.

5 Hemming, *Die If You Must*, 157.

6 Ibid., 226.

7 Norman Lewis, "Genocide," *Sunday Times of London,* February 23, 1969.

8 Grandin, *Fordlandia*, 368.

9 In 2000, the U.S. Army rebranded the School of the Americas as The Western Hemisphere Institute for Security Operation.

10 Matt Sandy, "'Sole Survivor' Recalls Jungle Conflict with Military in Brazil," *BBC News*, January 17, 2016.

11 Colonel Alvaro de Souza Pinheriro, *Guerrilla in the Brazilian Amazon*, Foreign Military Studies Office, July 1995, http://fmso.leavenworth.army.mil/documents/amazon/amazon.htm.

12 Larry Rohter, "Long After Guerrilla War, Survivors Demand Justice from Brazil's Government," *New York Times*, March 28, 2004.

13 Skidmore, *The Politics of Military Rule in Brazil*, 146.

14 Robert G. Hummerstone, "Cutting a Road Through Brazil's 'Green Hell,'" *New York Times,* March 5, 1972.

15 Loren Moss, "Interview: Colombia's Skynet Bringing Broadband Internet Trunking to Leticia, Amazonas via 03b Earth Orbit Satellites," *Finance Colombia,* September 24, 2015.

18. City of Vultures

1 Tom Phillips, "I'd Lost the Strength to Carry On," *The Guardian*, May 21, 2008.

2 Jonathan Watts, "Brazil Salutes Chico Mendes 25 Years After His Mur-

der," *The Guardian,* December 20, 2013, https://www.theguardian.com /world/2013/dec/20/brazil-salutes-chico-mendes-25-years-after-murder.

3 Elaine Bloom and Thais Santi, "Belo Monte: A anatomia de um etnocídio," *El Pais Brasil,* December 1, 2014.

4 Todd Southgate, *Belo Monte: After the Flood,* Documentary, 2016.

5 Friends of the MST, "Need and Basis for Agrarian Reform," http://www .mstbrazil.org/content/need-basis-agrarian-reform.

6 Felipe Milanez, "Madeiras de Sangue," *Rolling Stone Brasil,* June 2008.

7 Roseanne Murphy, *Martyr of the Amazon: The Life of Sister Dorothy Stang* (Maryknoll, NY: Orbis Books, 2007).

8 Larry Rohter, "Brazil Promises Crackdown After Nun's Shooting Death," *New York Times,* February 14, 2005.

9 Michael E. Miller, "Why Are Brazil's Environmentalists Being Murdered?" *Washington Post,* August 27, 2015.

10 Rohter, *Brazil on the Rise,* 209.

11 "MPPA investiga se grupo encontrado na Transamazônica era escravo," *G1 Pará,* April 26, 2016.

12 Greenpeace UK, *The Amazon's Silent Crisis: Night Terrors,* October 2014, http://m.greenpeace.org/belgium/Global/belgium/report/2014/gp_amz _silent_crimefile_final.pdf.

13 Anastasia Moloney, "Brazil Slave Labor Victims Seek Justice at Americas' Top Rights Court," Reuters, February 24, 2016.

14 "A Batalha de Belo Monte," *Folha de S. Paulo,* December 16, 2013.

19. Soul Counts

1 Hemming, *Die If You Must,* 328.

20. Guardians

1 Hemming, *Die If You Must,* 482.

2 Davi Kopenawa and Bruce Albert, *The Falling Sky: Words of a Yanomami Shaman* (Cambridge, MA: Harvard University Press, 2013), 165.

3 Hemming, *Die If You Must,* 497.

4 Peter C. Baker, "Fight Clubs: On Napoleon Chagnon," *The Nation,* May 15, 2013.

5 American Anthropological Association, "El Dorado Task Force Papers," vol. 2, May 18, 2012, 103.

6 Kopenawa and Albert, *The Falling Sky: Words of a Yanomami Shaman,* 8.

7 Ibid.

8 Hemming, *Die If You Must*, 506.

9 Emily Eakin, "How Napoleon Chagnon Became Our Most Controversial Anthropologist," *New York Times Magazine*, February 13, 2013.

10 Hemming, *Die If You Must*, 507.

11 Kopenawa and Albert, *The Falling Sky: Words of a Yanomami Shaman*, 262

12 Ibid.

13 Ibid., 507.

14 Tim Golden, "Talk About Culture Shock: Ant People in Sky-High Huts," *New York Times*, April 17, 1991.

15 Hemming, *Die If You Must*, 518.

16 Kopenawa and Albert, *The Falling Sky: Words of a Yanomami Shaman*, Appendix D.

17 Ibid, 406.

18 Dom Phillips, "Defending the Amazon," *Washington Post*, October 6, 2015.

19 Luana Lila, "Indigenous Lands Are Going Up in Smoke in the Amazon—Because of Illegal Logging," *Greenpeace International*, October 23, 2015.

20 Sarah Shenker, "Giving a Platform to the Tribal Guardians of the Natural World," Survival International, n.d.

21. Last Dance

1 Brad Haynes and Eduardo Simões, "Brazil Prosecutors Seek Lula's Arrest for Money Laundering," Reuters, March 10, 2016.

2 Secretaria de Segurança Pública do Estado do Amazonas, *Relatorio Final de Operaçao Alcateia: Inquérito Policial*, November 27, 2015, 017/2015-UAIP/PC/AM; 128.

3 Joana Queiroz, "Dos 36 homicídios do último final de semana, 20 das vítimas não tinham passagens pela polícia," *A Critica*, August 8, 2015.

22. The Torch and the Jaguar

1 "Investigação mostra que governador do AM usou PM para intimidar eleitor," *Fantástico*, June 5, 2016.

2 Reinaldo Azevedo, "Governo do Amazonas negocia apoio de traficantes para o 2º turno," *Veja*, February 11, 2017.

3 Oswaldo Neto, "Estresse de cerimônia pode ter eliminado efeito de tranquilizante em onça-pintada," *A Critica*, June 21, 2016.

Selected Bibliography

Bishop, Elizabeth, and Emanuel Brasil, eds. *An Anthology of Twentieth-Century Brazilian Poetry*. Middletown, CT: Wesleyan University Press, 1972.

Diacon, Todd A. *Stringing Together a Country: Cândido Mariano da Silva Condon and the Construction of a Modern Brazil, 1906–1930*. Durham, NC: Duke University Press, 2004.

Goodman, Jordan. *The Devil and Mr. Casement: One Man's Battle for Human Rights in South America's Heart of Darkness*. New York: Farrar, Straus and Giroux, 2009.

Goulding, Michael, Ronaldo Barthem, and Efrem Ferreira. *The Smithsonian Atlas of the Amazon*. Washington, DC: Smithsonian Books, 2010.

Grandin, Greg. *Fordlandia: The Rise and Fall of Henry Ford's Forgotten Jungle City*. New York: Henry Holt, 2009.

Hemming, John. *Red Gold: The Conquest of the Brazilian Indians*. London: Papermac, 1995.

———. *Amazon Frontier: The Defeat of the Brazilian Indians*. London: Papermac, 1995.

———. *Die If You Must: Brazilian Indians in the Twentieth Century*. London: Macmillan, 2003.

———. *Tree of Rivers: The Story of the Amazon*. New York: Thames and Hudson, 2008.

Jackson, David K., ed. *Oxford Anthology of the Brazilian Short Story*. Oxford: Oxford University Press, 2006.

Kopenawa, Davi, and Bruce Albert. *The Falling Sky: Words of a Yanomami Shaman*. Cambridge, MA: Harvard University Press, 2013.

Levine, Robert M., and John J. Crocitti, eds. *The Brazil Reader: History, Culture, Politics*. Durham, NC: Duke University Press, 1999.

Lévi-Strauss, Claude. *Tristes Tropiques*, trans. John and Doreen Weightman. New York: Penguin, 1992.

Millard, Candice. *The River of Doubt: Theodore Roosevelt's Darkest Journey*. New York: Anchor, 2005.

Pearson, David L., and Les Beletsky. *Traveller's Wildlife Guides: Brazil—Amazon & Pantanal*. Northampton, MA: Interlink, 2010.

Rohter, Larry. *Brazil on the Rise: The Story of a Country Transformed*. New York: Palgrave Macmillan, 2010.

Skidmore, Thomas E. *The Politics of Military Rule in Brazil, 1964–85*. New York: Oxford University Press, 1988.

Southgate, Todd. *Belo Monte: After the Flood*, Documentary, 2016.

Stam, Robert. *Tropical Multiculturalism: A Comparative History of Race in Brazilian Cinema & Culture*. Durham, NC: Duke University Press, 1997.

Wallace, Scott. *The Unconquered: In Search of the Amazon's Last Uncontacted Tribes*. New York: Broadway, 2012.

About the Author

CHRIS FELICIANO ARNOLD has written for *The New York Times*, *Harper's*, *The Atlantic*, *Foreign Policy*, *Outside*, *Sports Illustrated*, *Playboy*, *Vice News*, and other outlets, including *Folha de S. Paulo*, Brazil's largest newspaper. He is the recipient of a 2014 creative writing fellowship from the National Endowment for the Arts. Born in Brazil and raised in the United States, he now resides in Northern California.